STOP Plagiarism

A Guide to Understanding and Prevention

Edited by
Vibiana Bowman Cvetkovic
Katie Elson Anderson

Neal-Schuman Publishers, Inc.

New York

London

Published by Neal-Schuman Publishers, Inc.
100 William St., Suite 2004
New York, NY 10038

Printed and bound in the United States of America.

The paper used in this publication meets the minimum requirements of American National Standard for Information Sciences—Permanence of Paper for Printed Library Materials, ANSI Z39.48-1992.

Library of Congress Cataloging-in-Publication Data

Stop plagiarism : a guide to understanding and prevention / edited by Vibiana Bowman Cvetkovic and Katie Elson Anderson.
     p. cm.
  Includes bibliographical references and index.
  ISBN 978-1-55570-716-3 (alk. paper)
    1. Plagiarism.   I. Cvetkovic, Vibiana Bowman, 1953-   II. Anderson, Katie Elson, 1973-

PN167.S76 2010
808—dc22

2010024860

Contents

Chapter 11. Professional Organizations' Recommendations Regarding Intellectual Honesty   137

Frances Kaufmann and Julie Still

Chapter 12. Inoculating against Plagiarism: Resources for Teaching and Learning   151

Leslie Murtha

Chapter 13. Write It, Then Cite It: Guiding Students toward Reliable Techniques and Resources for Effective Scholarly Writing 173

Robert J. Lackie

See this book's companion CD-ROM to access:
Live links to websites discussed in the book
Plagiarism tutorials
(developed by the Reference Department of the Paul Robeson Library,
Rutgers–The State University, Camden, New Jersey)

Don't miss the wiki that keeps this book up-to-date:
stopplagiarism.wikispaces.com

Preface

Stop Plagiarism: A Guide to Understanding and Prevention is about honesty: how to teach it; how to model it; and how to promote it. Its basic premise is that intellectual honesty is the foundation of good scholarship. It is the keystone upon which rest all new advances in the academy. Plagiarism, on the other hand, is theft—the theft of an idea.

Regardless as to whether an act of plagiarism is a result of deliberate deception, poor research habits, or ignorance, the outcome is the same—a harm is perpetrated. The magnitude of that harm can range from careers and reputations being ruined; inaccuracies being perpetrated in scholarly literature; loss of financial considerations for the originators of plagiarized material; to faulty intelligence being gathered and used for major policy decisions. This book and its accompanying CD-ROM are tools educators can use to teach their students the basics of intellectual honesty and to stop plagiarism.

Stop Plagiarism: A Guide to Understanding and Prevention is a sequel to *The Plagiarism Plague* (Neal-Schuman, 2004). Many of the original authors have returned, but there are new voices here as well. A majority of the new contributors represent the next generation of librarianship, the Web 2.0 professional—librarians who have come of age with the PC. They grew up gaming and socializing online and were learning during transitional times of increased technology use in education. Their perspectives contribute greatly to this edition, whose goal is to update and reenergize the fight against plagiarism.

Like the original book, this work addresses the problems and concerns facing librarians and educators involved in the process of teaching academic honesty to high school and college students. Over the past six years, there has been a spate of legal rulings, technological innovations, and new online resources that have had a direct impact on the plagiarism debate. There have also been seismic changes in the ways that the Internet is both accessed (through mobile and hand-held devices) and utilized as a social networking tool.

Cell phone use by students has become nearly ubiquitous. A cell phone culture of constant connectivity has given rise to for-fee text-messaging services that deliver information directly to phones. Wikipedia has become the main Internet research tool for students. These developments raise questions regarding the authority and accuracy of the information used by students in research and writing. Educators are also concerned because students often use the materials from such sites without proper attribution—cutting and pasting the information directly into their papers. The idea of intellectual ownership is lost on students when materials are either freely available or purchased. While many of these concerns existed when the first edition appeared, the problems have been increasingly exacerbated.

Accusations of plagiarism involving notables are on the rise. Recent examples include the 2006 Dan Brown/*The Da Vinci Code* trial; the Kaavya Viswanathan/*How Opal Mehta Got Kissed, Got Wild and Got a Life* debacle, also in 2006; and, in early 2008, accusations of serial plagiarism aimed at University of Florida English professor James Twitchell. In 2008 presidential candidates Barack Obama and John McCain were accused of plagiarizing speeches, and the story of Joe Biden's law school plagiarism incident was resurrected. These incidents have heightened public awareness of plagiarism and serve to underscore what the legal, social, and professional ramifications are for academic dishonesty.

This work is intended as a practical handbook. The material it contains is designed to be of use to all levels of educators working with students—from high school to postgraduate college students. For the most part, the contributors are instructors or librarians working daily in the trenches with students. Authors were asked to keep the tone of their chapters conversational, as if they were conferring with a colleague. The dedication, professionalism, and humor of the authors are apparent in their contributions. The various sections are based on their own research, experience, and resourcefulness. *Stop Plagiarism* contains background material, web resources, a collection of sample exercises, and an interactive CD-ROM so that users of this handbook can immediately access the web materials and utilize the sample exercises. The authors have also established an antiplagiarism wiki, available at stopplagiarism.wikispaces.com. Readers are encouraged to add to the sources and participate in the ongoing conversation on plagiarism.

"Part I: Understanding the Problem" gives the reader background material about the topic of plagiarism. In Chapter 1, Katie Elson Anderson and Vibiana Bowman Cvetkovic give an overview of the cultural milieu in which the notion of intellectual ownership currently exists. Laura B. Spencer discusses the concept of the originality of ideas in both the public and private sectors in Chapter 2. In Chapter 3, Nick Cvetkovic traces the history of papermills (sites for downloading papers) and their current business practices. Vibiana Bowman Cvetkovic and Luis F. Rodriguez play devil's advocate in Chapter 4 by examining whether the fight against plagiarism is a losing battle. Author Sarah F.

Brookover provides the undergraduate perspective regarding academic writing and intellectual honesty in Chapter 5.

"Part II: Finding Remedies" offers some practical solutions for the practitioner concerned with creating antiplagiarism resources. Vibiana Bowman Cvetkovic and John B. Gibson draw upon their experience in creating an award-winning online tutorial to provide a "how-to" in Chapter 6. Gillian A. Newton and Jeffrey J. Teichmann provide best practices and an overview of the "first-year" experience in Chapter 7. Dolores Pfeuffer-Scherer examines public and private university and college intellectual honesty policies in Chapter 8. Considerations regarding the nontraditional student are discussed by Dawn Amsberry in Chapter 9.

"Part III: A Practitioner's Toolkit" is intended to provide the reader with resources for developing policy and for further scholarship. In Chapter 10, Robert Berry discusses legal issues regarding plagiarism and academic cases of intellectual dishonesty. Chapter 11, by Frances Kaufman and Julie Still, examines the intellectual honesty policies of professional organizations. Robert J. Lackie provides a guide to resources for educators to use in teaching scholarly writing skills in Chapter 13. Chapters 12 and 14, by Leslie Murtha and Patience L. Simmonds, respectively, represent webographies of antiplagiarism resources (Murtha) and articles and scholarly resources not discussed in previous chapters (Simmonds).

The companion CD-ROM for *Stop Plagiarism: A Guide to Understanding and Prevention* provides easy access to the websites discussed in the book. It also contains the suite of plagiarism tutorials developed by the Reference Department of the Paul Robeson Library, Rutgers–The State University, Camden, New Jersey. These tutorials are licensed through Creative Commons and are intended to be freely used by educators.

The companion wiki at stopplagiarism.wikispaces.com also provides easy access to the websites mentioned in the book as well as a place for readers to provide their own links and tips for stopping plagiarism.

The production of this book has been a collaborative process. Both the editors and the chapter authors are concerned about plagiarism and hope that their contributions to this volume will help to solve the problem. We hope that *Stop Plagiarism: A Guide to Understanding and Prevention* will be useful to our readers and help to educate our next generation of scholars.

Acknowledgments

V.B.C. would like to thank her kind and patient husband, Nick, and her children, Elizabeth, Tatiana, Anna, Natasha, Michael, and David, for their love and support.

K.E.A. would like to thank her husband, Chris, for his patience and support and her mother, father, and sister for their support and extra hours spent with Petr while "mommy was working." She would also like to thank V.B.C. for her enthusiastic and inspiring guidance.

V.B.C. and K.E.A. thank all the authors for contributing their talents to this project. They also thank Sandy Wood, their Project Development Editor at Neal-Schuman, for shepherding the book through the publication process with both patience and consummate professionalism.

Part I

Understanding the Problem

1

Teaching Intellectual Honesty in a Parodied World

Katie Elson Anderson
Vibiana Bowman Cvetkovic

Some Thoughts about Plagiarism

A search for the term *plagiarism* on the microblogging website Twitter (twitter.com) at any given time often results in several instances of some version of this statement: "To steal ideas from one person is plagiarism. To steal from many is research." Not surprisingly, few, if any of these instances are properly attributed to the originator of this quote, Wilson Mizner. The original quote and any attribution are difficult to find; however, a Google or Wikipedia search does quickly identify him with the concept. The fact that this statement appears so often and is shared by so many indicates that the topic of plagiarism is on the minds of microbloggers. The fact that the statement is not properly attributed to the author indicates that plagiarism continues to be a problem.

Microbloggers are not the only ones with plagiarism on their minds. In recent years, news stories regarding accusations of plagiarism have been frequent. Musicians, artists, writers, journalists, and politicians are consistently under the scrutiny of a society attuned to plagiarism. While many of these accusations are dismissed, the fact that they are being asserted shows that the problem of plagiarism has gone well beyond the classroom.

Proof that concerns over plagiarism have gone mainstream can be seen in the list of names accused. The nation's current President and Vice President have both been accused of plagiarism. While on the campaign trail, Obama was criticized for his use of Governor Deval Patrick's words during a speech. Biden's plagiarism occurred before this most recent campaign and played a pivotal role in the end of his presidential bid in 1988 (Greenberg, 2008). The popular, award-winning band Coldplay has been targeted at least twice in recent years; other musicians claimed that the group had stolen their music (Varga,

3

2009). J.K. Rowling, author of the Harry Potter series, and Stephanie Meyers, creator of the teen vampire series *Twilight*, are among the best-selling authors who have been called upon to defend their writing's originality. *Wired* editor Chris Anderson's book *Free* was found to have included sections of Wikipedia without citations (Vaidhyanathan, 2009). Columnist Maureen Dowd was criticized for her use of a blogger's words without attribution (Hoyt, 2009).

Accusations of plagiarism occur in the sciences as well, with Stanford researchers accused of stealing an idea for an artificial knee (Mangan, 2009). Perhaps one of the more interesting accusations is the ironic accusation that Southern Illinois plagiarized Indiana University's policy on plagiarism (Bartlett, 2009a). Making this even more interesting is that fact that both universities have had plagiarism concerns previous to this one. While each of these cases has its own nuances and conclusions, ranging from denial to dismissal to apology and retraction, the fact that so many continue to occur is of concern to educators and scholars.

These are just some examples of recent instances of plagiarism that have followed one of the more infamous cases which took place in 2001 when Doris Kearns Goodwin was charged with plagiarism. An accusation of plagiarism is damaging for any scholar, but especially one of Goodwin's standing. Goodwin has impeccable credentials: best-selling author; recipient of the Pulitzer Prize for History; and member of various prestigious societies such as the Harvard Board of Overseers, the Society of American Historians, and the American Academy of Arts and Sciences (Academy of Achievement, 2003). The problem arose when critics noticed that portions of her book *The Fitzgeralds and the Kennedys* (St. Martins Press, 1991) bore a remarkable resemblance to passages from Lynne McTaggart's work, *Kathleen Kennedy: Her Life and Times* (Dial, 1983). Goodwin publicly apologized for the error. She explained that she had done copious research but had neglected to properly footnote her source material and that this lapse in scholarly protocol was a source of professional embarrassment: "What made this incident particularly hard for me was the fact that I take great pride in the depth of my research and the extensiveness of my citations" (Goodwin, 2002: 69).

Goodwin's woes were exacerbated by the fact that the incident came quick on the heels of accusations of plagiarism for another popular and well-respected historian, Stephen Ambrose. Ambrose was criticized for using whole passages from Thomas Childers's work *The Wings of Morning* (Da Capo Press, 1996) in his book *The Wild Blue* (Simon & Schuster, 2001). Critics were harder on Ambrose than Goodwin mainly because his apology seemed cavalier and self-serving. Ambrose told the press that while he may have had lapses in scholarly procedure by failing to use quotation marks around direct quotes, he did indicate source materials through the use of notes in the work (Tolson, 2002: 52). Jay Tolson (2002) of *US News & World Report* called this remark a *"mea sorta culpa"* and noted that few university professors would have accepted this excuse from an undergraduate student caught in the same situation.

Many of the accused in the aforementioned instances find themselves explaining how the plagiarism occurred. These explanations include Goodwin's failure to footnote properly, Ambrose's leaving off quotes, and Obama's neglecting to provide attribution. Chris Anderson explained that the endnotes he had used were removed from the final document by the publisher (Vaidhyanathan, 2009). These apologies and retractions are generally viewed by the public as acceptable with limited consequences to the accused and their reputations. These limited consequences by famous writers cannot go unnoticed by students of today who are often introduced to the concept of plagiarism via their school's code of plagiarism. These codes detail the punishment for plagiarism, which is often dismissal from the institution. These attempts to scare students into not plagiarizing are being thwarted by such real-world examples where there are light penalties. Charles McGrath (2009) observes that it is not surprising that young people are confused and continue to plagiarize if they see that once they are out of school the punishment for plagiarism depends on "who you know and how well you pull it off."

While the real-world examples of scholarly plagiarism should be viewed as problematic in their watering down of the severity of committing plagiarism, they can also be viewed as illustrative of the high stakes involved in the art of good scholarship: the stress and pressure to meet deadline dates versus the time and discipline required to maintain academic integrity.

The troubles of these authors serve to emphasize the plight of the undergraduate student. If eminent scholars can become overwhelmed by the detail work required for scholarly writing, what of the poor novice? Educators need to be concerned with not only teaching students the mechanics of good scholarship, such as using footnotes to properly credit another person's intellectual property, but also with giving students a clear understanding of the ethics and meaning behind these seemingly arcane academic practices.

There are some sobering statistics and studies about undergraduates that give educators pause. In response to a 2001 Rutgers University survey, three out of four high school students stated that they cheated on a test at least once during that academic year, and the same number confessed to handing in another person's written work (Sohn, 2001). Plagiarism.org reports similar findings from the Center for Academic Integrity (Plaigarism.org, 2010a). The actual 2005 study is not currently available but is referred to often in articles (Jackson, 2006), websites, and presentations. The numbers are not getting smaller.

The ease with which student papers can be purchased is disconcerting. Plagiarism.org, the website that hosts the plagiarism-buster service Turnitin.com, reports that hundreds of papermills exist that offer hundreds of thousands of academic papers for sale:

> The fact that many of these sites have become profitable ventures (complete with paid advertising!) only attests to the unfortunate truth that plagiarism has become a booming industry. (Plagiarism .org, 2010b)

A recent cover story from the *Chronicle of Higher Education* explores the growing number of these profitable and increasingly international companies. Among these companies are some who provide essays that are "custom" and supposedly go undetected by plagiarism-checking software (Bartlett, 2009b).

At the other end of the spectrum, faculty and administrators feel at a loss about how to appropriately address the issue of academic honesty and what to do when confronted with situations in which student cheating is apparent. In a national survey of psychology professors, 71 percent of the respondents reported that "dealing with instances of academic dishonesty was among the most onerous aspects of their profession" (Keith-Speigel et al., 1998: 215). Literature in scholarly journals underscores the concern and a sense of urgency for understanding and dealing with a seeming erosion of academic integrity: "Most students want to be honest; dishonesty is not innate; it is learned. Preemptive instruction, role modeling, and rewards must precede the learning of cheating" (Petress, 2003: 624). The importance of preemptive instruction is further emphasized in the results of a recent look at students' perceptions of plagiarism where it is noted that while every student in the study knew that a plagiarism policy existed, only one out of 31 students had actually read it (Power, 2009). Awareness that plagiarism is a punishable offense and that a school has policies against it do not in any way guarantee prevention.

Those who have worked with undergraduate students generally agree that most do not set out to deliberately cheat or plagiarize. Rather, most students are unaware and uncertain about how to go about writing an appropriate, scholarly paper. Educators should keep in mind that our students (i.e., those young adults in their late teens and early twenties) have very different cultural attitudes and perspectives than educators (especially those of us who are in the thirty-something-on-up category). To teach our students about intellectual *honesty*, it is important to understand this generational divide in background experience toward research and toward the concept of intellectual *ownership*. Power (2009: 655) found that "only a handful of people seemed to have an internal sense of plagiarism as an undesirable behavior in the sense that plagiarism is unfair to the original author."

Plagiarism and Technology

While personal computing dates back to the 1970s, the rise of PCs as the recognizable household device that we know today begins in the early 1980s with the introduction of affordable, easy-to-use, IBM products (Long, 2003). The early 1980s is also when those in Generation M were being born. Gen M is the demographic group to which current undergraduates belong, so named because of their end of the millennial births as well as their heavy use of media. Members of Gen M have been characterized as "adept multitaskers, adroit with technology, and abysmal at sustaining long attention spans" (Cvetkovic and Lackie, 2009: xii). Current undergraduates have grown up with computing technology, analogous to the way baby boomers grew up with television. It is one of their defining popular culture influences.

According to the U.S. Census Bureau's (2007) "2007 Internet and Computer Use Supplement to the Current Population Survey," the percentage of households with access to the Internet increased from 18 percent in 1997 to almost 62 percent in 2007. It is a safe assumption that that number has increased since that survey. Of the children aged 3 to 17 living in these households, 56 percent have accessed the Internet. This is an increase from 47 percent in 2000 (U.S. Census Bureau, 2001).

Use of the Internet is also no longer restricted to a hard-wired desktop computer sitting on a desk. The Internet provides teenagers with a volume of mixed media. They are watching television shows on their iPods and PSPs (PlayStation Portables) and movies on their phones and reading e-mail on desktops, laptops, PDAs (personal digital assistants), and phones. The Kaiser Family Foundation (2010) reports that today's 8- to 18-year-olds spend an average of 7.5 hours a day, seven days a week, using mixed media. During those 7.5 hours using media, they actually cram in 10.75 hours worth of content by multitasking. These numbers represent an increase of almost 2.25 hours since 2004. All forms of media use (TV, music, computer, video games, movies) by this age group are increasing with the exception of reading (Kaiser Family Foundation, 2010).

For teenagers, personal computers and other technologies that provide access to the Internet are a source of entertainment and communication; they are devices to download "free" movies and "free" music and watch "free" television shows. Such ease of access does not foster much consideration as to copyright or ownership of artistic material. While previous crackdowns by the music industry (e.g., the lawsuits brought against individuals by the RIAA) significantly altered the landscape of downloaded music (less free, more paid), it did not alter the attitudes. Instead, it seems that while the industry was focused on audio, the youth culture had already moved on to video. The ease with which one can find a multitude of copywritten videos on shared video sites such as YouTube (www.youtube.com) points to this shift.

The problem is that there exists a deeply ingrained sensibility that if it is on the Net, it is free:

> [T]he convenience and anonymity of file sharing have made it a remarkably guilt-free form of plunder. In effect, the masses of Americans have joined the previously small chorus of hard-core hackers in chanting the credo "Information wants to be free." (Terrell and Rosen, 2003: 43)

It is not surprising that this credo has been embraced. The Internet has provided more opportunities for sharing, copying, and customizing. Along with the ease of downloading materials, copying and pasting, and sharing, open source software, freeware, and shareware have always been a part of these students' lives. Add to this mix the fact that our students have grown up gathering most of their information exclusively from the web. It therefore becomes a daunting task for educators to help their students to differentiate between the "infotainment" and commercial purposes of the web that they utilize daily and the scholarly resources that they are expected to utilize and utilize correctly.

Gloria J. Leckie (Graduate School of Library and Information Science, University of Western Ontario) did an analysis of the undergraduate research process. She concluded that undergraduates gather information for college-level research papers according to the strategies that they used for previous projects and papers. This includes using public libraries and asking family and friends for information. "They are also likely to use whatever sources are most familiar . . . even if they are not appropriate" (Leckie, 1996: 204). Among those familiar resources are the Internet sites and web search engines that students are accustomed to using on a day-to-day basis. This fact is supported by the results from a Project Information Literacy Progress Report on how students seek information. The findings are that almost all of the students surveyed go to Google for course-related research and to Google and Wikipedia for everyday life research (Head and Eisenberg, 2009).

By the time they reach college, most undergraduates have spent a lot of time surfing the web and consider themselves to be computer savvy. For the most part, this is true. As freshmen, they arrive with many skills essential for computer literacy: a facility for keyboarding; a familiarity with a number of software packages; knowledge of chat software and instant messaging; and a background experience in navigating the World Wide Web. However, skill at using personal computers and familiarity with searching the Internet do not equate with research skills or knowledge of standard research practices. This differentiation of skills should be part of our educational objective in teaching students about the research process.

Word Processing and Scholarly Writing

In addition to a familiarity with Internet searching, Gen M has grown up using word processing software to write their research papers. Word processing software has become a ubiquitous office tool, and many of us take it for granted. There is a school of thought that holds that the act of word processing, including the software tools it utilizes and the ease with which the words appear on the screen, is influencing the way that we as a society think and write. Scholars from various fields (e.g., psychology, linguistics, and literary criticism) are concerned with this question (Norris, 1989: 277).

Prolific author Stephen King has also commented on the phenomenon of the relationship of writing tool to writing style. King wrote his early best-sellers on a typewriter, moved to word processing, and then reverted to writing in longhand after his near-fatal accident in 1999. He stated, in an interview, that writing on a computer is like ice skating and writing in longhand is like swimming. In the former you glide across the surface, and in the latter you are totally immersed in the process (Baker, 2003).

Observations from librarians and educators show that undergraduate students will usually begin a research project by browsing the Internet for source material on a topic, often searching Google and Wikipedia. They will next cut and paste the material that they need for their paper into the document on which they are working. It is in the subsequent steps, reworking the material into their own words, using quotations for exact quotes, and citing the material that is not their original intellectual property, where students typically run into problems. The act of cutting and pasting material from one source to another is a wonderful tool, but it is one that needs to be used with caution. The ease with which a writer can physically transfer the written word is offset by the burden of keeping good records of what came from where and what needs to be properly credited. Goodwin (2002) noted, in her apologia, that she lost track of her source material in her final book manuscript through the process of cutting and pasting from her notes. Once again, it is of note that if a professional writer can get into trouble via technology, how much more vulnerable to mistakes is the student researcher?

Plagiarism and Popular Culture

For educators and students to have a shared value about what constitutes plagiarism, one must also assume a shared understanding as to what constitutes an individual's right to ownership to an intellectual or an artistic concept. Social critics are positing that there has been a generational shift of attitude with regard to the ownership of ideas. First, there is an emerging construct that all information and ideas are data and should flow freely in the intellectual community (Anestopoulou, 2001). Second, in popular culture there is an increasing tendency to reference or "sample" previous works, be they musical, written, or visual. Allusion to other cultural phenomena, or quotationalism, has been called "the dominant trend of thought of the twentieth century" (Matheson, 2001: 123). Referencing, or sampling, has become so prevalent that it is hard to tell where homage stops and rip-off starts.

One area where referencing is prominent and has gained a lot of media attention is in popular music, most particularly with hip-hop artists. While hip-hop has a complex history, it is safe to say that it erupted on the popular scene in the mid-1970s and started to gain real prominence in the mid-1980s. The trajectory of hip-hop music is roughly analogous to that of the rise of the PC. Hip-hop culture is now couture, and it deeply influences all popular media, including film, music videos, and literature. Sampling music, a staple of hip-hop DJs, has been heavily influenced by technology. As the technology got better the sampling became easier to do and utilized more by artists. Of the current popular music scene, philosophy scholar Carl Matheson (2001: 118) writes: "The musical world is a hodge-podge of quotations of styles where often the original music being quoted is simply sampled and re-processed." Some artists give proper credit (and royalties) to the creator of the material that is sampled. Other artists consider sampling to be a political statement—one that is both in defiance of a corporate, capitalist culture and a direct, cultural descendent of the oral traditions of the African diasporic tradition (Bartlett, 1994).

Evidence of referencing, quotationalism, or plagiarism (depending on your philosophical perspective) can be found in all aspects of popular culture, not just music. Couturier Nicolas Ghesquiere of the House of Balenciaga recently admitted to "borrowing" designs from a San Francisco designer, Kaisik Wong, for his spring collection for 2002. Wong, who died in 1990, was little known but had a cult following that included Ghesquiere. The similarity was noted in the March 27, 2002, "Chic Happens" column on the fashion website Hintmag. com. When interviewed about the similarities, Ghesquiere freely admitted to "referencing" Wong; however, he gave no credit—either verbal or written—to Wong as the source of his inspiration when the collection debuted. In an article in the *New York Times*, fashion writer Cathy Horyn posed the question as to whether copying another's work is plagiarism or just part of the creative process. Horyn quotes Metropolitan Museum of Art costume curator Harold Koda regarding Ghesquiere's designs:

> I think that it is a phase of our time. Part of it is post-Warhol. It's just rummaging through extant material culture and juxtaposing it with other things to create something different. Postmodernism has really pervaded our culture. (Horyn, 2002: B10)

As with costume designers, furniture designers often "reference" others in the creative process, and there is little protection or support for the original designer (Chu, 2010).

This sampling and referencing continues to be an important part of today's culture. Web 2.0 has allowed for easier creation, sharing, and modification of original material. The rise of social media has further blurred the lines of ownership with the ease in which items can be shared and distributed. While there is a lot of copywritten material illegally shared on the video-sharing site YouTube, there is also an abundance of original content. In many cases, other users are encouraged to take the original material, modify it, and re-post it. The gaming industry has begun to acknowledge the creativity of gamers and is beginning to embrace and allow modifications, or "mods," of their games. This hacking of the games is something that has been going on since the early 1980s but is now being recognized as a way to harness the power and creativity of the user to improve the game (Postigo, 2007).

Today's students have grown up with "free" content, and now they are being encouraged to make that free content their own. The lines between homage and rip-off are increasingly fuzzy in a culture of parody and quotationalism. Today's students are surrounded by parody; from something as trivial as an amazon.com review of a gallon of milk that parodies Edgar Allan Poe's *The Raven* (www.amazon.com/review/RXXPVOUH9NLL3) to entire movies based on parody, such as the *Scary Movie* series, that make a habit of spoofing the previous year's most infamous movie scenes. The popular show *The Simpsons* recently celebrated its twentieth anniversary, making it older than today's college freshmen. Relying heavily on allusion for humor, it references dozens of movies, novels, and television shows often so quickly that it is difficult to catch all the references in one sitting. Matheson (2001) notes that in just one *Simpsons* episode, "A Streetcar Named Marge," the writers managed to squeeze in visual and verbal references to a Tennessee Williams play, Ayn Rand's *Fountainhead*, the movie *The Great Escape*, and Hitchcock's *The Birds*. Matheson (2001: 119) finds the multitudinous use of references, this "hyper-irony," culturally significant: "I think that, given a crisis of authority, hyper-ironism is the most suitable form of comedy." Deconstructionist humor for a deconstructed world.

In watching media like *The Simpsons*, it becomes apparent that today's students are being introduced to cultural allusions for the first time often in parody or remake. Hollywood studies continue to pump out remakes of classics and even nonclassics. The popular videogame Guitar Hero, while lauded for introducing younger generations to older music, originally provided only remakes (some poorly done) of the original songs. The sheer number of parodies available through YouTube videos, blog posts, and other social media make it a very real conclusion that some people are being exposed to even recent cultural allusions first through parody and then the original.

The fact that students are being introduced to concepts and ideas in ways other than through original is significant when it comes to teaching students about plagiarism. Educators assume a common cultural understanding that is decreasing with each new batch of freshmen. Philosophers and pop-critics William Irwin and Lombardo (2001: 87) write: "Cultural literacy is essential for successful communication and comprehension as is clear in condensing allusions."

If a phrase, an idea, or another item of intellectual property has imbedded itself deeply into pop culture, students might be totally unaware of its origin or the fact that it needs to be referenced in a scholarly work. In an increasingly hip and ironic world, students are becoming further removed from cultural source material. Educators need to be aware of their own assumptions and reference points and how these differ from the students'. Good scholarship requires good work ethics, a working knowledge of accepted procedures, and the ability to recognize and keep track of the origins of numerous pieces of information. These can be taught. Cultural, technological, and philosophical touchstones of educators may be very different from those of the students. Still, they can be effectively communicated if approached with an open mind, sensitivity, and a respect for the students' differing background knowledge and experiences.

Thoughts, Hopes, and Conclusions

While many new technologies have been held accountable for the rise in plagiarism, they can also be used as tools to combat plagiarism. There are websites where students and teachers can check documents for instances of plagiarism. Web 2.0 citation tools provide students and scholars alike with easy ways to track their sources and generate bibliographies. New technologies allow for better tutorials, more engaging education, and the ability to share these with other educators and students.

It is obvious that plagiarism is a problem that continues to grow. It is apparent to educators that previous methods have not been as effective as hoped. The fear of being caught plagiarizing is not a large enough deterrent. Breaking the rules seems to have become passé for Gen M. There is a stronger need for educators to explain why plagiarism is wrong and who it hurts. Recent findings concur, showing a change in student behavior regarding plagiarism after educational tutorials (Jaschik, 2009). Teaching students about the importance of ownership will help more students gain that internal sense that plagiarism is unfair to the original author that was found to be lacking (Power, 2009).

This education along with the increased ability of students to post their own original content should lead to a better understanding of plagiarism. The Internet provides everyone a forum in which to express their creativity through words, music, video, and pictures. The students of today are themselves contributing to the vast amount of information available on the Internet. Perhaps as they see their ideas, pictures, and words being shared and distributed without attribution or permission for modification, they will form a better understanding of the importance of citing. It is encouraging to see examples on social networking sites were plagiarism is not tolerated and the offender is often humiliated or reprimanded by other users (Mapes, 2009). While fear of punishment by a school may not be as strong a deterrent as desired, fear of humiliation among peers on social networking sites might. It is hoped that students will realize the importance of attribution as they themselves become the people who might possibly be plagiarized.

References

Academy of Achievement. 2003. "Doris Kearns Goodwin: Biography." Available: www.achievement.org/autodoc/page/goo0bio-1 (accessed January 29, 2010).

Anestopoulou, Maria. 2001. "Challenging Intellectual Property Law in the Internet: An Overview of the Legal Implications of the MP3 Technology." *Information & Communications Technology Law* 10, no. 3 (October): 319–337.

Baker, Dorie. 2003. "Best-Selling Author Stephen King Says 'Everyday Life' Inspires Him." *Yale Bulletin and Calendar* 31 no. 28 (May 2). Available: www.yale.edu/opa/arc-ybc/v31.n28/story4.html (accessed January 29, 2010).

Bartlett, Andrew. 1994. "Airshafts, Loudspeakers, and the Hip-hop Sample: Contexts and African American Musical Aesthetics." *African American Review* 28, no. 4 (Winter): 639–642.

Bartlett, Thomas. 2009a. "2 Universities' Plagiarism Policies Look a Lot Alike." *Chronicle of Higher Education* (January 28). Available: chronicle.com/article/2-Universities-Plagiarism-/1486 (accessed January 27, 2010).

———. 2009b. "Cheating Goes Global as Essay Mills Multiply." *Chronicle of Higher Education* 55, no. 28 (March 20): A1–A25.

Chu, Jeff. 2010. "A Modern Mess." *Fast Company* (December 2009/January 2010): 92–97.

Cvetkovic, Vibiana Bowman, and Robert J. Lackie, eds. 2009. *Teaching Generation M: A Handbook for Librarians and Educators.* New York: Neal-Schuman.

Goodwin, Doris Kearns. 2002. "How I Caused That Story." *Time* 59, no. 5 (February 4): 69.

Greenberg, David. 2008. "Friends, Romans, Countrymen, Lend Me Your Speech." *The New York Times* (February 28): WK.

Head, Alison J., and Michael B. Eisenberg. 2009. "How College Students Seek Information in the Digital Age." Project Information Literacy Report (December 1). Available: projectinfolit.org/pdfs/PIL_Fall2009_Year1 Report_12_2009.pdf (accessed January 28, 2010).

Horyn, Cathy. 2002. "Is Copying Really Part of the Creative Process?" *The New York Times* (April 2): B10.

Hoyt, Clark. 2009. "The Writers Make News. Unfortunately." *The New York Times* (May 24): WK.

Irwin, William, and J.R. Lombardo. 2001. "*The Simpsons* and Allusion: 'Worst Essay Ever!'" in *The Simpsons and Philosophy: The D'oh! of Homer* (pp. 81–92), edited by William Irwin, Mark T. Conrad, and Aeon J. Skoble. Chicago: Open Court.

Jackson, Pamela A. 2006. "Plagiarism Instruction Online: Assessing Undergraduate Students' Ability to Avoid Plagiarism." *College and Research Libraries* 67, no. 5 (September): 418–428.

Jaschik, Scott. 2009. "Plagiarism Preventing Without Fear." *Inside Higher Ed Blog* (January 26). Available: insidehighered.com/news/2010/01/26/plagiarize (accessed January 28, 2010).

Kaiser Family Foundation. 2010. "Generation M2: Media in the Lives of 8- to 18-Year-Olds" (January 20). Available: www.kff.org/entmedia/mh012010 pkg.cfm (accessed January 28, 2010).

Keith-Speigel, Patricia, Barbara G. Tabachnick, Bernard E. Whitley, and Jennifer Washburn. 1998. "Why Professors Ignore Cheating: Opinions of a National Sample of Psychology Instructors." *Ethics and Behavior* 8, no. 3: 215–227.

Leckie, Gloria J. 1996. "Desperately Seeking Citations: Uncovering Faculty Assumptions about the Undergraduate Research Process." *Journal of Academic Librarianship* 22, no. 3: 201–208.

Long, Major Dale J. 2003. "A Brief History of Personal Computing, Part 1." Available: www.chips.navy.mil/archives/02_summer/authors/index2_files/ briefhistory.htm (accessed January 28, 2010).

Mangan, Katherine. 2009. "Small University Accuses Stanford U. of Cribbing Idea for New Artificial Knee." *Chronicle of Higher Education* 56, no. 15 (December 15): A9–A10.

Mapes, Diane. 2009. "Net's Plagiarism 'Cops' Are on Patrol." msnbc.com (September 10). Available: www.msnbc.msn.com/id/32657885/ns/ technology_and_science-tech_and_gadgets (accessed January 29, 2010).

Matheson, Carl. 2001. "The Simpsons, Hyper-irony, and the Meaning of Life," in *The Simpsons and Philosophy: The D'oh! of Homer* (pp. 108–125), edited by William Irwin, Mark T. Conrad, and Aeon J. Skoble. Chicago: Open Court.

McGrath, Charles. 2009. "Plagiarism: Everybody into the Pool." *The New York Times* (January 7): 4A.

Norris, Christopher. 1989. "Review Essay—'Electric Language: A Philosophical Study of Word Processing by Michael Heim.'" *Comparative Literature* 41, no. 3 (Summer): 270–277.

Petress, Kenneth. 2003. "Academic Dishonesty: A Plague on Our Profession." *Education* 123, no. 3 (Spring): 624–627.

Plagiarism.org. 2010a. *Facts about Plagiarism.* Available: www.plagiarism.org/plag_facts.html (accessed January 7, 2010).

———. 2010b. *Plagiarism and the Internet.* Available: www.plagiarism.org/plag_article_plagiarism_and_the_Internet.html (accessed January 7, 2010).

Postigo, Hector. 2007. "Of Mods and Modders: Chasing Down the Value of Fan-Based Digital Game Modifications." *Games and Culture* 2, no. 4 (October): 300–313.

Power, Lori G. 2009. "University Students' Perceptions of Plagiarism." *The Journal of Higher Education* 80, no. 6 (November/December): 643:662.

Sohn, Emily. 2001. "The Young and the Virtueless." *U.S. News & World Report* 130, no. 20 (May 21): 51.

Terrell, Kenneth, and Seth Rosen. 2003. "A Nation of Pirates." *U.S. News & World Report* 135, no. 1 (July 14): 40–45.

Tolson, Jay. 2002. "Whose Own Words?" *U.S. News & World Report* 132, no. 2 (January 21): 52.

U.S. Census Bureau. 2001. "Children's Access to Home Computer and Use of the Internet at Home: 2000." Series P23-107. Available: www.census.gov/prod/2001pubs/p23-207.pdf (accessed January 15, 2010).

———. 2007. "2007 Internet and Computer Use Supplement to the Current Population Survey." Available: census.gov/population/www/socdemo/computer/2007.html (accessed January 15, 2010).

Vaidhyanathan, Siva. 2009. "Anderson's Wiki-versy." *Publishers Weekly* 256, no. 26 (June 29): 132.

Varga, George. 2009. "The Song Remains the Same: Rock Artists Find It's a Fine Line between Borrowing and Stealing." *The San Diego Union-Tribune* (July 12): Final edition.

The Onus of Originality: Creativity and Accomplishment in a Digital and Competitive Age

Laura B. Spencer

Introduction: Themes and Settings

This chapter is not about ethics. It will not put forward a single rule regulating scholarly behavior in the presence of scholarly work. While a proscribed behavior, such as plagiarism, is easy to engage in, rules prohibiting it are not in themselves typically sufficient to stop the behavior. A better approach is to create conditions under which the proscribed behavior makes no sense and confers no benefit. What conditions need to exist in order for plagiarism to make no sense? This chapter considers four elements present in conditions that encourage intellectual honesty: originality, imitation, expertise, and engagement. Three of these are examined in real-world environments: imitation in business, expertise in science, and engagement in the arts. The impetus for looking beyond academia was to see if there are problems or issues out in the world that parallel or resemble the problem of plagiarism in the educational setting and if any efforts to solve or manage those problems can be adapted for or applied in the classroom.

The opening section, "Originality and Imitation," introduces the tense, paradoxical, and closely bound relationship that these two concepts have with each other. The next section, "Copycat Commerce," explores that relationship as it plays out on retailers' display shelves. The third section, "Of Pilots and Plagiarists," reports on what researchers in aviation have learned about mitigating the effects of overdependence on technology. The last section, "Research Remixes," drawing on contemporary sound recording techniques, proposes an unusual method to promote students' engagement with their subject matter.

There are many degrees of plagiarism, from the most egregious kinds such as outright purchasing of term papers to minor infractions such as omitting data in a footnote. The plagiarism focused on in this chapter is of the moderately egregious kind, such as cutting and pasting of large chunks of text without attribution and then inserting them into a paper to which the student signs his or her own name. This particular method of plagiarism, while clearly wrong in many educators' minds, has intriguing parallels in the aforementioned worlds of business and the arts. Examining these parallels allows us to think anew and differently about what plagiarism is and does.

Originality and Imitation: A Difficult but Lasting Relationship

What is originality? At this late date, can there be any such thing? It is written that "there is nothing new under the sun" (Ecclesiastes 1:9, Revised Standard Version). An attentive student and careful reader aware of the sweep of history might be inclined to agree. Problems recur and patterns repeat. Societies in every era struggle with allocations of power and wealth; individuals in every age express love and experience loss. While the locus of power and sources of wealth might bounce among government, business, and private individuals, the location of death move from home to hospital to hospice, and expressions of love vary in tone and by degrees of openness, the basic contours, problems, and pleasures of human society remain consistent over time. In one sense, then, Ecclesiastes is right; yet the changes over time are substantial, profound, transformative. The follower of scientific or technological developments can observe that new things arrive under the sun all the time, from the combustion engine to the microchip. While the scientific principles behind such inventions might have been discovered in ancient Rome or seventeenth-century Europe, the application of those principles, combined with the discovery of new ones, bring about inventions that clearly are new. Originality in science, at least, is most certainly possible; it would be absurd to suggest it is not, even while observing that innovations owe a debt to previous work. The new and familiar, the original and the derivative, and the innovative and traditional are closely bound together. It appears that we cannot have the one without the other. In his *Stolen Words*, Thomas Mallon (1989: 24) writes: "Originality—not just innocence of plagiarism but the making of something really and truly new—set itself down as a cardinal literary virtue sometime in the middle of the eighteenth century and has never since gotten up."

Originality, as newness unfettered by tradition, is an idea but a few centuries old. The idea that tradition is nothing to escape from, but rather something to embrace and follow, is a good bit older. An undergraduate can readily perceive that the notion of the "cardinal literary virtue" of newness is at odds with her own sense of the difficulty in achieving that newness. Assigned readings in philosophy and literature can reinforce any doubts that she, or anybody else, could add anything new and worthwhile. She is not alone in this doubt. Indeed, she has much company—from the author of Ecclesiastes in the third century BC to Samuel Johnson in the eighteenth century AD. As Thomas L. Jeffers (2002: 59), Associate Professor of English at Marquette University, puts it: "There is something annoyingly unoriginal about harping on the impossibility of originality."

Originality may be possible, but it is certainly paradoxical. A writer must blend the familiar with the new; the challenge and the difficulty are in how this blend is accomplished. Thomas McFarland (1985: 31) observed in his *Originality and Imagination* that this paradox "stems from the larger paradox of human existence" in which "our social natures on the one hand and our individual natures on the other" are ever in conflict. An individual is at once an autonomous self and a member of a community. The autonomous selfhood and the community membership exist in tension with one another, in a paradoxical and complementary relationship. At any given time, within a single society, one will be stronger or more ascendant than the other. The ascendancy of the one is not permanent. The struggle between the two, however, is. "Neither individuality nor communality can be felt without the other, although each strains against its complement" (McFarland, 1985: 1). As our social and individual natures strain against each other, while yet remaining bound together, so in a similar manner do the original and derivative aspects of our work (e.g., written papers) struggle together. They must both exist, in all their tension and paradox. "Any attempt to resolve the paradox is unsuccessful" (McFarland, 1985: 1). The trouble comes when we do not agree on how best to balance the two.

That disagreeing "we" can be society as a whole, fighting over how to balance personal autonomy with communal responsibility, or simply a teacher and student discussing how well the latter wrote her paper. Did the student fail to credit her sources? Did she dutifully credit her sources but relied on them too heavily, thus drowning out her own voice or masking the fact that she hasn't developed one yet? Relying overmuch on sources might or might not be plagiarism, but it certainly can be a sign of poor writing or insufficient thinking. Our cardinal rule requires that student writers put matters in their own words. We want our students to have thought through what they've read so that when they write about it, they understand the material enough to use words that come more or less naturally to them, to use their own unique voice.

This is the heart of the matter: to have read and thought and digested well enough and carefully enough to have made the material enough your own to say it your way yet simultaneously and scrupulously to maintain the distinction between "yours" and "theirs." This creates a tense paradox. Keeping that distinction is very difficult for beginners whose own voices are not yet well-developed. It takes time and practice to strike the right balance. In a culture that values speed and efficiency as much as ours does, taking one's time is often punished. Even an educator who advocates the taking of time has only 16 weeks in which to inculcate this value.

I am not certain that a clear, fat, and bright line can always and easily be drawn between acceptable borrowing and unacceptable theft or between original and derivative work. My view of the territory between "original" and "derivative" is that they are two areas on a continuum, and it is not always clear when one bleeds into the other. Incorporation of properly credited sources into one's own work can certainly be indulged in overmuch, but determining when quantities exceed acceptable limits is not a simple, straightforward calculation of a constant, nonnegotiable value. The next section explores an environment where the original and the derivative mingle and rub elbows and asks us to think about the implications of that mingling.

Copycat Commerce: Trade Dress, Imitation, and Acknowledgment

The plagiarism that angers us most, I suspect, is when the writer deliberately intends to deceive. Our society values transparency and honesty. Readers, like consumers, do not like to be fooled by appearances. In the marketplace, one way to distinguish one's company's goods from another is with distinctive trademarks and a distinctive packaging, which is called "trade dress." Trade dress is defined as "a product's physical appearance, including its size, shape, color, design, and texture"; and it can "also refer to the manner in which a product is packaged, wrapped, labeled, presented, promoted, or advertised" (Lehman and Phelps, 2005: 66–67).

Thou shalt not deceive—or confuse—thy customer base. The purpose of trademarks, trade dress, and logos is to distinguish the product from a competitor's—to brand it—so that customers immediately think of a particular product when they see a particular label. Companies are very aware of the value of brand recognition and work to distinguish their brands from their competitors. An exception to this practice appears to occur in the packaging of over-the-counter (OTC) store brand drugs.

CVS Pharmacy is a chain store that sells prescription drugs, OTC medicines, and health-care products such as vitamins and first-aid supplies. At CVS, the store brand OTC drugs are placed directly beside a national brand. The store brand product is referred to as an "equivalent" of the national brand and is usually significantly cheaper. The list of ingredients in both tends to be very similar, and the active ingredients are often identical in both kind and amount. The package design of the equivalent usually bears a strong resemblance to the national brand, particularly in its use of color. A national brand cough syrup, Whitehall-Robins' Robitussin CF, for example, is packaged in a white, green, and pink box. CVS's Tussin CF is likewise packaged in a white, green, and pink box.

In 2003, there were horizontal white pinstripes in the green and pink areas of the Robitussin but not in the store brand equivalent. The green and pink areas were square or rectangular on the Robitussin. On CVS's, those areas had a wavy, rather than straight, top edge. The labels on several other CVS store brand OTC products, from plastic bandages to pain relievers, usually had that wavy top edge, thus creating a characteristic CVS trade dress. That wavy top edge remains on their packages for many of their products in 2009. CVS distinguished its packaging in other ways. For instance, plastic bandages from Johnson and Johnson were pictured horizontally, against a background of dark blue and light blue. CVS plastic bandages were displayed vertically, against a hazy blue background (with wavy top edge) with reddish elements. In 2009, not much has changed with this product's package design. Johnson &

Johnson's bandages are still displaying horizontally, while CVS's are displaying vertically. Both have simplified their background colors: Johnson & Johnson uses a dark blue background, while CVS uses a medium blue, and has dispensed with the reddish elements. Are their package designs different enough, or is CVS "plagiarizing"?

This practice of similar trade dress is a common one and not limited to CVS. Most major supermarket and drugstore chains have store brand products. The names and packaging of these products frequently mimic the names and packaging of a well-known brand. When the major brand finds the similarity too close, suits are filed and changes are made. A manufacturer and packager of many store brand OTC pharmaceuticals, including CVS's, is Michigan-based Perrigo Co. Perrigo has been the subject of several suits. Schering-Plough, a maker of allergy tablets, nasal spray, and other products, sued Perrigo in federal court in 1984, alleging that Perrigo's packaging was "confusingly similar" to Schering-Plough's. It wanted Perrigo to stop, and it sued for "triple damages, recovery of Perrigo's profit from those products' sales and legal fees and expenses" (*Wall Street Journal*, 1984). Perrigo agreed to stop and settled with Schering-Plough for $125,000 (*Wall Street Journal*, 1985). On the topic of trade dress, Perrigo's chairman and CEO, Michael J. Jandernoa, stated that: "the challenge is not getting too close, to where you're copying the packaging, which raises the legal issue of trade dress . . . our focus . . . is on being similar but not being the same" (Stern, 1993).

While it does not appear that Whitehall-Robins has filed suit against Perrigo, the packaging for both products has changed significantly from 2003. While the CVS packaging continues to echo Whitehall-Robins', the difference between them is greater in 2009 than it was in 2003. The color schemes for both continue to be white, green, and pink. The green background behind the product name in the CVS Tussin CF has, again, the wavy top edge characteristic of many CVS store brand products. Robitussin has done away with pinstripes and has uncoupled the CF from the product name; the name Robitussin is in white print on a black background, while the CF is about an inch lower in pink print on a white background. CVS continues to call its product Tussin CF. On the front of the package, each brand enumerates the symptoms its product relieves. While the symptoms on their lists are nearly identical, Robitussin lists them in white print on pink ovals on a green background. Tussin CF, by contrast, provides a bulleted list in black print on a white background. The increased difference is intriguing, though it doesn't appear to extend to other CVS products, such as the plastic bandages mentioned earlier.

This lengthy discussion of package design does not intend to cast aspersions on Perrigo or similar companies. The practice of creating a similar trade dress for a lesser known product sheds a light on the issue of deliberate plagiarism by students. Often, the store brand packaging explicitly instructs the consumer to compare the product inside with the national brand of which it is an equivalent. In so doing, the store brand equivalent makes it clear that it is not the national brand, but it is similar to it. Imitation is the sincerest form of flattery; perhaps it is also the sincerest form of commerce. At the very least, it is a shrewd form of retailing: imitate a national brand's packaging closely enough to catch the consumer's eye, but not so closely as to incur the producer's wrath.

How does that sit with educators who strive to inculcate the virtues of originality and ownership of one's work in their students? Is a store brand equivalent's close imitation of a national brand's package design too much like a student's use of a well-known scholar's entire framework of thought in a paper in which he footnotes only a single quote from the source? Does the student plagiarist understand that he takes more than exact words but also ideas and carefully researched trains of thought? If educators agree that "putting it in your own words" is not enough when acknowledgment needs to be made for adopting a train of thought or a framework of understanding, what do we make of the relatively peaceful coexistence of national brand products and their store brand equivalents as they sit beside each other on retailers' shelves?

The close resemblance of store brand to national brand packaging can serve to remind us that much of good scholarship is derived from following the established procedures and authoritative literature—including frameworks and trains of thought—of a particular discipline. Laboratory science students demonstrate good technique by measuring characteristics of a metal and getting the same results as the experts have established to be correct. Humanities students demonstrate familiarity with material by writing about it in such a way as to make it obvious that they have done a close reading of the material. They need to be ready to demonstrate that they have really read it for style and meaning and not just passed their eyes over the pages or dragged their mouse over the text to copy and paste it into their own paper. This familiarity is accomplished in part by citing or quoting the material, of course, and also by more or less restating it—freshly and in their own words. Here is a troublesome, paradoxical area. An undergraduate need not be expected to break new ground in the discipline, because he is too inexperienced, but neither is he permitted to merely parrot the authorities in the field.

The undergraduate, like the rest of us, must inhabit a region that combines the old with the new, the derivative with the original. Negotiating the terrain requires acknowledging the authorities in the field without being subservient to them. Subservience in this instance would be repeating mindlessly what they wrote. The plagiaristic technique of cutting and pasting huge chunks of text without attribution is, ironically enough, a kind of subservience. Students don't see it in these terms; to them this technique of quickly assembling papers is a kind of freedom. But to writers in the English Renaissance, copying was viewed as slavish and subservient, and they frowned upon it (White, [1935] 1965). The modern day equivalent, cutting and pasting, is frowned upon as well.

Yet, a good student cannot defiantly ignore the authorities in his field. To present a well-informed argument, a student needs authoritative source materials. He cannot rely solely on his own knowledge to write his term paper, even if his conclusions jibe with the established authorities in the field. He must consult and cite them, at the very least to support his own views. This can be exasperating to the bright, impatient student, who feels dragged down by what feels like petty pedantry. Our culture does not suffer authorities gladly;

our egalitarianism often encourages us to doubt "they" know more than "we" do about any but the most technical of subjects. Our drive to focus on "results" makes us impatient with mere "process." These cultural tendencies are at odds with the classroom requirements for proper research and writing methods.

The successful writer will be neither wholly slave nor wholly rebel, but draw upon authorities as needed for support or insight. Perhaps she will present them in a fresh way, or find a new relevance, or come up with a new or intelligent critique. She will not escape the paradox of needing to be at once both familiar and new. If she lives in the paradox long enough, she has a better chance than her plagiarizing classmate to engage with her subject matter and develop expertise in handling it. The next two sections explore how the relationship between people and technology can impact the development of that expertise and engagement.

Of Pilots and Plagiarists: When Technology Undercuts Expertise

What do student plagiarists and commercial airline pilots have in common? Such a question might sound absurd and perhaps offensive. How could an experienced, well-trained pilot utilizing carefully designed autopilot or flight deck technology to fly a plane safely have anything whatsoever in common with a college student inappropriately exploiting electronic databases and word processing software to assemble a plagiarized paper? The answer comes from a field called *human factors research*. Human factors research explores how humans interact with technology, and it examines whether the design of automated computer or machine technology has taken into account human perception, cognition, and behavior (Graves and Jones, 2003). Studies of automated systems in aviation have uncovered problems that can adversely affect the skills of the pilot and the safety of the flight. The findings provide intriguing parallels to student–database interactions that result in plagiarized papers. Perhaps the analysis and suggested solutions to the problems in aviation will offer a fresh way for educators to think about how to reduce the incidents of plagiarism.

Technology is supposed to help people do a better job, not cause them to do a worse job. Exasperated office workers suffering through a computer upgrade, however, know all too well that automation can cause problems and decrease productivity as well as solve problems and enhance productivity. Even when the bugs and glitches are minor and bearable, it's clear enough that the best expert system, like the best human expert, isn't accurate 100 percent of the time. Setting up a simulator study in which flight deck automation was designed to be unreliable, human factors researchers discovered that pilots' performance suffered more when the automation offered bad decision advice than when it merely offered bad data (Sarter and Schroeder, 2001; Parasuraman and Wickens, 2008). Put another way, the pilots were in worse shape when they let the computer do their thinking for them than when they let it do their fact gathering for them—even when the facts were wrong. Pilots—or any other human operator utilizing the decision-making features of automation—risk a number of things when they rely too heavily on this technology; two of them are automation complacency and skill degradation. In automation complacency, the human operator pays inadequate attention to how well the automation is performing its job. She is placing more trust in the automation than is warranted. When the automation makes decisions for the human operator over a long period of time, it limits the opportunities she has to improve or maintain her own skills. Given enough time, her skills will degrade. This skill degradation risks putting her in a weak position when the system fails. She must then perform the work manually, when she is out of practice (Parasuraman, 2000).

It turns out that an excellent remedy for the problems of complacency and skill degradation is to "insert periods of manual task performance after a long period of automation and then return to automation" (Parasuraman and Riley, 1997: 242). Performance thereby improves. While there might be a short-term reduction in efficiency, it pays off in the longer term performance of the personnel in charge of monitoring system performance. Can we adapt this solution—and its rationale—to the problem of student plagiarism? Can we frame the problem of plagiarism as less of an ethical lapse to be prevented or punished and more as a result of the student placing too much trust in an expert system that he needs instead to monitor and understand—and, in time, critique and improve upon? Granted, the electronic databases that provide full-text scholarly articles aren't, strictly speaking, expert systems; but when student plagiarists commandeer large chunks of text from them, they are using them as if they were. They consequently run similar risks of complacency and poor performance as the pilots in the simulator study ran when they relied on the decision-making capabilities of faulty software. Might the observation that plagiarism is an example of naïve trust get the attention of students who, in all likelihood (and possibly even accurately), perceive themselves as savvy and sophisticated people? Would the observation that plagiarism denies the student the opportunity to interact effectively with an expert system pique the interest of those eager to make their mark in the world?

What would "insert periods of manual task performance" mean in this setting? Surely it would not mean to return to the onerous act of writing out papers in longhand; that would be roughly comparable to recommending that pilots flap their arms periodically to keep the aircraft aloft. Nor could it mean refraining from accessing research articles in electronic form. More and more important scholarly research is accessible only in electronic form. It would be an unreasonable burden on the students and harmful to their education to deny access to the databases. But student plagiarists are relying on the databases and word processing software too heavily and uncritically. In human factors terms, they are engaging in automation complacency, which needs to be addressed and corrected. If we think of plagiarism as an automated process whose basic steps include accessing articles in databases, transferring chunks of data from them to a word processing file, and then sending that file to the professor, we can then argue that the student plagiarist is failing to sufficiently oversee or monitor the process, by trusting overmuch in the automation.

If we can't completely turn off the automated process, then we will need to interrupt or break the process to force the student to make a more careful review of the material. The means to achieve this could be as simple as having the instructor review notes, outlines, and drafts of student papers or to breaking out the blue books. In a blue book, written in real time with real ink on real paper, the only cutting and pasting of text a student can do is with material already inside her head. To those who find blue books and printouts tired, quaint, passé, or worse, it will be helpful to bear in mind that human factors researchers understand that "conditions exist for which the optimal choice is *not* to use the automation" (Parasuraman and Riley, 1997: 236; italics in the original). Even though the technology exists to automate a task or process, there are times when it is best not to employ it. One such time is when technology undercuts expertise.

The appealing part of drawing on the findings in human factors research to shed light on how incidents of plagiarism might be reduced is in how the problems of automation complacency and skill degradation are not perceived primarily as flaws in the character or lapses in the ethics of the pilots. The problems grow out of the *nature of the relationship* between the pilots and the technology they use in the cockpit. The solutions, then, will likewise focus on the relationship between students and the technology they use to perform their jobs of reading, writing, thinking, and learning. While this section has considered the value of disengaging periodically with the technology for the sake of developing expertise, the next section will take a different tack. It will ask if engaging with the technology—even to the extent of indulging in what could be perceived as a shady practice—could confer the benefit of more engagement with subject matter.

Research Remixes: Can Technology Enhance Engagement?

Recording artists and DJs live the paradox of innovation and tradition when they engage in the practice known as sampling, "a technique of extracting a recorded passage from a previous musical work and inserting that passage into a new recording" ("Will Case Change Law on Sampling?" 2002). It's roughly comparable to a block quote in a scholarly article. Why does a writer, whether student or professional, quote a source in the first place? She quotes because it supports her argument, because the quotation sheds light or is phrased superbly, or because the source is an established authority with a stellar reputation. Sections of musical pieces are sampled for comparable reasons. With sampling, authority is about good music rather than solid scholarship. It's about the listener being moved rather than the reader being enlightened. Christopher "DJ Premier" Martin describes sampling as "repeating a part of a record that grabs you. Sampling is all about placement, where it emotionally grabs you and makes your head nod" (Mitchell, 2000). The sampled piece lends an emotional power to the new recording just as a well-chosen quote lends scholarly power to the research paper.

In both the sound recording and the research paper, the quality of the final product is enhanced. As Rick James, who has "made millions from musicians sampling his tracks" (Taraska, 1998: 13), puts it: "Yes, it's their rap," he says. "But it's our fucking music. [People] have danced to it, made love to it. If [these musicians] think their rap is what's really getting it over, try playing it without our shit" (Taraska, 1998: 13). Here is an argument for the vital power of the sampled pieces and the cachet or authority they bring to the new recording that incorporates them.

One can sample well or badly. Grabbing a great guitar riff from a great rock song, a compelling bass line from a classic rhythm and blues recording, and a soprano solo from an opera, then mixing them together, while quite easy to do with the right software, won't necessarily result in a pleasing new recording. More than likely, it will result in a musical mess. Digitally juxtaposing the elements is not sufficient to blend their sounds into a musically coherent whole. Plagiarists who think their term papers will read well if they crib from various sources by rearranging the paragraphs of published articles and altering some phrases, should consider hip-hop DJ Edward "Eddie F." Ferrell's observation on the art of good sampling: "If you don't really fine-tune what you're doing and are just trying to throw something together, it won't sound good" (Mitchell, 2000). The attentive ear will be able to hear the difference between a good sample and a bad one. Digital technology makes sampling easy; it doesn't necessarily make it good. Individual judgment, talent, and expertise make sampling good and make money (the real-world version of getting an A) for both the sampler and the sampled.

Likewise, the attentive eye will be able to read the difference between a good borrowing from sources and a bad one. In a 1920 essay on the Elizabethan playwright Philip Massinger, T.S. Eliot (1950: 182) wrote: "Immature poets imitate, mature poets steal; bad poets deface what they take, and good poets make it into something better or at least something different." Serious listeners to hip-hop and other musical genres that employ sampling techniques will recognize the parallels between Eliot's good poets and their good musicians.

Student writers will, in one way or another, incorporate what they read into what they write. Educators want them to do so properly, whether by correct footnoting techniques or by the thorough reading and hard thinking that are the necessary preludes to putting matters in their own words. Educators today might not wish to use Eliot's terminology of stealing and theft, lest their students be confused over when stealing is right and when it is wrong. On the other hand, however, the stark terminology might get students' attention, a necessary prerequisite for both students and educators to perform the hard work of thinking about the close and dynamic relationship between honest writing and plagiaristic writing, between being properly influenced and improperly enriched by one's sources, between the kind of taking that makes material your own through deep familiarity with it, and the kind of taking that prevents that familiarity, by keeping the taken material at too great a distance.

A student's plagiarized paper is the latter kind of taking. Students who hack off large chunks of text from authoritative works and drop them alongside one another into their own term papers don't realize that their professors can often tell they've done so, because style and tone change from one chunk to another. The individual chunks blend as well as the aforementioned rock guitar riff, R&B bass line, and opera vocal. While a clever plagiarist might take a little trouble to smooth out a choppy transition, or alter some phrases here or there, he leaves much of what he shanghaied into his paper intact. He didn't read what he borrowed or stole closely enough to come to understand whether the disparate chunks could blend together in a scholarly whole or which components of those chunks of text were most worthy of including in the first place.

What if we made our student plagiarist pay more attention to what he's doing? A good recording artist or DJ knows the music he samples from and chooses what he samples based on aesthetic and emotional criteria. Can there be a scholarly counterpart? Here's a hypothetical assignment: for a draft of a 15-page research paper, require the students to perform cut and paste plagiarism. Call it, though, scholarly sampling or, if you prefer, a research remix. Make it clear that, while they can borrow as freely and as heavily as they want from as many or as few sources as they want, they absolutely must include complete citations for all borrowed works. Furthermore, they are free to include as little or as much of their own words as they wish.

The catch, and the point of the exercise, comes with the next step in the assignment: ask them to explain and defend their choices of sources and arrangement, and grade them on their choices and rationale behind them. DJs don't have to be experts on a musical instrument, but they do need to know and feel the music they are sampling and incorporating into their recordings. Likewise, undergraduates can't be expected to be experts in a subject area, but they do need to understand and absorb the material they are incorporating into their papers. DJs and recording artists who are good at what they do are intelligently engaged with the music. Can a student doing a research remix, a.k.a. cut and paste plagiarism, become engaged with the material he is sampling, a.k.a. stealing, by paying attention to the content of what he is taking and taking care to fit the pieces together to make something new that is itself good?

West Chester University Professor of History Dr. Charles Hardy has spent nearly 20 years teaching undergraduates. I asked him if this hypothetical research assignment was an example of intriguing innovation, ruinous insanity, or something in between. He found it an intriguing idea, agreed that it would certainly engage a student's creativity, and allowed that, "if done skillfully, it should work," but pointedly asked how and when the students would learn the basic techniques of rigor and good writing, the scholarly equivalents of playing scales and developing chops (Hardy, 2009). I conceded that a research sampling exercise wouldn't teach those techniques. It might, however, promote engagement, which is the goal. One of the many reasons deliberate cut and paste plagiarism is wrong is that it inhibits engagement. The plagiarist remains at arms' length from the material she is appropriating. Her use, or more accurately misuse, of technology—electronic databases and word processing software—exacerbates her disengagement. Rather than prohibit a means to facilitate disengagement, which an antiplagiarism decree would in effect do, this research sampling exercise permits the misuse of the technology but then counteracts the disengagement effect of that misuse by having the student explain and defend her results. For her to mount a creditable defense, she will have to engage with the material, her instructor, and the thought processes in her own head—triple play, so to speak. Will it work? Any faculty member who elects to assign this exercise in any classes has a standing invitation to contact the author with accounts of whether it worked or not.

A Final Thought: Think a Little Differently

Plagiarists are missing out on all the fun. Plagiarism denies students who practice it opportunities to develop their own voice, expertise in a subject, and engagement in that subject. This chapter has endeavored to view plagiarism from unusual perspectives in order to highlight aspects of the practice, the better to help educators find new ways of thinking about the problem.

References

Eliot, T.S. 1950. *Selected Essays*. New York: Harcourt Brace.

Graves, Gaye, and Patricia M. Jones. 2003. "Human Factors 101." NASA (June 26). Available: human-factors.arc.nasa.gov/web/hf101/index.html (accessed May 27, 2010).

Hardy, Charles. Conversation with author. Philadelphia, September 30, 2009.

Jeffers, Thomas L. 2002. "Plagiarism High and Low." *Commentary* 114, no. 3 (October): 54–60.

Lehman, Jeffrey, and Shirelle Phelps (eds.). 2005. *West's Encyclopedia of American Law*. 2nd ed., vol. 10: 66–68. Detroit, MI: Thomson/Gale.

Mallon, Thomas. 1989. *Stolen Words: Forays into the Origins and Ravages of Plagiarism*. New York: Ticknor and Fields.

McFarland, Thomas. 1985. *Originality and Imagination*. Baltimore: Johns Hopkins University Press.

Mitchell, Gail. 2000. "Where'd You Get That? The Further Evolution of Sampling." *Billboard* 112, no. 50 (December 9): 56.

Parasuraman, Raja. 2000. "Designing Automation for Human Use: Empirical Studies and Quantitative Models." *Ergonomics* 43, no. 7: 931–951.

Parasuraman, Raja, and Victor Riley. 1997. "Humans and Automation: Use, Misuse, Disuse, Abuse." *Human Factors* 39, no. 2: 230–253.

Parasuraman, Raja, and Christopher D. Wickens. 2008. "Humans: Still Vital After All These Years of Automation." *Human Factors* 50, no. 3: 511–520.

Sarter, Nadine, and Beth Schroeder. 2001. "Supporting Decision Making and Action Selection under Time Pressure and Uncertainty: The Case of In-Flight Icing." *Human Factors* 43 no. 4: 573–583.

Stern, Gabriella. 1993. "Cheap Imitation: Perrigo's Knockoffs of Name-Brand Drugs Turn into Big Sellers—Its Versions of Advil, Listerine Are Sold as Store's Own at Rock Bottom Prices—'Pink Bismuth' for Indigestion." *Wall Street Journal* (July 15): Eastern edition.

Taraska, Julie. 1998. "Sampling Remains Prevalent Despite Legal Uncertainties." *Billboard* 46, no. 12 (November 14): 12–13.

Wall Street Journal. 1984. "Schering-Plough Unit Files Trademark Suit" (April 12), Eastern edition. Available (registration required): global.factiva.com (accessed December 9, 2009).

———. 1985. "Schering-Plough's Suit against Perrigo Is Settled" (February 6), Eastern edition. Available (registration required): global.factiva.com (accessed December 9, 2009).

White, Harold Ogden. [1935] 1965. *Plagiarism and Imitation during the English Renaissance: A Study in Critical Distinctions.* New York: Octagon Books.

"Will Case Change Law on Sampling?" 2002. *National Law Journal* 24, no. 56 (October 14). Available (registration required): global.factiva.com (accessed December 9, 2009).

The Dark Side of the Web—
Where to Go to Buy a Paper

Nick Cvetkovic

Introduction: A Short History of "Papermills"

A plethora of sites on the web provide term papers for sale. Despite professors' attempts to deter and punish students who turn in papers not their own, the papermill industry has continued to evolve and prosper. The purpose of this chapter is twofold: first, to instruct the instructors where these sites are and how the students find them; second, to provide links to these sites as a resource for teachers to use in exposing plagiarized papers. Sample paper requests and links are also included. "Papermill" is a term used to describe an Internet website that students can access in order to obtain a term paper on virtually any topic. The electronic versions are the logical progression of the old fraternity term paper file. They began appearing on the web very shortly after the Internet itself was born, possibly right after that driving force of technological change, pornography. This chapter looks at the origin and history of Internet papermills, and how to find them, and it defines the different types that exist.

There is no conclusive evidence about which was the first Internet papermill. However, it is widely agreed that Schoolsucks.com not only was one of the first but also was instrumental in raising the awareness and popularity of papermills. Schoolsucks.com was founded by Kenny Sahr, who gained a lot of attention by circulating an e-mail announcement (see sidebar) to a large number of fraternities and sororities in June 1996. Schoolsucks.com grew by leaps and bounds to the point of getting 10,000 unique visitors per day. Progress in fighting plagiarized papers as well as more sophisticated professional competition led to the site being taken offline early in 2009.

The evolution of papermills has reached the point in time where the mills have become increasingly sophisticated. Papermills generally fall into one of two broad categories: a student can purchase an existing paper or pay to have

---

Dear Frat or Sorority:
Greetings from Miami, Florida
www.SchoolSucks.Com

School Sucks is a new web site which will no doubt interest you. It is the Internet collection of College Term Papers. All papers are organized by topic (i.e. College of Arts and Sciences, etc.).

School Sucks is a FREE service, allowing college students (all of whom have free Internet access across the globe) to DOWNLOAD THEIR WORKLOAD.

School Sucks has been asked more than once, "How can we HELP School Sucks grow? Start a campaign to encourage students to submit papers they've written. IMAGINE MILLIONS OF STUDENTS WITH MILLIONS OF PAPERS. What a library!

As School Sucks is new, we need submissions. They can be sent to termpapers@schoolsucks.com. Students built the Internet and now it's their turn to benefit from it.

School Sucks needs any links, attention or articles that you can provide. It will ALWAYS remain free. It is sitting on a T1 line (1,500k) and the owners will gladly hire students to work on it when enough papers are submitted!

Next time you have a paper to write, it may have already been written. At least you'll be able to use someone else's sources or see how OTHER students attacked the problem!

School Sucks is run by Kenny Sahr. Kenny currently lives in Miami and spent seven years in Israel (three in Israel Defense Forces) working as a journalist. His Jordan Travel Guide was the first Hebrew language travel guide about that nation.

www.SchoolSucks.Com

(*Source:* Kenny Sahr; letter reprinted with permission.)

---

one custom written. Today one is most likely to find hybrid sites that combine the features of these two types. This seems to appeal to a broad audience, and many sites now pay contributors, frequently graduate students, to attract even more papers and more paying customers. These models evolved from the earliest sites that offered papers for free. Before examining the detailed workings of specific sites, the next section will first explore how students typically find online papermills.

Finding Papermills

There are many ways to locate an online papermill. Just entering "term paper" (including the quotes) on www.google.com will produce over two million "hits." This is about a tenfold increase in results returned since the appearance of the earlier version of this book (September 2004). In addition to "term paper," students can search on the sites by subject area and/or enter keywords to find papers that relate to the topics for which they are searching. Bowing to pressure from the academic community, Google banned the use of Google AdWords for "term papers" effective June 1, 2007 (Coughlan, 2007). Students have found a way around this dilemma. For faculty interested in locating papermills there are various strategies that can be used; these are explored in the next two sections.

Specific Resources for Finding Papermills

The easiest way to find a number of sites is to look for "directory list" webpages. There are many of these available. A highly regarded, comprehensive list of them can be found at www.coastal.edu/library/presentations/mills2.html. This presentation evolved from the popular original "directory" list created and maintained by Margaret Fain, Reference Librarian at Kimbel Library, Coastal Carolina University, located in Conway, South Carolina, and intended as a "plagiarism-busting" tool. When she started the list, in 2000, it had 35 sites on it; it now contains over 300 sites. The original page is no longer online. The new resource is maintained by Margaret Fain and Peggy Bates of the same library and updated twice a year. It is by no means an exhaustive list; rather, it is a representative one and includes the current most popular and visible sites.

The tradition of academic librarians helping to track term papermills continues. Another popular page that has a "directory list" of term paper sources is located at www.library.csustan.edu/lboyer/plagiarism/plagiarism3sources .htm. Titled "Sources of Plagiarism Used by Students," it is maintained by Laura Boyer (2007), CSU Stanislaus Library. As acknowledged on that page, it's impossible to keep a comprehensive list, but it lists some of the more common sites.

Using Search Engines to Find Papermills

Knowing how search engines "work" can make using the returned results more useful. Students turn to search engines like Google to find term papers and papermills. For example, Google uses a proprietary search algorithm expanded from their original PageRank (a trademark of Google) mechanism to determine popularity. The following are some of the most popular sites from a Google search for "papermills" in November 2009. The websites and their addresses are included, along with promotional/informational quotes taken from the sites.

Best Essays
www.bestessays.com
From the site's description: "Welcome to Bestessays.com, your source for
    original writing and research. For the last 10 years we have helped many
    students just like you with their custom essay demands."
Superior Papers
www.superiorpapers.com
From the site's description: "When you choose superiorpapers.com you can
    relax knowing that you will receive a custom written paper that is true

quality. Your original academic paper will be written by a professional with MA or PhD degree in the specified subject that you request. Each member of our research and writing team are professionals with proven writing experience. Let us provide you with a custom essay that meets your requirements."

Best Term Paper

www.besttermpaper.com

From the site's description: "We know that academic plagiarism can harm your reputation and academic future. Our professional writing team ensures that our papers are 100% custom original and written from scratch. We take original writing serious and make sure that your order matches your instructions."

Essay Town

www.essaytown.com

From the site's description: "Even if you don't choose EssayTown, we must warn you about sites that scam students. Never buy from 'monthly access' sites with a database of old, plagiarized essays. Avoid sites that sell 'custom writing' for less than $16/page. Those FOREIGN sites deceive students by selling the exact same, low-quality papers repeatedly to millions of students. To increase profits, they hire cheap, foreign writers who write terrible papers."

These sites showed up as the most linked, but the PageRank can be manipulated to show sites with a high ranking that may, in fact, not be the most visited. More information about Google's patented search algorithm as well as an explanation of PageRank is provided by Phil Craven (accessed 2010). Google conveniently has a directory page that lists some of the fee-based papermills and also has links to articles critiquing some of the leading sites at www.google.com/Top/ Reference/Education/Products_and_Services/Academic_Papers/Fee_Based. Yahoo Directory also offers a list of papermills located at dir.yahoo.comBusiness_and_Economy/Shopping_and_Services/Writing_and_Editing/Academic_Services/Research_and_Term_Papers/?skw=term+paper+directory+yahoo. How students proceed from this point will vary greatly, depending on whether they want a prewritten paper or are willing to pay much more for a custom paper. Most sites now offer both types of papers, but, generally, there are two main types of papermill sites as explained in depth in the following sections.

Types of Papermills

Papermills could originally be easily classified into one of three major types: free, per page, and custom. Over the years, many papermill sites have evolved to try to be a "one size fits all" site. In addition, we now find "networks" or "mega sites," which are meta-sites from which a number of sites can be accessed at once. There are still a smattering of "free sites" that will allow downloading a paper in exchange for a real term paper upload.

Free Papermills

These claim to be the purest form of papermill, with a direct lineage back to the old fraternity paper files. The original totally free sites have fallen out of favor. A few remain that require uploading papers in order to obtain downloading credits. Many sites claim to be free, but when one goes to download an actual paper one finds that there is payment required to download the paper. Here are some examples:

Cyber Essays
www.cyberessays.com
From the site's description: "Cyber Essays is your one-stop source for free, high-quality term papers, essays, and reports on all subjects." This is one of the few remaining really free sites. In 2004, this was a blended site offering both free and "for pay."
Free Essays
www.freeessays123.com
From the site's description: "Free Essays offers the best free essays, term papers and book reports from the brightest high school and college students" but requires uploading a paper in order to download one ("you must submit one complete, good quality essay or term paper of your own to us"). Offers download without a need to upload for $12.99.

For-Fee Sites: Existing Papers

These sites require payment to obtain any of their many term papers. The fee structure varies, with some sites requiring a flat membership fee, either lifetime or per month, and others charging fees depending on various attributes of the requested paper. The sites with fixed fees for unlimited access evolved from the free sites with a larger selection of slightly better papers. Unlimited access fees can be as little as $9.95 for a lifetime membership up to $29.95 per month and even higher. The higher priced sites seem to provide higher quality papers. Some of the sites in this category charge a fee for each paper. The fee varies from a fixed amount per paper to an amount per page. The fixed amount per paper will vary with the complexity of the paper as will the amount per page. These are some of the more popular for-fee sites:

12,000 Papers
www.12000papers.com
From the site: "All Papers Are Only $9.95/page + FREE Bibliography."
Cheat House
www.cheathouse.com
Prices range upwards from $ 9.95 for three days. This automatically renews at $14.95 a month with an option of $ 69.95 for six months.

For-Fee Sites: Custom Papers

This last category of term paper sites claims that they write each particular paper on a "custom" basis based on strict specifications supplied by the purchaser. The fee structure is generally a fixed amount per page. The sites charge significant surcharges for papers that are requested with a tight deadline. Many sites advertise that their papers are written by actual schoolteachers or moonlighting college teachers. While obviously more expensive, these custom paper sites will provide the closest thing to a real paper that a student might create on his or her own. There is no way to verify that these custom papers actually are written totally anew for each requestor. These are some of the more prominent sites:

Cheap Term Papers
www.cheaptermpapers.info
Normal delivery cost is $9.95 per page. Urgent delivery cost is $14.95 per page delivered within three days.
Accepted Term Papers
www.acceptedpapers.com
Custom papers cost $12.95 per page up to $ 29.95 if need is immediate.
Itchy Brains
www.itchybrainscentral.com
Custom-written papers are $29.95 per page. The site states: "Itchy Brains never plagiarizes. Many other companies that promote research material in the form of papers, recycle pre-written papers. We use professional writers who provide custom-written papers, guaranteed."
Papers Inn
www.papersinn.com
Prices range from $12.95 per page to $26.95 for "next morning."
A1 Termpaper
www.essaytown.com/custom/
Rates range from $18.00 to $38.95 (8 to 23 hours). The site states: "All work offered is for research purposes only."

The Current Trend

Term paper sites continue to evolve. Many appear and then quickly disappear. Some change from one model to the other (Cyber Essays). There is a trend toward consolidation under an umbrella site. There are also still very specialized sites that do not directly offer complete papers but provide dissertation and thesis "assistance" generally at a fairly high minimum or fixed rate. Here are some examples:

Associated Writers
associatedwriters.com
From the site's description: "Associated Writers is a confidential, professional writing service for doctoral and masters candidates with needs

in the areas of writing, research, and editing. Post-graduate assistance is also provided in the publication of dissertations and theses and the preparation of articles for scholarly journals and periodicals." No prices are listed on the website.

Dissertations and Theses: Custom Research

www.dissertationsandtheses/comcustomreports.html

The site offers "more than 25,000 quality research papers, experimental studies, and even examples of entire theses to download, study from, and cite in the body of your own thesis or dissertation!" Unmodified pages are $ 9.95 per page and can be customized for $ 19.95 per page. Custom research is also available.

Graduate Papers

www.graduatepapers.com

The site offers prewritten papers, but the primary focus is on original papers at $19.95 per page for 7 days' turnaround and $44.95 for "same day" service.

Specialty Sites

Specialty sites offer term papers by subject. Some of these sites may be blocked on university computers as known "phishing sites," but they are still accessible via public computers. Sites include the following:

Africanlit.com: Essays on African Literature

www.africanlit.com

The site charges $9.95 for papers in a database with free bibliographies/ works cited. Custom work is $19.95 per page.

Aristotle Papers

www.aristotlepapers.com

Prewritten papers are $9.95 per page; custom papers are $19.95 per page.

EthicsPapers.com

www.ethicspapers.com

The per-page charges are $9.95 for prewritten and $19.95 for custom.

Jane-Austen-Essays.com

www.jane-austen-essays.com

This site charges $9.95 per page for papers on file and $19.95 per page for custom work.

Literature Papers

www.literaturepapers.com

The cost is $12.95 per page unless it is a rush job. "We guarantee that our term papers will not be available in any database online. All orders are custom made and confidential."

Philosophypapers.com

www.philosophypapers.com

The site charges $9.95 per page for on-file papers; custom papers cost $19.95 per page.

"We Don't Encourage or Condone Plagiarism"

Virtually all papermills contain disclaimers disavowing any intent to encourage or even condone any form of plagiarism by the use of the materials available on their sites. While some of the disclaimers are minimal, some are informative and very direct in terms of what they tell the students. Cyber Essays (www.cyberes says.com) states that the papers on its site are available free of charge. On the "Frequently Asked Questions" page, the folks at Cyber Essays state that their service is meant to challenge "the lazy teacher" who gives his or her students "the same assignments year after year" (Cyber Essays, 2010). The implication is that by using Cyber Essays, students will cause teachers to rethink their methodology and thereby improve the kind of assignments that they are given.

Student Reviews of Papermill Sites

There are many sites that a student can use to shop for a term paper online, including offshore sites out of reach of U.S. law enforcement agencies. Students tend to get peer recommendations from classmates, or they reach out to the social networks such as Facebook and MySpace. One site, aptly titled EssayScam (2009), allows public posting in their forums. Founded in 2005, its raison d'être seems to be to encourage students to do their own writing. The homepage states: "Will you find out which essay writing companies or writers are trustable and which should be avoided? Probably not. Will you have a good time and be entertained? We should think so! Will you start writing essays on your own? We do hope so!" Their forums cover such topics as essay-writing services, essay-writing jobs, stolen papers, and general discussions that include "general talk for students, writers, and others interested in academic essay writing and researching" (EssayScam, 2009). Comments in these forums have to be read closely to filter out postings from disgruntled term papermills employees as well as from people who just don't understand how term papermills operate.

Conclusion

A 2001 article in the online magazine *Slate* examined term papermills. The author actually purchased and then graded papers, including custom ones, from them and came to the following conclusions. For the prewritten papers the author states that this is "not a bad strategy" for a "smart but horribly lazy student." His review of the custom paper was: "When the custom paper came back, it was all I'd dreamed. Representative sentence: 'The novel's diverse characters demonstrate both individually and collectively the fixations and obsessions that bind humanity to the pitfalls of reality and provide a fertile groundwork for the semiotic explanation of addictive behavior.' Tripe" (Stevenson, 2001).

Thus, it's very clear that papermill websites will continue to flourish and to grow as long as students believe that there is no downside to using them. A number of factors conspire to ensure that students can still turn in these papers, little changed, as their own work. These include overly large classes and overworked faculty. As faculty become more knowledgeable about papermill sites and the ease with which students can purchase papers, they will be better equipped to attack the problem of plagiarism on many fronts.

References

Boyer, Laura M. 2007. "Plagiarism in Cyberspace." Turlock: California State University, Stanislaus Library (November 19). Available: www.library.csustan.edu/lboyer/plagiarism/plagiarism3services.htm (accessed May 27, 2010).

Coughlan, Sean. 2007. "Google Bans Essay Writing Adverts." *BBC News* (May 22). Available news.bbc.co.uk/2/hi/uk_news/education/6680457.stm (accessed May 27, 2010).

Craven, Phil. "Google's PageRank Explained and How to Make the Most of It." WebWorkshop. Available: www.webworkshop.net/pagerank.html#how_is_pagerank_calculated (accessed May 27, 2010).

Cyber Essays. 2010. "Frequently Asked Questions." Available: www.cyberessays.com/faq.htm (accessed July 12, 2010).

EssayScam. 2009. "EssayScam Forum." Available: www.essayscam.org/Forum (accessed May 27, 2010).

Stevenson, Seth. 2001. "Adventures in Cheating: A Guide to Buying Term Papers Online." *Slate* (December 11). Available: slate.msn.com?id=2059540 (accessed May 27, 2010).

4

The Academy versus Plagiarism: Rearranging the Deck Chairs on the *Titanic* or the Stand at Thermopylae

Vibiana Bowman Cvetkovic
Luis F. Rodriguez

Introduction

In 2006, National Public Radio correspondent Mike Pesca delivered a commentary about plagiarism. It was a musing brought on in part by the intellectual honesty cause célèbre of that moment. Young adult author Kaavya Viswanathan lost a lucrative book deal and endured a public shaming when it was discovered that her novel, *How Opal Mehta Got Kissed, Got Wild, and Got A Life* (Little, Brown, 2006), borrowed liberally from the Megan McCafferty's novels *Sloppy Firsts* (Three Rivers Press, 2001) and *Second Helpings* (Three Rivers Press, 2003). Pesca's point was that as new media move into the millennium, the notion of plagiarism will become passé:

> The last big institution holding the line against plagiarism is the Academy. . . . I predict that in 20 years, whatever version there is of Wikipedia will refer to plagiarism as a short-lived concept in the history of communication. Eventually, the open source reference guide will say "Plagiarism, once seen as a dire pitfall, came to be discounted as a sin. Eventually, plagiarists were treated like hack comics. You can steal a joke, but you can't steal a career. (Pesca, 2006)

Although the segment was delivered with tongue firmly in cheek, Mr. Pesca raised an important and thought-provoking point: is the Academy clinging to an antiquated model of scholarship? Are we, the members of the Academy, rearranging the deck chairs on the *Titanic*, i.e., are we agonizing about minor details in the face of a world-changing event, or are we making a valiant stand against overwhelming forces like the 300 Spartans at Thermopylae? Or perhaps the truth lies somewhere in between.

The stated purpose of this book is to help educators teach high school and undergraduate students about intellectual honesty. The contributors to this work have uniformly constructed their arguments on the premise that plagiarism is an act of intellectual *dis*honesty. This premise's logical corollaries are that plagiarism undermines academic integrity; the people who engage in such behavior should be censured and punished; and educators are responsible for teaching the next generation of scholars that such behavior is unacceptable. There is, however, a 500-pound gorilla lurking at the corners of this premise: Is it correct, or is the entire antiplagiarism endeavor a moot point?

Various media critics contend that the world has moved into a postplagiarism era. The argument advanced goes like this: because information is web-based, fluid, hyperlinked, and collaboratively authored, citations to source documents are irrelevant; therefore, it is not only pointless but futile for the Academy to adhere to print-based standards of scholarship. Why then does the Academy still wage war on plagiarism, and is it time to lay down arms? Which stance—anti- or postplagiarism—best serves the public good and the advancement of knowledge? To explore these questions, it is necessary to have a clear definition of plagiarism and an understanding of what it is and what it is not.

What Is Plagiarism?

The history of the concept of plagiarism can be traced back at least until the seventeenth century. It is closely associated with the Enlightenment thinkers and the rise of individualism. (Note: for readers interested in an in-depth discussion of the development of plagiarism as an intellectual concept, we recommend Thomas Mallon's [2001] history of the topic, *Stolen Words*). *The Oxford English Dictionary* cites as one of the earliest users of the term the cleric Richard Montagu in his *Diatribae on the First Part of the Late History of Tithes* (1621). Discussions of plagiarism often note that authors through the ages, up to and including the Elizabethan (most famously Shakespeare), stole, borrowed, and swapped plots lines, characters, and dialogue in their creative endeavors. Around the mid-1600s, intellectual works began to be thought of as "belonging" to an individual; the accompanying notion was that these intellectual works could then be "stolen." When the written word became an emblematic expression of "self"—an expression that could enrich the individual both literally and figuratively—the notion of plagiarism firmly took root.

The author as creator and therefore owner of an intellectual property is central to plagiarism debates, because the plagiarist lays claim to something that is not his (or hers). Related to, but not synonymous with, the concept of plagiarism is the concept of copyright infringement. Simply put, plagiarism is about honesty and proper attribution to the creator of intellectual works. Copyright is about property rights and revenue. Plagiarism is an ethical question; copyright is a legal one.

Plagiarism and Copyright

According to *Merriam-Webster's Encyclopedia of Literature*, plagiarism is "taking the writings of another person and passing them off as one's own." The author of the entry makes a distinction between copyright infringement and plagiarism: "The fraudulence is closely related to forgery and piracy—practices generally in violation of copyright laws. There is no breach of copyright laws if it can be proved that duplicated wordage was arrived at independently." In many discussions, copyright infringement and plagiarism are conflated; however, there are significant differences between the two.

Article I, Section 8, of the U.S. Constitution gave Congress the power to "promote the Progress of Science and useful arts, by securing for limited times to Authors and Inventors the exclusive right to their respective Writings and Discoveries." Copyright law gives the author of an original work, or those authorized by the author, the exclusive right:

- to reproduce the work;
- to make derivative copies based upon the work;
- to distribute the work by selling, renting, lending, or leasing it or by transferring ownership of the work; and
- in the case of literary, musical, dramatic, and choreographic works, pantomimes, and motion pictures and other audiovisual works, to perform the work publicly;
- in the case of literary, musical, dramatic, and choreographic works, pantomimes, and pictorial, graphic, or sculptural works, including the individual images of a motion picture or other audiovisual work, to display the work publicly; and
- in the case of sound recordings, to perform the work publicly by means of a digital audio transmission. (U.S. Copyright Office, 2008)

The Digital Millennium Copyright Act added another wrinkle to these rights by making illegal most reverse engineering of technology that prevents the copying of a digital work (Ogden, 2003: 473–481; U.S. Copyright Office, 1998).

Not all things or all works are copyrightable. Facts are not copyrightable, but the language used to describe facts, if original enough, is (Ogden, 2003). An idea is not copyrightable, but the use of unique language for the expression of that idea is. According to various authorities, the unattributed use of an idea is plagiarism (Gibaldi, 2009). The plagiarism policies of many colleges and universities specifically require a student to cite the source of the idea, no matter how original the student's manner of expression.

In addition to ideas, procedures, methods, systems, processes, concepts, principles, discoveries, or devices are not copyrightable. Descriptions, explanations, and illustrations of these—if original enough—are. Originality and creativity are key concepts in copyright law. Thus, the traditional, printed phone book is not copyrightable, because it uses a commonplace and traditional method of arranging raw data (subscribers' names, towns, and telephone numbers), and the raw data are arranged in a way that "lacks the modicum of creativity necessary to transform mere selection into copyrightable expression" (*Feist v. Rural Telephone*). Works of the U.S. government are not copyrightable, but those of foreign, state, and local government are.

To be copyrighted, a work must be fixed in a tangible form. Thus, improvisational speeches and performances are not copyrightable, but recordings and written transcripts of those performances are. However, these same improvisational speeches and performances can be plagiarized. To promote the "Progress of Science and the Useful Arts," the U.S. Constitution did not make copyrights perpetual; they are granted for a limited time. Thus, copyrighted works eventually pass into the public domain, meaning that they are free for the public to use without permission of the work's creator. Neither the acts of copying a work in the public domain or of making oneself the author of such a work is an infringement of copyright. However, such acts are acts of plagiarism. An example of a work in the public domain is a photograph of the deck chairs that were used on the sister ships *Olympic* and *Titanic* (Figure 4.1). Because it is in the public domain, it can be freely used. One could lay claim to authorship

Figure 4.1.   Deck chairs used on the *RMS Olympic* and sister ship *RMS Titanic*.

This photograph and other images in the public domain are available through Wikimedia Commons (commons.wikimedia.org). According to the image description, "This media file is in the public domain in the United States. This applies to U.S. works where the copyright has expired, often because its first publication occurred prior to January 1, 1923." Wikimedia lists the puplication date as 1912 and the photographer as "unknown."

of the image. To do so would make one a plagiarist, well over 100 years old (the *Titanic* sunk in 1912), but not a copyright violator.

Thus, while copyright and plagiarism are often treated as equivalent, in many important aspects, they diverge. Understanding this divergence is important for developing a working understanding of both concepts. As Stuart Green (2002: 200–201) notes, plagiarism can occur "when a writer fails to acknowledge the source of facts, ideas, and specific language; copyright infringement occurs only when specific language is copied or used in a derivative work."

Fair Use Is Not Plagiarism

U.S. copyright law allows for certain exceptions and limitations on the rights of copyright holders. Arguably, the best known exception, at least for those involved in education, is "fair use." What constitutes "fair use," i.e., a use that does not infringe the rights of a copyrighter holder, is weighed against four factors: purpose of use; nature of use; amount copied; and the effect on the value of the original work (U.S. Copyright Office, 2009).

The fourth factor, effect on the value of the original work, is sometimes called the "tipping" factor. This means that courts will consider the first three factors

---

U.S. Copyright Office: Excerpt from "Fair Use Statement"

One of the rights accorded to the owner of copyright is the right to reproduce or to authorize others to reproduce the work in copies or phonorecords. This right is subject to certain limitations found in Sections 107 through 118 of the copyright law (Title 17, U.S. Code). One of the more important limitations is the doctrine of "fair use." The doctrine of fair use has developed through a substantial number of court decisions over the years and has been codified in Section 107 of the copyright law.

Section 107 contains a list of the various purposes for which the reproduction of a particular work may be considered fair, such as criticism, comment, news reporting, teaching, scholarship, and research. Section 107 also sets out four factors to be considered in determining whether or not a particular use is fair:

- The purpose and character of the use, including whether such use is of commercial nature or is for nonprofit educational purposes
- The nature of the copyrighted work
- The amount and substantiality of the portion used in relation to the copyrighted work as a whole
- The effect of the use upon the potential market for, or value of, the copyrighted work

The distinction between fair use and infringement may be unclear and not easily defined. There is no specific number of words, lines, or notes that may safely be taken without permission. Acknowledging the source of the copyrighted material does not substitute for obtaining permission.

to determine if fair use of a copyrighted work applies. If the use of a work is fair, based on an examination of the first three factors, then courts will usually not consider the effect of copying on the market for the work. However, if an examination of the first three factors indicates that the use of a copyrighted work is not fair, then the effect on the market for a work will be considered (Office of Intellectual Property, 2005). While there are exceptions in copyright law—"fair use" among them—there are no exceptions granted in the world of professional writers for plagiarism (Green, 2002: 167).

As discussed earlier, one cannot copyright an idea, but one can plagiarize an idea. Because copyright does not extend to works in the public domain, an author cannot be charged with a copyright infringement for utilizing that work as her own. That author would, however, be a plagiarist unless she properly attributed the source of the exact words that she "borrowed" from the original work. This is the heart of plagiarism: failure to attribute authorship for an expression or idea. Proper attribution is not a defense against copyright infringement. Intent to deceive is often an issue in plagiarism cases. Intent is not an issue in copyright.

Information Wants to Be Free

In discussions about plagiarism the topic often gets conflated with other concepts and movements, such as open access, collaborative authorship (e.g., Wikipedia), file sharing, and "copyleft," the copyright reform movement. These concepts tend to be lumped together in the public imagination under the rallying cry of "Information wants to be free." This phrase, according to Wikipedia (2010b), is the "unofficial motto of the free content movement" and was used by Stewart Brand at the first Hackers' Conference in 1984. The "information wants to be free" argument is used by media critics as a justification for advancing a postplagiarism era. Online content, hyperlinked and collaborative in nature, should be freed from the constraints of footnoting, attribution, and the seeking of permissions. Content creation has moved beyond such quaint notions. This section will examine these arguments, the various digital reform movements, and how they relate to the concept of plagiarism.

Richard T. Kaser, former Executive Director of the National Federation of Abstracting and Information Services, posed the question: "If information wants to be free . . . then who is going to pay for it?" Kaser (2000) condensed the arguments of the free-content proponents into three broad categories: information should be "free of structure, free of usage restrictions, and/or free for the taking." His main contention is that the notion of "free information" is a myth: "Though librarians know that information is anything but free, those who use libraries have come to believe that it is free. Unfortunately for those who sell information, there are far more users of libraries than there are librarians in the world." He goes on to state that "'Free information' is a cultural perception. 'Free information' is an illusion . . . a figment of our collective imagination. We have all contributed to this myth." The "we" in this instance is the creators of information: government, corporate, and academic researchers. Kaser suggests that the true cost of information is best defrayed by partnerships between the public and private sectors.

The open content movement was formed in response to what many in the sciences, arts, and digital community view as increasingly restrictive copyright laws. The Free Software Foundation (www.fsf.org), developers of the GNU operating system, Creative Commons (creativecommons.org), and Wikimedia Commons (commons.wikimedia.org) are all proponents of open content. FSF and Creative Commons offer "copyleft" licensing (Figure 4.2) by which the creator of intellectual content can make her work freely available (sometimes with specific restrictions such as a request for attribution).

The open content licensing available through not-for-profits like FSF and Creative Commons is not in opposition to copyright. Rather their purpose is to provide content creators with a broader range of possibilities in licensing their work from traditional copyright protections to "no rights reserved" (Creative Commons, accessed 2010). Creative Commons' mission statement notes:

> We work to increase the amount of creativity (cultural, educational, and scientific content) in "the commons"—the body of work that is

---

Figure 4.2. The Copyleft Licensing Symbol

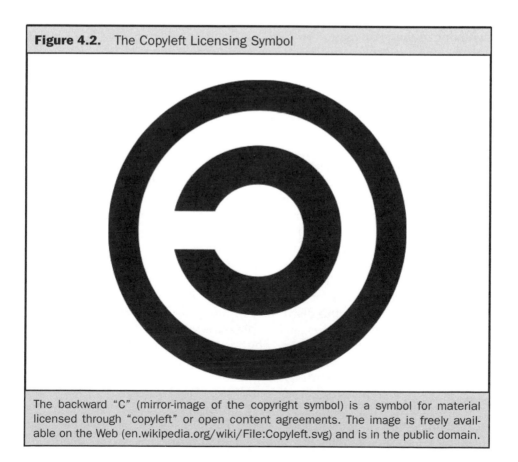

The backward "C" (mirror-image of the copyright symbol) is a symbol for material licensed through "copyleft" or open content agreements. The image is freely available on the Web (en.wikipedia.org/wiki/File:Copyleft.svg) and is in the public domain.

available to the public for free and legal sharing, use, repurposing, and remixing.

The movements and concepts discussed so far are primarily concerned with legal ownership and financial responsibilities of and for intellectual properties. To return to Kaser's (2000) argument summary of the "information wants to be free debate," these are issues related to the concepts that information should be "free of usage restrictions, and/or free for the taking." What of the third argument: "information should be structure?" Has the time come for information to be set free from a print-based system of attribution and record keeping?

Standing on the Shoulders of Giants . . . Sort Of

The quote "If I have seen further it is by standing on the shoulders of giants" is frequently found in resources about plagiarism and intellectual honesty. Its origin was the subject of a similarly-titled book by sociologist Robert K. Merton (1965). According to blogger and independent filmmaker Brad Lichtenstein (2009), while this quote is widely attributed to Sir Isaac Newton, its actual origins date back to the twelfth-century scholar Bernard of Chartres. Lichtenstein writes that the content of the quote and its misattribution to Newton are symbolic of the creative process:

> What I love here is the double insight, the effort to describe creativity in a commons-sense, and the journey of the description itself through the commons of knowledge and creativity. Art and knowledge are derivative and generative. We take what we know and build on it. (Lichtenstein, 2009)

The conundrum of whether any work can be uniquely original or if all creative content is derivative is a matter of philosophical debate. It is also at the heart of the issue of plagiarism. The Academy's attempt to provide a practical solution was to develop a system of citation. With variations in style based on discipline, the formal process of attribution is the basis for all good scholarly writing. Footnotes, "Works Cited," or "References" pages and in-text citations serve as a genealogy chart for the ideas that authors contribute to the world of scholarship. Part 3 of this book explores in-depth the Academy's guidelines, procedures, and rationales for the importance of these practices. However, the question posed earlier in this discussion still remains. Is, as Mr. Pesca suggests, the Academy alone in its war against plagiarism, and has the rest of society moved on? Can arguments for the attribution of sources be found outside of the Ivory Tower? The answer comes interestingly enough from the anti-Academy, Wikipedia, in an article regarding its guidelines for entries:

> Wikipedia articles should be based on reliable, published sources, making sure that all majority and significant-minority views that have appeared in reliable, published sources are covered. . . . Reli-

able sources may therefore be published materials with a reliable publication process; they may be authors who are regarded as authoritative in relation to the subject in question; or they may be both. (Wikipedia, 2010c)

The philosophy behind Wikipedia is that through collaborative authorship a process of "open and transparent consensus" would be reached in the articles that appear in this free, online encyclopedia. Although subject to controversy and abuses, Wikipedia has emerged over the past decade as the most widely used encyclopedic resource on the web (Wikipedia, 2010a). In is interesting to note that this model of successful Web 2.0 publishing still utilizes the standards of "authenticity, validity, and reliability" found in the Association for College and Research Libraries' (2000) *Information Literacy Competency Standards for Higher Education.*

Other proponents of new media, including blogger, poet, and musician Nick Courage, still give a tip-of-the-hat to the mechanics of attribution. In a series of blogs, "Rethinking Plagiarism," Courage (2009) questions the continued validity of the notion of plagiarism:

> Traditionally, originally—at least in contemporary western culture—plagiarism was understandably stigmatized. Once the idea of Authorship, distinct and iconic, emerged from the nascent, lobe-finned cult of the individual—well, it was only natural to start attributing. To do otherwise would have been tantamount to bending—if not outright breaking—a previously established societal rule, one with gravitas . . . with a long and venerable history that cut to the proprietary quick: cuckoldry. Stealing another man's wife. This language that I'm using, the roots of contemporary copyright—it's archaic. It's phallocentric and condescending.

Courage (2009) goes on to state that he is against neither author's rights nor documentation. He advocates copyright reform and a rethinking of the process of attribution. He writes that "all our web-writing is a fragile mélange of e-source detritus. So long as there's an understanding, from the outset, that the cultural artifact you're encountering is curated rather than Authored." (Note: Courage uses "Authored" as opposed to "authored" traditional, individualistic writing.)

Conclusion

Based on a closer examination of the arguments against the war on plagiarism, what critics are actually proposing is not a cessation but a restrategizing of that war. The web has revolutionized the way information is created and disseminated. Blogs, wikis, and other formats for information aggregation are based on a new paradigm. As Mr. Courage suggests, the information found in these resources is "curated" rather than "authored." Standards and conventions for these forms of content creation will eventually be held to a now evolving standard of attribution through linkage and other methods of information embedding.

Good scholarship is still good scholarship. Even in a Web 2.0 world, after examining the rhetoric, there is a consensus that authors still need to provide a roadmap for the attribution of the ideas they present in a piece of formal, scholarly writing. Doing so is critical in order to establish the validity and authority of the author's work.

So perhaps the comparison between educators in the battle against plagiarism to the 300 Spartans at Thermopylae is apt; we are at the forefront, and reinforcements are on the way. But perhaps, if we listen to the new media critics, we need to rethink our battle plan.

References

Association for College and Research Libraries. 2000. *Information Literacy Competency Standards for Higher Education*. Chicago: American Libraries Association. Available: www.ala.org/ala/mgrps/divs/acrl/standards/standards. pdf (accessed January 30, 2010).

Courage, Nick. 2009. "Rethinking Plagiarism: The Death of Text as Authorial Icon Pt. 1." A Mutual Respect Blog. (August 6). Available: amutualrespect.org/words/2009/08/06/rethinking-plagiarism-the-death-of-text-as-authorial-icon-pt-1 (accessed January 30, 2010).

Creative Commons. "What Is Creative Commons?" Available: creativecommons. org/about/what-is-cc (accessed January 30, 2010).

Feist Publications, Inc. v. Rural Telephone Service Co., Inc., 499 U.S. 340 (1991), 362.

Gibaldi, Joseph. 2009. *MLA Handbook for Writers of Research Paper*, 7th ed. New York: Modern Language Association of America.

Green, Stuart P. 2002. "Plagiarism, Norms, and the Limits of Theft Law: Some Observations on the Use of Criminal Sanctions in Enforcing Intellectual Property Laws." *Hastings Law Journal* 54 (November): 167–232.

Kaser, Richard, T. 2000. "If Information Wants to Be Free . . . Then Who's Going to Pay for It?" *D-Lib Magazine* 6 (May). Available: www.dlib.org/dlib/may00/kaser/05kaser.html (accessed January 30, 2010).

Lichtenstein, Brad. 2009. "Standing on the Shoulders of Giants." Brad Lichtenstein's Blog (January 26). Available: bradlichtenstein.wordpress. com/2009/01/26/standing-on-the-shoulders-of-giants (accessed January 31, 2010).

Mallon, Thomas. 2001. *Stolen Words*. San Diego: Harcourt.

Merriam-Webster's Encyclopedia of Literature, s.v. "Plagiarism." Available (through Rutgers University subscription): go.galegroup.com/ps/start .do?p=LitRC&u=Rutgers (accessed January 23, 2010).

Merton, Robert K. 1965. *On the Shoulders of Giants*. Glencoe, IL: Free Press.

Office of Intellectual Property. 2005. "Fair Use of Copyrighted Materials." University of Texas. Available: www.utsystem.edu/ogc/intellectualproperty/copypol2.htm (accessed January 25, 2010).

Ogden, Robert S. 2003. "Copyright Issues for Libraries and Librarians." *Library Collections, Acquisitions and Technical Services* 27, no. 4: 473–481.

Oxford English Dictionary, s.v. "Plagiarism." Available (through Rutgers University subscription): dictionary.oed.com.proxy.libraries.rutgers.edu/cgi/entry/50180576? (accessed January 23, 2010).

Pesca, Mike. 2006. "Cribbing Through the Ages." On the Media. National Public Radio (May 19). Available: www.onthemedia.org/transcripts/2006/05/19/08 (accessed 23 January 23, 2010).

U.S. Copyright Office. 1998. *The Digital Millennium Copyright Act*. Washington, DC: U.S. Copyright Office. Available: www.copyright.gov/legislation/dmca.pdf (accessed January 23, 2010).

———. 2008. *Copyright Basics*. Washington, DC: U.S. Copyright Office. Available: www.copyright.gov/circs/circ1.pdf (accessed January 23, 2010).

———. 2009. *Fair Use*. Washington, DC: U.S. Copyright Office. Available: www.copyright.gov/fls/fl102.html (accessed January 23, 2010).

Wikipedia. "About." 2010a. Available: en.wikipedia.org/wiki/Wikipedia:About (accessed January 30, 2010).

———. "Information Wants to Be Free." 2010b. Available: en.wikipedia.org/wiki/Information_wants_to_be_free (accessed January 30, 2010).

———. "Reliable Resources." 2010c. Available: en.wikipedia.org/wiki/Wikipedia:Reliable_sources (accessed January30, 2010).

An Undergraduate's Perspective

Sarah F. Brookover

Introduction

It wasn't until the third year of my undergraduate career, when I transferred to Rutgers University, that I understood the gravity of punishment for plagiarism. I was taking an art history class, and we were assigned a research paper. A librarian came into our classroom to give a demonstration on how to use academic search engines for our papers. There was then a presentation about plagiarism, and an example was given about someone who had lost his entire academic career when he was found to have accidentally plagiarized a small paragraph of his PhD dissertation research. I never knew it could ruin your whole academic career; I thought you would just get an F on the paper and that would be all. I never realized the extent to which it could affect a student's academic career or the importance of the academic structure of research, built on previous research.

When I began my undergraduate career at a community college, my professors certainly discussed plagiarism. The discussion was mostly couched in terms of aversion for fear of consequence. What wasn't taught to us was the value of academic research or how the whole academic world functions. It wasn't until I began really seriously writing an increasing number of academic papers for my major in history that I began to see how my research was built on top of previous research. I realized that by not giving credit or citing the previous research along the way, I would contribute to eroding the value of the whole system. The concept of how original work and new theories are built upon verifiable scholarship was never explained to me when I began academic life as a freshman. From what I've experienced, the majority of the conversation about plagiarism is about the punishment for doing it, not about why it is wrong. The credentials that allow my professors the positions they have are based on credit and/or copyright. Their academic value is in the research and original thought they've worked on for years. Credit and citation are imperative for the whole academic system to continue existing and growing.

Technology and Writing

The technology available today makes conducting academic research very different. Though there may have been incremental advances in the speed and ability to access research information in the past, nothing compares to the technology of the Internet and computer-based research. The ability to conduct online searches and find full-text information today is exponentially more rapid and efficient than any tool in the past. Periodical literature searching is a good case in point. Before computers, research involved being physically present in the library, using a paper index to find the citation, and then leafing through bound periodicals in the library to locate the article. Typically, indexes and periodicals did not circulate, so the researcher was limited to library hours to do the work. The researcher was restricted in both time and place. However, the whole process of handling the material helped to solidify the experience of "synthesis." Students had to physically engage in the act of research, ingest and digest it, and thereby formulate and synthesize their own ideas. I believe that this process of physical interaction with the actual artifacts worked to help maintain the idea behind citation and due credit.

However, modern technology has been a mixed blessing. By creating a quick, easy, and seamless interface to digitized information, online resources have worked to undermine the notion of origin of the material, thereby eliminating the necessity of proper attribution to the content. Technology has been embraced by Generation M, today's undergraduates, who use iPods, cameras, and mobile phones. Even for those without the Internet literally in their pocket, there is an overall assumption that information over the Internet is available anywhere, all the time. This idea has become not only an assumption but an expectation; this is where the problem begins. It is very common for people to use the Internet to watch and instantly share music mp3s, music videos, movies, television shows, books, and newspaper and magazine articles. Some of the content is legal and the viral spread of which is actually aided by the original owners of the content. For example, the *New York Times* has links on its articles' webpages to instantly share them through e-mail, blogs, Facebook, and Twitter. Once the link is shared from a site like this, proper credit is given to the author and owner of the article. But this is done automatically; the user never even has to look at or know the author's name. Other times, and very often, when content is shared, there is no regard for source. There are plenty of HBO shows that are illegally downloaded and made available freely on the web. The sites making them available have no legal right to do so, but that seems irrelevant to the people posting and viewing. On the authorized front, when I want to read a book, I can log onto Google Books (books.google.com/books) and read an entire book for free. I can still go to a library and check out the book for free, but the access on the Internet is constant and immediate, right along with access to all those other free media—both authorized and unauthorized.

So now we have a generation of college students with this kind of assumption about free media with little or no regard to ownership. They sit down and use the same computers and kinds of Internet tools to do their academic research, such as EBSCO and other library online tools. Conducting research this way is both convenient and efficient, but it appears and feels just like searching for any other content on the Internet, which is, for the most part, available free when you find it. This creates an environment for students to easily disregard or simply forget to use citations and to be careful not to cut and paste, whether purposefully or accidentally. Along with education about how to use Internet-based research engines, a distinction needs to be made clear between casual Internet searching and academic research using Internet-based tools.

Another element that contributes to the degradation of the concept of intellectual content ownership is the way advertising and branding is used push technological devices. The products that have the most status are the fastest and the ones that best lend themselves to the art of multitasking. For example, the iPhone has not only promoted our desire for media and information on demand, regardless of the quality or validity of the source, but also our need to be downloading music while we search the web and navigate our driving route all at once. The emphasis is now placed on doing many things at the same time rather than focusing on fewer things but doing them well. Sometimes it feels as if that world of information being sold to us puts no value on the content itself, but rather the speed in which it is accessed.

This concept is packaged as part of a larger paradigm of disposable consumerism. Technology, music, and fashion, which are now linked together, are all disposable. Cell phones and computer systems, programs, and tools regenerate so much more rapidly than ever in the past. The creators of a lot of the content itself, say, pop musicians, are required to morph themselves into a brand of themselves in order to be sellable to the younger generation. They sell themselves as an image, which is more important than the quality of their music or performance skills. These brands and images are purchased and tried on by young people to identify themselves until all that creative content doesn't belong to anyone—as if the artists are more a brand than they are the owner of the content as property. The music industry itself continues to be embroiled in debates over intellectual property. Ever since the onset of Napster, the free music file-sharing program, the question of rights protection has been at the forefront of cultural debates.

An element of modern college life is the pressure to physically show up and to attend. It is common to hear students talk about how they don't care about being in school or about learning anything. Many students put out just enough effort to skate by with a passing grade; their motivation is to get a degree in order to compete in the marketplace. Their motivation for being there has little to do with learning or participating in the academic world; they are there for the bullet point on their resume under "Education." These students are also often the same students who openly admit to cutting and pasting papers together rather than developing writing or research skills. That conversations about how to cut and paste or where to purchase academic papers occur in the classroom indicates that while students know that such behavior is wrong, they believe they won't get caught.

More importantly, they are not taking advantage of the opportunity to learn. This kind of student I am sure is not new, but it seems that because these days a college degree is the equivalent of a high school diploma for our parents, such attitudes about higher education are more common. I have heard other concerns about the lack of academic preparation and lack of study skills in members of today's undergraduate classes. I have many people in my life who are teachers, and a common concern they all discuss is the No Child Left Behind policies enforced in their schools. Although the concept seems to be ideal, they are concerned about how it is executed, including how academic integrity is brushed off. They often refer to the way children are pushed through the public education system in order for the teachers to meet their quotas of passing children—a process that undermines the whole learning process. The pressure to pass children shifts the focus from the teaching of positive learning skills, such as plagiarism avoidance and the integrity of one's own work, to teaching to the test. It creates a large section of students who become a population of cogs in the wheel for the work force who simply uphold the status quo, not a group of critical thinkers who contribute intellectually to our society.

The inconsistency of requirements for citations in class assignments, I believe, also contributes to the habit of copying. Students are confused about what should be cited and what constitutes intellectual property. I've had the experience in lower level classes of being assigned papers and expected to simply regurgitate the information that had been taught in the class. Such papers serve more as exams than represent academic writing. In these instances students are often required to cite the textbook or other required readings within the paper. However, in some of my classes, we were also allowed to quote the professor word for word from class notes with no citation. Because it can be difficult to cite lecture notes, it might be better in these instances to require paraphrasing rather than cut and paste or copy verbatim into papers. It might even be good practice to rephrase concepts into the students' own words, which is often necessary in order not to plagiarize. The lack of a consistent set of standards from high school to college, and from class to class once in college, adds to the sense of confusion. Of course it would be difficult to require the same citation form for every class, as different disciplines require different formats, but adherence to a standard practice would allow for an opportunity for good research habits to start to become second nature when writing papers.

For many students, going to college is a responsibility to their parents or to society, not to themselves. Sometimes this kind of student doesn't really want to be there doing the work, so he or she often looks for shortcuts. In addition to plagiarizing sections from books or articles, students have other tools to use to avoid doing their work. Many websites offer to write papers for a fee, and others have papers "in stock" available for browsing by subject or category and downloading for a price.

Websites that offer a virtual store of papers available for download, where the students simply add their names to them, is pretty black and white cheating. One assumes that students utilizing these websites are aware that they are breaking rules and trying to get away with it. However, what's both more deceiving and more alarming about the websites that will write a "custom paper" for the student is that this practice can appear less like cheating. Websites such as www.bestessays.com offer their writing experience to students not to help students improve their writing skills but rather to write them a paper that fits the description of the assignment exactly. Using phrases such as "truly unique" and "custom" foster the impression that they are not helping students cheat or plagiarize but rather just helping students complete their assignments.

The website www.superiorpapers.com is so customer service oriented that it creates the appearance that there is nothing wrong with what it is selling. This website claims that your paper will be written by someone with a master or PhD degree, giving the impression that it is a sanctioned practice to have papers written for students rather than the students going through the research and writing processes themselves. This completely disregards the importance of the learning process that occurs when doing the work assigned. Such websites support the idea that cheating is an easy way out of the work, a concept valued by students who just want to skate through college to get a degree, and therefore a job, not to become part of the thinking, cultural class in our society.

However, let's assume we can give students the benefit of the doubt that they had no intention of cheating or plagiarizing when they came across these websites. The way the websites sell themselves makes it sound legitimate to utilize their services. Many of them focus on how they can help relieve some of the everyday stress of school assignments and "save your time, efforts and help you succeed in your academic life" (www.besttermpaper.com). Some even claim that what they are offering is not plagiarism, to rest assured that the paper you are purchasing is "100% custom original and written from scratch" (www.besttermpaper.com). These kinds of services are part of a large grey area of understanding about cheating and plagiarism for students. Some students may be looking for a shortcut or help writing their papers by utilizing these sites. Even with permission by the author from the website to submit work that is not theirs, students embark on a slippery slope from cheating themselves to plagiarism. If they feel it is appropriate to submit that kind of work, what's the distinction that will stop them from cutting and pasting content from other sources? When this grey area of what's allowed and not allowed increases, there is more room for plagiarism and cheating.

One solution to this, which is twofold, is to talk about it in the classroom. First, professors need to discuss the tools that students use for cheating and to make clear that they won't put up with this use. I have had professors who did this, and their honesty and openness about the subject put us students on the same level with them. By explaining that the expectations and purpose of the assignment are to improve our abilities to research and learn, and that these ways of cheating will not get us there, was helpful for some students. Other students simply think of all homework and assignments as hoops they have to jump through and want to do so as fast and effortlessly as possible. But when students are spoken to as peers on this subject, the reaction I've heard is that the teacher is reasonable. When combined with an incredibly, and frighteningly, strict no tolerance policy, many more of the students I've been in class with reacted by just doing the work. When presented honestly, not just strictly, the option to cheat seems less plausible.

Second, professors have a responsibility themselves to not use clearly copyrighted materials found on the Internet, such as on YouTube and other movie websites. I have had professors who sent the class students links to websites to stream movies and television programs that should have been purchased legally. These instructors are sending a nonverbal message that they feel the boundaries of intellectual property are grey and that it's acceptable to use this to our advantage. It is true that the Internet makes some boundaries unclear, and there is a lot of work to be done to secure those boundaries again. In the meantime, professors should not openly participate in spreading the acceptance of content usage without permission. Professors need to demonstrate what the rules are by example; utilizing illegal websites to instruct undermines this.

Another important part of avoiding plagiarism that isn't often specifically discussed in the high school or college classroom is the function and skill of citing sources in research papers. The information that is cited in papers is meant to be used to support the argument being made, and unoriginal material must be attributed correctly. However, such material is sometimes used to construct an argument rather than support it. The author sometimes uses cited material as a substitute for developing his or her own ideas. Some students use research information that they gather as an outline. This is a process by which articles are found, and, instead of using the information to support their argument, the students figure out the outline of the article and end up paraphrasing most of it and calling it their own set of ideas. It is not explicitly taught that using another person's argument construction and thought outline without attribution is also a form of plagiarism.

I have struggled in the past with trying to find my own so-called voice when writing papers. At the undergraduate level, it is rare for students to be expected to write anything that is actually 100 percent original content. The majority of what we do is read about research that's been done by the scholars in our field, and the papers we produce are meant to demonstrate that we understand the research that already exists. Other times the papers involve us forming opinions about the research. When it came time for me to produce a higher level of academic writing, one that required me to develop my own original argument and my own voice, I felt that I had received little previous guidance and that the process had not been clearly explained. I had received a good foundation in the mechanics of writing (how to write grammatically, how to construct a thesis statement, etc.), but the process of how to conduct research, read the information, and synthesize it to produce a well-written academic paper was not explained. What I have learned about this process I have learned on my own through trial and error.

At the outset, I recall being concerned about overciting in my papers for fear that they would appear cut and pasted. I was also concerned about the process of paraphrasing, which I do not feel was ever clearly defined to me. Many professors have defined plagiarism as "two to four words or more used exactly verbatim"; such situations require citations. Though this may sound specific, when you sit down and attempt to paraphrase, it all of a suddenly becomes amazingly vague. Rather than teaching student writers through the use of such prescriptive statements, it would be more useful to teach them to be critical thinkers who understand where information comes from and how it is supposed to be honestly used. That's what scholarly research and writing is really all about, isn't it? To look into the source of something, to gain perspective by learning through what others have discovered, and to build upon that knowledge? If this overarching concept were more prevalent in the college curriculum, students could better understand the processes they are participating in. And certainly the more people who think critically about the world in which they exist, the better off we all will be. This skill serves us well both when students and long after into the rest of our lives if we want to become lifelong critically thinking learners.

Conclusion

The world that students inhabit now, in the twenty-first century, is very different from the world of any previous generation. This of course is an old adage, but it's important to realize that the gap between generations now is much larger than ever before. The cultural impact of technology on the ways Generation M works, plays, and learns needs to be included in conversations about academic writing skills and plagiarism. Plagiarism, what it is and how it erodes the scholarly community, needs to be emphasized along with the notion of personal consequences in order for students to have a clearer understanding of the effects their actions have. Finally, arming students with tools that will not only help them to avoid plagiarize but also show them how to develop their own writing process and their own voice when writing might be enough to start turning the tide away from the growing rates of plagiarism in the academic community today.

Part II
Finding Remedies

Creating a Tutorial: Background, Theory, and Practical Application

Vibiana Bowman Cvetkovic
John B. Gibson

Introduction

In the early 2000s, as part of a university-wide initiative to curb the rise of plagiarism, the Reference Department of the Paul Robeson Library (accessed 2010) decided to create a packet of web-based teaching modules as part of its bibliographic instruction program. The design team included the library director, an instruction librarian, the library's information technology specialist, and a part-time computer-graphic artist. The plagiarism tutorial that was produced was specifically geared to undergraduates and was intended to instruct the students about intellectual honesty, its importance in the process of scholarly writing, and how to avoid the pitfalls of plagiarism. It consists of a series of modules that utilizes web-based cartoons. The rationale for the use of webtoons was that if the tutorial was entertaining and interactive the undergraduates would become more engaged in the online learning process.

The response from the target audience—both students and faculty—was very positive. The tutorial, which is continually tweaked and updated, is still in use. Over the past ten years it has garnered recognition and awards. More important, high school and college educators, nationally and internationally, report that their students find the modules engaging and that they (the educators) consider them to be effective tools for teaching intellectual honesty. The modules are freely available on the web (library.camden.rutgers.edu/EducationalModule/Plagiarism). Educators are welcome to capture the tutorials and customize them for their own use.

When the first version of the plagiarism webtoons debuted in the early 2000s, there was some reluctance in the academic community to utilize cartoons for teaching purposes. Over the intervening years, particularly since the arrival of Web 2.0 and the proliferation of gaming culture, such reluctance has—for the most part—dissipated. Educators at all levels have come to embrace a wide variety of learning objects (teaching tools that encompass various media and platforms) as part of their methodology. These tools range from traditional print-based resources (handouts and pathfinders) to the creation of virtual worlds via Second Life to educational computer games such as *LittleBigPlanet* [*sic*]. Webtoons represent just one teaching strategy that an educator can use to engage students in participatory learning.

This chapter presents some suggestions on how to plan and execute an on-line tutorial. The projects that the authors have worked on and have used to illustrate this discussion are web based; however, the underlying pedagogical principles that were used in their design are applicable for learning objects in any format. The framework that the authors used for the plagiarism tutorial is based on the structure of a traditional lesson plan combined with basic marketing and advertising principles. The marketing techniques cited have been used for decades and are the underpinning of advertising campaigns for all manner of consumer goods from Apple iPods to Burger King Whoppers as well as for Public Service Announcements (PSAs) like "This Is Your Brain on Drugs." For those interested in more information about basic marketing techniques, the U.S. Small Business Administration (SBA) offers an excellent, online resource guide (Hudson, 2009). Information about lesson plans and samples that can be used for modeling can be found at educational websites such as Federal Resources for Educational Excellence (2009). A seminal work on educational planning is R.F. Mager's (1962) *Preparing Instructional Objectives*. Finally, an excellent overview, eminently useful to those new to writing educational objectives, is provided by the UCSD School of Medicine (Winegarden, 2005).

In this chapter the authors provide samples of their own work as they go through the step-by-step process of creating a tutorial. They do not offer these selections as examples of excellence but rather as a starting point for conversation. The authors encourage the readers to use the information as a springboard for creating new tools to educate the next generation of scholars, leaders, and citizens.

Designing a Tutorial: Step-by-Step

Step One: Establish a Mission and a Message

A clear mission statement makes project planning easier. It defines the project's underlying philosophy and delineates its goals. Ideally, it also reflects the values and aspirations of the stakeholders involved with the project—the administration, the faculty, and the creative team. Good mission statements are short and positive in tone. It is both necessary and appropriate to reference school policy and disciplinary measures when crafting a mission statement with respect to plagiarism. However, wherever possible, the emphasis should be on the importance of intellectual honesty and how learning to write in a clear, scholarly manner is a skill that will serve students well throughout their professional lives.

Excerpt from the "How to Avoid Plagiarism" Mission Statement
The Paul Robeson Library Reference faculty recognize that undergraduate students struggle with the concept of plagiarism. "How to Avoid Plagiarism" is intended to give students a clear understanding of what is plagiarism using clear language and concrete examples. (Paul Robeson Library, accessed 2010)

The value of a positive tone throughout the project, starting with the mission statement, cannot be emphasized enough. People are more receptive to a positive message than to a negative one. When planning an antiplagiarism tutorial, shift the focus to a list of "thou shall" rather than "thou shall not." Intellectual honesty implies that a writer is playing by the rules of good scholarship—defined as gathering, assessing, utilizing, and documenting the information that she has gathered, processed, and presented in a written or oral format. Scholars-in-training need to understand the importance of documenting their work so that the results can be independently verified and reproduced for the advancement of the discipline in which they are working. This is part and parcel of the "scientific process" and a cornerstone in every discipline that they might choose to pursue, from culinary arts to genetic engineering. Part of a broader mission for a tutorial in plagiarism is to give students specific skills for producing the formal, nonfiction style of writing required at the academic level. Students learning these skills need a clear understanding of what is required for this kind of prose.

Step Two: Identify Goals and Measurable Outcomes

A goal differs from a mission statement by its degree of specificity and intent. A mission statement is a general description of a broad purpose—the philosophical underpinnings. Goals are derived from the mission statement but are intended to describe specific, measurable outcomes. In designing the plagiarism tutorial for the Paul Robeson Library, the authors utilized macro and micro sets of goals and outcomes. At the macro level were the goals and outcomes for the entire project. Micro level goals and outcomes were established for each specific tutorial. The overall educational goals of the plagiarism project were to:

- promote the values of intellectual honesty;
- teach good scholarly writing skills, especially with regard to the importance of documentation; and
- promote information literacy skills, specifically with regard to what constitutes intellectual property.

Outcomes are based on the stated goals. An outcome statement defines an observable, measurable skill or action that the student will be able to perform as a result of the learning process (Lignugaris-Kraft, Marchand-Martella, and

Martella, 2001). Well-written outcome statements aid with assessment of both what the student has learned and how effective the tutorial is. The outcomes established for the plagiarism project were that, upon completion of the modules, the student would be able to:

- accurately define plagiarism;
- recognize what kind of source materials needed to be cited in a research paper; and
- demonstrate an understanding of the Rutgers University policies, procedures, and guidelines regarding academic integrity.

Plagiarism is a complex issue with many components. For the purposes of clarity and effectiveness, it is advisable to keep tutorials short and simple. To this end, a packet of modules on the topic of plagiarism might serve to make the project more manageable. The modules will all share the same mission; each module will have its own goal; and each module may have several educational objectives.

Step Three: Identify the Target Audience

Market research is used to customize advertising campaigns for all kinds of goods and services, from Rice-A-Roni to reality shows. This research in undertaken with the understanding that the more knowledge one has about a target audience the better a product can be pitched. After writing the mission statement, goals, and outcomes, identifying the target audience is the logical next step in the process of creating an educational campaign. A clear message to a targeted audience increases the chances that the message will not only be heard but also absorbed.

The SBA states that "successful marketing requires timely and relevant market information." The SBA also underscores the importance of research, which "can often uncover dissatisfaction or possible new products or services" (U.S. Small Business Administration, accessed 2010). Assuming that there is some lead time for research before the project is due and some access to the potential user group, standard survey tools like interviews, focus groups, and questionnaires are fairly inexpensive and can provide researchers with the kind of written documentation that is useful for planning goals and objective. This paper trail will also serve as a baseline for assessment by providing the designers with a staring point for establishing whether documented user needs were met. Of course, conversations with students, in both formal and informal settings, are a valuable resource for providing insights. Instructors can also use scholarly indexes, databases, table of content services, and government statistics and surveys to stay current with trends, demographics, and scholarly literature regarding their target audience.

As mentioned previously, the plagiarism tutorial that the Paul Robeson Library team created was web based. The target audience was undergraduate students at Rutgers University, Camden, New Jersey—a large, diverse, urban

**Academic Information Page from "How to Avoid Plagiarism"
(www.libraries.rutgers.edu/rul/libs/robeson_lib/
HAPACADINFO.html)**

Educational Goals and Outcomes:

The goals for this tutorial are that students will use information in an ethical manner and will recognize the art of citation as part of the scholarly communication process.

The educational outcome is that the student will produce a college-level paper with correct citations for all research materials.

The standards and performance indicators for the modules are based on the Association of College and Research Libraries Information Literacy Competency Standards for Higher Education (see: http://www.ala.org/ala/acrl/acrlstandards/informationliteracycompetency.htm).

ACRL Literacy Standard Five:

"The information literate student understands many of the economic, legal, and social issues surrounding the use of information and accesses and uses information ethically and legally."

Performance Indicators:

"The information literate student follows laws, regulation, institutional policies, and etiquette related to the access and use of information resources."

Educational Outcomes:

- Student accesses and assimilates the Rutgers University Guidelines for Academic Honesty.
- Student properly attributes sources materials when writing academic papers.

Performance Indicators:

"The information literate student acknowledges the use of information sources in communicating the product or performance."

Educational Outcomes:

- Student identifies when to use a citation.
- Demonstrates an understanding that all non-original information needs to be acknowledged.
- Identifies intellectual honesty as part of the scholarly communication process and as part of good scholarly writing.

campus. Background information about the intended user group was drawn from the design team's work with students in bibliographic instruction classes, reference desk exchanges, and general interactions with students in the library setting. In addition to informal information gathering, questionnaires were used and interviews were conducted. As each portion of the module was completed, the design team would have students preview and critique them. Student input was found to be invaluable; most of the students' critiques and suggestions found their way into the final product.

Step Four: Identifying an Appropriate Format for the Concept

A decision of appropriate format for presentation builds on the research gathered in the process of identifying the target audience. Again, what is feasible varies greatly according to individual circumstance. The choices for presentation format are constrained by the resources that the design team has at its disposal, particularly with regard to hardware, software, graphics capability, and available talent pool. The world of marketing offers an interesting context in which to frame these choices. The SBA gives this advice to beginning entrepreneurs:

> Your next step is to select the advertising vehicles you will use to carry your message, and establish an advertising schedule. In most cases, knowing your audience will help you choose the media that will deliver your sales message most effectively. Use as many . . . tools as are appropriate and affordable. (Hudson, 2009)

If one substitutes "educational vehicles" for "advertising vehicles" and "content" for "sales message," the advice seems particularly apt.

To aid in complex decision making it is often useful to create a decision-making chart. Enchanted Learning, a web resource for teachers, has printable decision charts at www.enchantedlearning.com/graphicorganizers/decision. In addition to clarifying available choices, charts can provide documentation on how decisions were reached and how they support mission statement, goals, and educational outcomes. This kind of documentation aids in the allocation of available financial and creative resources. In addition, the process of creating alternate scenarios facilitates planning for future purchases of instructional technology tools.

The next step in the planning process is to identify the appropriate format for the tutorial. As part of the consideration regarding various presentation formats, include planning for learning diversity. There is a wide variety of learning modalities; the most often used groupings are auditory, visual, and kinetic (learning by doing). Most students use a combination of strategies, but typically learners are stronger in one modality than another. An effective learning tool incorporates an awareness of different learning modalities into its design. This helps to ensure that all students have an opportunity to utilize their strengths. Incorporating different kinds of presentation strategies also makes the lesson more engaging. Talking heads, written materials, lectures, and graphics can become easy to tune out when overused. It is more attention grabbing when different skills or bits of information are imparted in a variety of ways. Examples of some different strategies and the learning modalities that they address include the following:

- Text passages are effective for short, important pieces of information such as definitions (for visual learners).

- Web-based movies (such as those done with Camtasia or Adobe Flash and can include a cartoon format, live actors, or stills) for pieces of information that require a lengthier explanation or are a little "dry" in content (for visual and auditory learners).
- Interactive quizzes can be used to reinforce a concept or to assess where the student is with regards to the information already presented (all learners—visual, auditory, and tactile learners).
- Role-playing especially involves the tactile/kinetic based learner.
- Peer editing again engages all three kinds of learners, especially if material is read aloud and the students are given the opportunity to move about the room.

For the Paul Robeson Library antiplagiarism project, much of the hardware, software, and training needed to create web tutorials were already in place. A robust web presence has been one of the goals of the library's strategic marketing plan for several years. Consequently, as funds became available, the library director was able to justify the purchase of educational technology tools because they had already been identified as necessary for meeting the goals established in the strategic plan.

Step Five: Creating the Tutorial

For this specific project, the decision was to create a web cartoon modeled after some of the more popular sites that the students watched (being very, very careful not to steal any ideas or step on any intellectual property rights). The library had a site license for Macromedia Flash (now Adobe Flash) software and had a high-end PC specifically configured for video creation. The instructional technology specialist had the skill set required to create the video, and the outreach librarian had the skill set for creating the educational content. The students supplied information regarding their own viewing habits and preferences that the designers used as the basis for a cartoon with educational content (Figure 6.1).

Macromedia Flash and Real One's video player were selected as the best software at the time to produce the final output. After the creation of this tutorial Adobe was purchased by Macromedia and rebranded. Since then, all the functionality is either unchanged or enhanced. To create content suitable for these mediums the graphic artist members of the team used Macromedia Freehand (Adobe Illustrator could now be used to perform the same tasks) and Adobe Photoshop. The objects were then animated using Macromedia Flash and captured from a Flash player using Camtasia. This allowed the team to output a raw AVI file to Adobe Premiere for editing. Adobe Premiere was used to export Real One content that could pseudostream from the server. This meant that the end user could begin to watch the video file before it was completely downloaded. Although the entire tutorial could have been developed with Macromedia Flash, these other external programs made it easier to harness the power of several tools to further tweak and maximize the final project for use

Figure 6.1. From the "Introduction" to the Cite Is Right

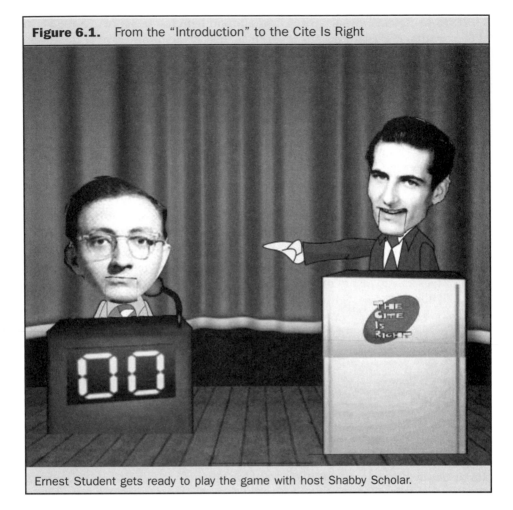

Ernest Student gets ready to play the game with host Shabby Scholar.

on the web. If this project were done today, we would likely use Adobe After Effects, instead of Premiere, and publish for use on more of the portable devices. The fact that the entire project had been storyboarded beforehand made the process of the actual production of the webtoon more efficient.

When planning out a tutorial, especially a graphics-based one, a storyboard, such as the ones animators and cartoon-strip artists use is very useful for plotting out ideas in a systematic fashion. Storyboards serve as a good communication tool, especially if a team is working on a project. They also serve as a way of documenting the project and reviewing changes, additions, and deletions. Drawings with an accompanying script make it easier for the creative talent doing voiceovers, music, and sound in a project (Figure 6.2).

Figure 6.2. Stick Drawing with Script

Shabby: OK, for the viewers at home let's review how to play the game:

Shabby: Ernest will type out the paper that he is working on. You the home viewer, will decide if the sentence that he typed needs a citation or not...

....

A rudimentary stick drawing (with script) serves as a storyboarding device.

Step Six: Assessment

The ability of the student who utilizes the tools to demonstrate the stated educational outcomes is one measure of the tutorial's effectiveness. The effectiveness of changing or influencing patterns of behavior over long periods of time is a more difficult outcome to assess. This is a topic that has been researched in relation to the effectiveness of PSAs, particularly those ads aimed at preventing illegal drug use by teenagers. In one study, researchers interviewed students, grades 5 through 12, after viewing a series of drug use– related PSAs. The students rated the ads that were specific with their message (e.g., possible consequences of heroin use) as effective and general message ads (e.g., those in the "Just Say No" campaign) as ineffective (Fishbein et al., 2002). The researchers cautioned that further evaluation of the topic is needed because of the difficulty of determining whether any behavioral changes actually came about as a result of viewing the PSAs. All they could claim to measure was the students' perceived effectiveness of the ad (Fishbein et al., 2002: 245). More recent studies (Langleben et al., 2009; Kang, Cappella, and Fishbein, 2009) indicate that the controversy over the effectiveness or perceived effectiveness of PSAs continues. Indeed, in their study of anti-marijuana PSAs, Kang, Cappella, and Fishbein (2009) concluded that the ads had a negative impact.

Skill assessment is perhaps a less daunting task than trying to assess changes in attitude. Specifically, it is easier for an educator to ascertain if a student can create a correct citation than to measure a change in a student's attitude toward intellectual property rights. A skill assessment tool in the form of an online game is included in "The Cite Is Right" module of the "How to Avoid Plagiarism" tutorial. The goal of this module is to teach students that different kinds of materials, in addition to exact quotes, need citations. The activity is a quiz that utilizes specific examples of various kinds of statements that a student might use in a paper, such as opinions, quotes (exact and paraphrased), "common knowledge," and statistics. The online interactive game provides assessment in the form of immediate feedback as to whether the answer given is right or wrong. The game also provides an explanation of "why" (Figure 6.3).

The tutorial itself also needs to be assessed to see if the students respond to it and if it is actually teaching them a skill that they can translate to a practical application. As mentioned earlier, the long-term effects of instruction are notoriously difficult to assess; however, it is crucial to try. Learning objects need to be refined and redone to respond to actual user need and effectiveness. Tools to asses a learning object's effectiveness include student and faculty surveys, questionnaires, and interviews. These evaluations can be used to refine and enhance a tutorial in order to better support the curriculum goals of the faculty and the information literacy needs of the students.

Conclusion

With the increased awareness in public schools, colleges, and universities about plagiarism and the increased resources being used to address the problem,

Figure 6.3. From the Cite Is Right

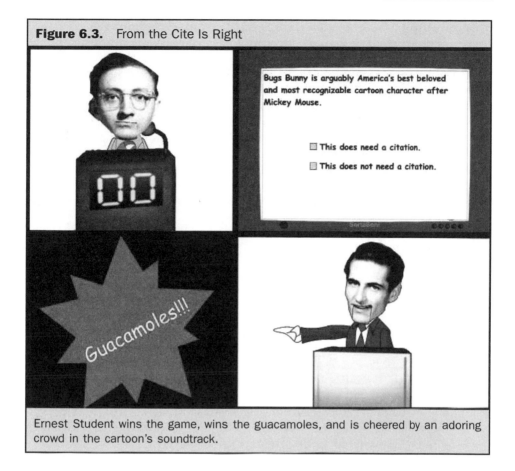

Ernest Student wins the game, wins the guacamoles, and is cheered by an adoring crowd in the cartoon's soundtrack.

new research will undoubtedly be forthcoming regarding outcomes of educational initiatives regarding intellectual honesty and their effectiveness. In the meantime, educators at all levels can continue to instill in their students the values and skills shared by the academic community with regard to scholarly writing and intellectual honesty. Educators can also contribute to this effort by producing and sharing learning objects and by making them freely available on the web. These works need to be shared fearlessly. Innovative projects often get stalled from fear of criticism. Teaching is a creative process, and teaching tools are by their very nature fluid, mutable, constantly changing, and tweaked through critiques. The more learning objects that a teacher has to choose from in her battle against plagiarism, the better her chances for success with her students.

Go forth and create!

References

Federal Resources for Educational Excellence. 2009. "Subject Map." Washington, DC: Office of Communications and Outreach. Available: www.free.ed.gov (accessed May 27, 2010).

Fishbein, Martin, Kathleen Hall-Jamieson, Eric Zimmer, Ina von Haeften, and Robin Nabi. 2002. "Avoiding the Boomerang: Testing the Relative Effectiveness of Antidrug Public Service Announcements before a National Campaign." *American Journal of Public Health* 92, no. 2 (February): 238–245.

Hudson, Vicki. 2009. "Advertising and PR." Washington, DC: U.S. Small Business Administration. Available: www.sba.gov/smallbusinessplanner/manage/marketandprice/SERV_ADNPUBLICREL.html (accessed May 27, 2010).

Kang, Yahui, Joseph N. Cappella, and Martin Fishbein. 2009. "The Effect of Marijuana Scenes in Anti-Marijuana Public Service Announcements on Adolescents' Evaluation of Ad Effectiveness." *Health Communication* 24, no. 6: 483–493.

Langleben, Daniel D., et al. 2009. "Reduced Prefrontal and Temporal Processing and Recall of High 'Sensation Value' Ads." *NeuroImage* 46, no. 1: 219–225.

Lignugaris-Kraft, Benjamin, Nancy Marchand-Martella, and Ronald C. Martella. 2001. "Writing Better Goals and Short-Term Outcomes or Benchmarks." *Teaching Exceptional Children* 34, no. 1 (September/October): 52–58.

Mager, Robert F. 1962. *Preparing Instructional Objectives.* Belmont, CA: Fearon Publishers.

Paul Robeson Library. "How to Avoid Plagiarism." Camden, NJ: Rutgers University. Available: library.camden.rutgers.edu/EducationalModule/Plagiarism (accessed January 10, 2010).

U.S. Small Business Administration. "Market and Price." Available: Washington, DC: U.S. Small Business Administration. Available: www.sba.gov/smallbusinessplanner/manage/marketandprice/index.html (accessed April 17, 2010).

Winegarden, Babbi. 2005. "Writing Instructional Objectives." San Diego: UCSD School of Medicine. Available: meded.ucsd.edu/faculty/writing_instructional_objectives.pdf (accessed May 27, 2010).

7

The First-Year College Experience

Gillian A. Newton
Jeffrey J. Teichmann

Introduction

This chapter explores and reviews current initiatives by academic libraries to assist first-year college students in the ethical use of information. In some cases librarians are working alone through information literacy programs, although collaboration with teaching faculty and college administrators is gaining in popularity. A discussion of recent trends in first-year programming and the impact they have on plagiarism prevention would not be complete without considering the past. A brief look back gives a historical perspective on the issue of educating students in the use of information and provides insight for the development of new initiatives in the future. Interestingly, the literature describing early library instruction does not specifically discuss the topic of plagiarism. Perhaps at the time it was not believed to be necessary, but today it is a topic that is of great concern to librarians and educators alike. Past experience has seen the pendulum swing from library-centered instruction to a more collaborative model. It is still in motion as librarians and educators continue to address the problem of how best to reach the first-year college students and provide them with the tools they need to avoid plagiarism and use information ethically.

The Past

Orientation Programs—For Better or Worse

College orientation programs date back over 100 years, with the first official programs being held by Boston University and Lee College in the 1880s, the first required general orientation program being held at Oberlin College in

1900, and the first credit-bearing program at Reed College in 1911 (Gordon, 1989; Ryan and Glenn, 2004). Library orientations and bibliographic instruction also date back into the latter part of the 1800s but were not a part of the overall college orientation process and certainly not a required element for the freshman class. In fact, some university libraries restricted freshman access to the libraries as recently as the 1930s (Denise, 1936). Today's freshmen certainly would not tolerate being excluded from any parts of the library.

Over time, academic librarians grew frustrated with the lack of library knowledge demonstrated by the students even as they offered library instruction classes. In 1926, Ada Jeannette English, the librarian at the New Jersey College for Women, questioned fellow college librarians to determine the breadth of the problem. As a result of her investigation, she learned that while almost half of the schools offered a program, less than 25 percent ran it during freshman orientation (English, 1926). At Rutgers College a mandatory freshman library instruction program was introduced in the fall of 1936, with positive evaluations by participants leading to this becoming a required component of freshman English courses (James, 1941). At the same time Suffolk University in Boston was running a series of five lectures on library instruction for the freshman class, with a reported 25 percent increase in freshmen's use of the library following the course (Newsome, 1940).

In 1939, the librarians at Williams College were given charge of the freshman orientation and felt this was the perfect opportunity to present library orientation to the freshman class before they were caught up in the rigors of coursework. The program combined lectures and visual displays and was declared a success (Stanford, 1939). However, by the mid-1940s popular thinking was leading librarians to question library orientation for the freshman class. Erickson (1949) called for library instruction to be integrated into credit-bearing courses in the English curriculum, thereby increasing the amount of faculty available to teach library instruction. This trend continued into the 1950s, when Devlin (1957) called for an increased level of collaboration among the students, the teaching faculty, and the library. Once again librarians were finding that the students would gain more from library instruction that was geared toward their coursework research needs (Ranstead and Spencer, 1959). In the 1960s, library instruction was part of the freshman orientation week schedule, but it again was being questioned for its validity in the college curriculum. Hartz (1965) called for library instruction to be a multipart, multiyear program, beginning with a general orientation session in the freshman year. Further instruction should wait until a research project is assigned, and a final session should be held in the junior or senior year to support the higher levels of research performed at these stages (Hartz, 1965).

Library Instruction—Innovative or Repetitive?

In 1926, the librarian at Princeton University reported that while he saw all the freshmen, he was allotted only 20 minutes with them. In this time he endeavored to cover the card catalog, book check out, and some major reference sources (English, 1926). In the summer of 2009, Rutgers University began a "new" freshman orientation program that included a library component. In speaking with the Instruction Coordinator of the Rutgers University Libraries about the content covered, she began by saying, "Well, we had them for 20 minutes, so we showed them the OPAC, how to look up a book . . . " (personal communication, Cassel, October 10, 2009).

Library instruction programs were usually held in the library where the resources were close at hand, but there is evidence of some forward thinking from a librarian at Vassar College in 1926. The librarian had the idea of producing a motion picture of the library instruction process, but she did not have any idea how this might be achieved (English, 1926). Hartz (1965) also called for librarians to utilize the new multimedia technologies available to solve the staffing problems of the larger colleges. By producing and distributing short films of research techniques, many students could be reached with a single librarian. Could these have been a precursor to the online tutorials of today?

The turbulence of the 1960s led to the development of a new type of freshman orientation course by the University of South Carolina in 1971, University 101 (Roach, 1998). This type of program became quite popular at smaller colleges and is even being adopted at large universities today. While University 101 does cover a broad range of topics, there is a research component that is built around library research. This is not the usual random exercise, but guided library research instruction on a topic with help available at every step. The students have commented, "this is one of the most significant events in the course" (Jewler, 1989: 204). To be truly effective, the library component needs to be comprehensive, not a light overview, which is likely to be quickly forgotten and not available when needed (Jewler, 1989). This carefully guided instruction approach used to connect to freshman students early in their collegiate careers can also help reduce feelings of library anxiety. Adapting library instruction to include greater amounts of technology (e-mail, instant messaging, etc.) and allowing the students to work collaboratively has also shown greater success rates (Kuh, Boruff-Jones, and Mark, 2007). By creating a bond with a librarian and the library in their first year of college-level research, the students will be more likely to use library resources in their later research projects.

First-Year Experience courses now number in the thousands in the United States. These courses or orientation programs have been patterned after the University 101 program at the University of South Carolina. Measures of success for these programs are mainly retention rates and the increased use of university services (Barefoot, 2000). The focal point of these programs has become strategy based, teaching learning skills; or socialization based, teaching life skills (binge-drinking prevention, health-related topics, the culture of the university). In turn these programs have bred a hybrid model that centers on a theme or topic of interest, similar to the first-year interest groups popular at larger universities. Currently most colleges and universities in the United States have some sort of First-Year Experience program in place. Ryan and Glenn (2004) looked closely at how the different types of programs fare with the freshmen. Using the common indicators of grade point average (GPA) and retention rate, they found that the strategy-based programs worked best for the students who found themselves in trouble academically in their first year of college. While it might be thought that the socialization-based models might aid some freshmen, this was not found to be the case; GPAs continued to decrease, and retention rates were not significantly different from those students not in a program. However, these results are not able to be generalized to the larger population of freshmen at four-year institutions due to the insulated population studied (Ryan and Glenn, 2004). While these results have some implications for the general direction of the First-Year Experience curriculums, they do not give much indication as to the best outline for information literacy or library orientation for first-year students.

The Present

A Closer Look at Today's Freshmen

The freshman class in the fall of 2009 was born in the final decade of the most technologically advancing century in history. These students have not known life without technology at their fingertips. In fact, according to the infamous Beloit College mindset list, students in the class of 2013 have never used a card catalog, always had text that is hyper, always seen a computer in the Oval Office, always had electronic books, and always known what would be on the evening news before the evening news—well, that is, if they cared to look (McBride and Nief, 2009).

In addition to growing up with more technology than any other generation, these freshmen have also grown up in the most child-focused era to date, where everyone gets a trophy just for their participation. Many of these students have juggled a schedule packed with academic, cultural, and sports activities that would have made personal assistants throw up their hands in dismay. They are probably able to multitask in their sleep. As these students progressed through school they continually collaborated and worked as teams, being educated primarily under the auspices of social development theory techniques.

As they grew into teenagers, these students were exposed to Napster, where they learned it was okay to "share" music without cost, even after the lawsuits began. They readily borrow and share photographs, links, and personal details via social networks—they literally are the "face" of Facebook. Throughout their teen years, these students were constantly exposed to a society where it was acceptable to cheat—at least until you got caught. Today's freshmen grew up with major scandals in government, sports, and business—Monica Lewinsky, performance-enhancing drugs in baseball and other sports, Enron, Bernie Madoff—just to name a few. Any lines that had been drawn had most certainly been erased (Bauman, 2009).

According to the National Center for Education Statistics (NCES), the freshman class of 2007 numbered over 2.7 million students. This number had been steadily rising for the previous ten years and is the highest enrollment in the past 50 years. In fact, the NCES predicts this number will continue to increase over the next ten years, topping out at well over 3 million persons (National Center for Education Statistics, 2008). Each year students inundate college campuses across the country, and the orientation process begins. But where does the college or university library fit into the technologically advanced student's life? How can information professionals convince these freshmen to grace the hallowed halls of the college library? And if they do, is it possible to reach out to them and show them how to use information ethically?

Today's freshmen have grown up with and are accustomed to technology in every aspect of their lives. Oseguera (2007) found that the majority spend between one and five hours per day using technology—surfing the web, instant messaging, e-mailing, etc. The second highest group spent between six and ten hours per day. In 2000, Olsen found that 90 percent of freshmen owned their own computer—today this number most likely would be higher. Campus housing provided hardwired Internet (today many are wireless) and campus wireless hotspots are easily located (Olsen, 2000). Today's undergraduates are used to having everything, including answers to their information needs, in an instant. Is this constant availability of the Internet further promoting this idea?

Barefoot (2006: B16) found that "students see the library as a museum—a place that belongs to the past, not the present." So if freshmen are not using the library, where are they obtaining information for their research projects? This tech-savvy generation is finding their information on the Internet, says Oseguera (2007), and this idea is supported by Harley, Dreger, and Knobloch (2001), who described undergraduates as consumers of information on the web. Barefoot (2006) calls for library instruction programs to have a common goal—to assist undergraduates in being savvy consumers of web information. But is this easier said than done?

In the late 1980s, Mellon (1989) coined the term "library anxiety" and used it to describe the feelings undergraduates had toward their college library. Feelings of hopelessness and embarrassment were said to plague undergraduates using their libraries. At that time, there were few alternate sources for researching available to undergraduates. Flash-forward 20 years—today undergraduate students do not need to leave their dorm rooms to become hopelessly lost in the virtual library or other Internet sources.

In the 1990s, McCabe, Trevino, and Butterfield (2001) reproduced a study first done in the 1960s that took an in-depth look at cheating in academic institutions. There were three major findings to come out of this study. First, students' definition of plagiarism had shifted in the 30 years since the initial study was done. Actions that students had considered plagiarizing in the 1960s were no longer being considered plagiarizing by the student body of the 1990s. This may be due in part to the ready access that the student of today has to information. It has already been mentioned that this year's freshman class is quite comfortable with technology and has come to expect information at its fingertips. Is it possible this comfort and ready access has blurred the lines of plagiarism?

The second finding to come from McCabe, Trevino, and Butterfield's (2001) study was that students' understanding of plagiarism and other aspects of academic cheating increased when the institutional expectations and penalties were clearly laid out before them. Simply placing the policy or a link to the academic integrity policy in the syllabus was found not to be sufficient; when the policy was discussed and supported by the teaching faculty, the students had a greater respect for, and an understanding of, the boundaries.

Third, McCabe, Trevino, and Butterfield (2001) had looked at possible individual factors for students cheating on exams and written assignments. Younger students, freshmen and sophomores, were found to have a higher level of cheating, possibly because of the large class sizes of these college levels. Students in the upper level courses have a closer relationship with the faculty and a more vested interest in the subject matter, so these factors may translate into a desire not to cheat. There were other factors that basically can be pared down to the following: pressure to get good grades, time constraints, gender, and personal integrity. While these factors were important, they were found to be less contributory than the contextual factors of the individual's definition of plagiarism, the institutional policy, and the institutional culture regarding academic integrity (McCabe, Trevino, and Butterfield, 2001).

The question of citations was addressed in a study by Davis (2003). From 1996 to 2001, he tracked student citations. During this period the number of citations climbed rapidly, as did the amount of ready information on the Internet. When citation guidelines were clearly expressed in terms of source and scholarly level, the number of citations dropped and the scholarly level of the individual citations increased (Davis, 2003).

Thompson (2003) attempted to determine if today's students are information illiterate or just plain lazy when it comes to their research needs. In her study, she attempted to determine if the Internet is to blame for the lower quality research of current students. After examining the question from several angles, her results were inconclusive but leaned decidedly toward the Internet not being at fault because, as we all know, there is quality information to be found on the Internet if one knows how and where to look. Unfortunately a majority of the students felt they were good to excellent searchers (Thompson, 2003). Clearly today's students are in need of guidance in terms of searching, retrieving, and using information found on the Internet.

In 2007, Stephens, Young, and Calabrese also surveyed undergraduates in an attempt to determine if there was a significant difference in the level of college students cheating using traditional methods versus digital methods. Approximately 1,300 undergraduate students were asked about six different forms of cheating, which included plagiarizing a few sentences and plagiarizing an entire paper. The results indicated no statistically significant difference between the instances of students plagiarizing via traditional or digital means. There was also no statistically significant difference in how the students felt about cheating via either means. This was a surprising result given the relative ease of "cut and paste" plagiarism; it had been expected that the students would be more accepting of cheating via the cut and paste method. Another interesting finding was that the students did not have a preferred method. It seemed that they would plagiarize by either means without preference. Last, the study looked at possible predictors of cheating behavior. One of the strongest predictors of digital cheating was the perception of peer acceptance of the digital cheating (Stephens, Young, and Calabrese, 2007). It seems as if the culture is a very strong influence on these students and their propensity to bend the rules.

The question of from whom or where students will receive guidance on performing their academic research is one that has plagued librarians and educators for a long while. This is not a new problem, nor a problem created by the Internet. What the Internet has done is to place the information closer to the students and the students further from those who can provide that guidance. When this problem is examined with regard to the first-year students, it is exacerbated by two issues. First, the large introductory classes taken by most freshmen in their first academic year, numbering anywhere from 75 to 1,000 students, do not require research papers. It has also been determined that college students learn most of the things they will need to know to survive college in their first year (Barefoot, 2006). Combining these facts with those mentioned previously—students' self-proclaimed efficacy in searching, the prevalence of library anxiety, and the wealth of information on the Internet—how will these students learn to use information ethically and legally? And what is our role in this process as education professionals?

First-Year Outreach and the Library

First-Year Experience programs run the gambit from mandatory one- or two-day orientations for new students, freshman seminars, 101 credit courses, and first-year interest groups (FIGS) to semester or year-long learning communities. Similarly the role of the academic library in these first-year initiatives may range from a quick library tour during orientation week to hiring a full time First-Year Experience librarian, as is the case at Bowling Green University where, in 1999, concerns surrounding retention and success of new students led to the creation of this unique position (Boff, Albrecht, and Armstrong, 2007). By 2006, a survey identified 15 librarians nationwide with responsibility for introducing new students to the library and providing support to first-year programming (Boff, Albrecht, and Armstrong, 2007). Although there was a slow and steady growth in librarians' participation in the lives of first-year students, through formal and ad hoc programs, collaboration between the two disparate but related fields of information literacy and freshman experience has become more of a force in the past five years, as concerns about student retention and success continue.

In 2003, at the annual meeting of the Association of College and Research Libraries (ACRL), John Gardner, founder and executive director of the Policy Center on the First Year of College and senior fellow at the National Resource Center (NRC), challenged librarians to become more active in first-year initiatives (Gardner and Koch, 2007). The ensuing collaboration between ACRL and NRC led to the production of the monograph *The Role of the Library in the First College Year* (Hardesty, 2007b), which includes analysis, models of instruction, and best practices and generally provides an excellent overview of where the academic library is currently positioned within the first-year movement. However, as noted by Hardesty (2007a: 170), while there has been interest in both camps to see increased collaboration, the "convergence of information literacy and the First Year Experience is not predetermined." Instead, establishment of stable and enduring programs requires continued discourse between library and nonlibrary faculty and creative use of staffing and technological resources to respond to the unique needs of the millennials who comprise today's freshman class. It has become increasingly apparent to librarians and teachers that students need not only to find information, which as we know is so abundant as to be overwhelming, but also be able to use it critically and appropriately. Assisting new scholars to avoid plagiarism is the responsibility of the whole college community working together and individually. Within that community the academic library has an important, and expanding, role to play in both welcoming new students and preparing them to be future scholars who can critically evaluate information and use it ethically.

Plagiarism, What Plagiarism?

New students often arrive on campus unclear as to what constitutes plagiarism. Many plagiarize through ignorance of the writing and research process rather than because of a determination to cheat. To be part of the solution, academic libraries need to become as integral to the First-Year Experience as possible, whether this means participating in an established campus program or by independent outreach of a group or even one librarian.

In this section the many ways that academic libraries and librarians have impacted first-year students' understanding of academic integrity will be considered. Librarians have been extremely innovative, using their expertise in collaboration with other teaching faculty to work directly with students in orientations, workshops, and tutorials and also with faculty either in the traditional policing role to uncover suspected plagiarism or by taking a more proactive stance in assisting teachers to plagiarism-proof their assignments. Although totally eliminating plagiarism is next to impossible, these collaborative efforts may reduce a student's desire to cut and paste or purchase papers and should lay an early foundation for improved scholarship. According to Watts (2005: 347), who advocates for positioning the library at the center of the First-Year Experience, "students will be more cognizant of the academic and ethical implications of plagiarism if they have been taught how to engage in scholarship in a meaningful way." In keeping with the "Standards of Information Literacy and Instruction" developed by the Association of College and Research Libraries (ACRL), which may be accessed at their website (Association of College and Research Libraries, 2000), it is a librarian's responsibility, in upholding Standard Five, to ensure the "information literate student . . . accesses and uses information ethically and legally." It is imperative to work with new students from day one to ensure they not only know how to access the information they need but also understand how to use it honestly.

Into the Future

Starting at the Beginning

To impact the scholarly lives of students, it is necessary first to reach them. For students to be willing to use the library physically or virtually, they need to trust in its ability to welcome them and help them as they adjust to their new environment. Developing the library as an anxiety-free zone is something that should start at orientation, or even earlier, and continue through the life of every student. Every encounter with a new student is an opportunity to demonstrate expertise and approachability, whether it is on a library tour, at the reference desk, or during online interaction. A solid first step in this process is to try to change first-year students' perception of the library from a place they see no use for to one that can help them succeed.

A quick tour of the library is often included on prospective students' campus tours, but in a rather unique venture Western Michigan University partnered with university admissions to produce a "Go for the Gold" program and provide an evening of "fun in the library for scholarship-seeking millennials" (Behr, Bundza, and Cockrell, 2007: 2). Part tour and part hands-on exploration of the website, the program included the online activity "The Plagiarism Puzzle" taken from a tutorial created by the librarians and the writing center at the University of Maine at Farmington (Writing Center and Mantor Library, accessed 2010). This program provided library staff the unique opportunity to work with other departments in the university and enhance the library's profile on campus while forcing a rethinking of the ways to conduct orientation instruction. It is noteworthy that the topic of plagiarism was included in this event. Although the opportunity to be a part of this type of recruitment event may be somewhat limited, it is food for thought for libraries wishing to make their presence and influence felt as early as possible in the lives of freshmen.

Becoming part of summer orientation activities for prospective freshmen is usually the starting point of many library initiatives. Often a stop on the campus tour provides a brief introduction to the library during an intense day or two of activities. In a new initiative at Rutgers University, New Brunswick/Piscataway Campus, librarians reached out to over 4,000 incoming freshmen this past summer at their main undergraduate library, where an online scavenger hunt using the libraries' website provided a brief introduction to library resources. According to Jeris Cassel, Instruction Coordinator for Rutgers University Libraries (personal communication, October 10, 2009), it was difficult to make a concrete assessment of the success of this brand new initiative, but there are plans to build on this experience to develop a program for next year.

Some schools have developed the resources and manpower to move beyond this model. In 2007, the University of Kentucky created a "Hubbub" during the university welcome week, with pizza, cupcakes, and many fun activities sponsored by outside companies (Wasielewski, 2009). This event was repeated in 2008 with over 700 students in attendance. The main aim, which they felt they achieved, was to dispel library anxiety and build approachability. In a similar vein, Penn State University libraries hosted a two-day interactive orientation Open House for around 2,000 students. A self-guided tour together with activities, prizes, and a focus on providing a personal experience for attendees contributed to the success and popularity of this event (Cahoy and Bichell, 2004). In 2004, with five Open Houses under their belts, they concluded that this model of orientation provided a "wonderful way to connect with students while dazzling them with [our] collections, services, and terrific faculty and staff!" (Cahoy and Bichell, 2004: 56). So start as early as possible and be as creative as you can within the bounds of the resources at your disposal. Those favorable first impressions go a long way toward ensuring that newcomers become frequent users of the library's many services.

Impressing with One Shot

Once orientation week is over and classes begin, some first-year students are given the opportunity to visit or revisit the library—many just for one class. A Freshman 101 curriculum often incorporates an introduction to the library, and typically staff will have around 50 minutes to reach out to new students in some meaningful way. A tour plus a quick overview of physical and online resources is still the most common format for this class. However, if this outpouring of information is not tied into any specific and immediately relevant research or writing assignment, it is debatable how much of the material is retained. Also considerable time may elapse between this introductory class and the scheduling of an assignment. Students often return to the library with little memory of their earlier instruction.

To provide a more meaningful and memorable experience within the limits of this short time frame, there have been attempts to change the typical tour and library website overview format to include more active learning or a more content-specific slant. One college library experimented with a self-guided treasure hunt for new freshmen and concluded that this more hands-on approach to learning led to improved skills and lessened library anxiety (Marcus and Beck, 2003). Another study compared three different methods of conducting a class about plagiarism (Moniz, Fine, and Bliss, 2008). Although not specifically directed at first-year students, this study at Johnson and Wales University, Charlotte Campus, included a significant number of younger students aged 17 to 19. Three types of instruction designed to increase a student's understanding of plagiarism were conducted. Traditional instruction using a lecture and short discussion looked at definitions of plagiarism and examples of paraphrasing; a PowerPoint presentation covered similar items to the traditional class with no deviation from the predetermined text; and one class employed what they labeled "a student-centered approach" (Moniz, Fine, and Bliss, 2008: 266), which included group activities and role-play exercises highlighting plagiarism violations. The desired result was not only for students to increase their understanding of what constituted plagiarism but also to determine if one type of instruction method would result in better understanding by the students. Surprisingly, they found that the more active learning class did not outperform the other two methods but that all three forms of instruction led to some improvement in the students' understanding. Students in all three classes demonstrated a need for further help with their understanding of plagiarism.

In her report of an eight-year longitudinal study at Abilene Christian University, Baker (2006) discussed how their 50-minute Freshman Seminar evolved from a Scavenger Hunt Model to a Research Model and finally to a Course Integrated Mini-Research Project. The librarians found that using a course-related topic added value and relevance to the instruction. By incorporating a worksheet on database use to be completed before the library class, they were able to concentrate on the conceptual rather than mechanical skills of completing boxes on the computer interface. This emphasis on discussing concepts rather than just demonstrating databases can lend itself to the teaching of plagiarism. Many students do know about citing and even have an idea of the rudiments of various citation styles, but teaching them when and why it is necessary to use these citations rather than merely how to use them is an area where librarians can demonstrate their expertise.

Leaping into More Teaching

In some cases librarians have had the opportunity to expand their involvement in the First-Year Experience beyond this one-shot deal. An example is the Library 101–type course, which usually counts for one credit and allows for a more in-depth exploration of access and use of information. At Delta State the one-credit course Fundamentals of Information Literacy included a session on plagiarism avoidance in conjunction with proper citation. The course was well received by students, according to a postclass survey. Using pre- and posttests the librarians determined where changes needed to be implemented for future years (Mounce, 2006). In 2005, at the University of Rhode Island, librarians became embedded in the distance learning program by offering their services to faculty as a way to assist students who study remotely. Instruction is given by e-mail, posting to discussion boards, or posting a whole lesson. As part of this program librarians taught a LIB 120, Introduction to Information Literacy, course both online and in person (Ramsey and Kinnie, 2006).

At Penn State–New Kensington a librarian partnered with a member of the teaching faculty to attend all class sessions of a freshman speech class (Hall, 2008). Although time consuming, this experiment was judged a success in terms of the relationships formed with the students and the opportunity gained to improve students' overall search and critical thinking skills. If time and budget permit, becoming "embedded" is a creative way to reach out to students and collaborate with faculty over issues of evaluating information and demonstrating its appropriate use. Most discussion of plagiarism happens in the classroom, so for a librarian to be available during each class is a golden opportunity to share expertise and encourage students to use their own voices.

Becoming integrated into the LEAP program was an exciting opportunity for librarians at the University of Utah. This program organizes first-year students on a voluntary basis into learning communities with other students who have similar interests (St. Clair, 2002). Twelve "LEAPing" librarians conduct a series of ten library sessions over the academic year. At each session the research skills of participants become more advanced. This collaboration between the librarians and faculty "places the library in the middle of a successful learning community" (St. Clair, 2002: 26). Although plagiarism was not specifically mentioned as a focus in these sessions, it would certainly be one way to take advantage of the spirit of collaboration between librarians and faculty. At Georgia State University, two librarians progressed from co-teaching the library section of the freshman orientation class to developing their own learning community, "Life in the information age" (Burtle and Sugarman, 2002: 277). This experience led to a better understanding of their freshman audience and an increased sense of their own value as faculty within the university community.

Increasing Collaboration

Collaboration seems to be a recurring theme in tackling the issue of plagiarism at the first-year level. Whether this takes the form of librarians working with faculty to select content for orientation sessions, teaching in a learning community, or becoming embedded in the classroom, forming relationships outside the library with other teaching faculty is essential when guiding freshman students through the research process. "In building assignments that focus on the information gathering process, information competencies are addressed and plagiarism is prevented" (Hurlbert, Savidge, and Laudenslager, 2003: 40). If the instructor requires students to turn in a preliminary bibliography together with an outline and rough drafts while working toward the finished product this will deter "procrastination, plagiarism, frustration and overload" (Hurlbert, Savidge, and Laudenslager, 2003: 47), which are surely four of the most common woes a freshman student has to bear. At the first-year level a partnering of librarians with writing professors to design meaningful assignments is a major step toward achieving academic honesty.

Buranen (2009), as Director of the University Writing Center at California State University, Los Angeles, endorses this kind of partnership. In addition to assisting with research design, librarians may also use their expert subject knowledge to guide students in the conventions of research within a discipline. For example, it is often difficult for the novice researcher to determine common knowledge on a topic as opposed to what does need to be cited. Citation practices vary among disciplines, and this can add to the confusion of new scholars. Librarians can help to demystify the citation process. In addition they can provide a censure-free zone where students may obtain advice on the how and why of citation (Buranen, 2009). According to Hurlbert, Savidge, and Laudenslager (2003: 49), "most faculty are glad for partners who help monitor the steps of the research process, with respectful attention to the particular challenges of their discipline."

There is an understanding that many cases of plagiarism, especially unintentional, may be prevented or at least diminished by teaching new students some of the skills required in writing a plagiarism-free paper: summarizing, paraphrasing, and citation. According to Harris (2005), with the changes in the teaching of writing that have evolved over the past few decades, some teaching faculty have moved away from focusing on how to use and cite sources. Librarians are helping to fill this void with their expertise in the ethical use of information.

Synthesizing multiple viewpoints and bringing these all together into a cohesive piece of text, with correct attribution, takes practice. It is a skill that is particularly difficult for new students to grasp. Teaching use of information should be an essential part of first-year curriculums whether it is integrated into library information literacy classes, covered in English class, or developed through a partnership of the two. Certainly a review of paraphrasing, summarizing, correct citation, and critical evaluation of information is within the standards of information literacy and the purview of the academic librarian. At Rasmussen College librarians decided to introduce paraphrasing exercises to freshman library instruction classes (Bronshteyn and Baladad, 2006). Although they found, during a literature review, that paraphrasing instruction is primarily taught within English education rather than in library instruction, a student self-assessment given to first-year students after the workshop suggested that an overwhelming majority found that this exercise in conjunction with citation instruction greatly helped their confidence in paraphrasing. Collaborating with the teaching faculty to ensure these skills are covered during the first year—whether as part of a formal program or through informal alliance—is essential in reducing plagiarism.

Offering Specialized Workshops

Another way librarians are fighting plagiarism among college freshmen is to provide stand-alone workshops. At Long Island University Library the Coordinator of Plagiarism Activities offers support to students and faculty across the campus (Madray, 2007). In student workshops on "Plagiarism Awareness" an active learning strategy is employed using exercises and discussion while keeping lecturing to a minimum. A survey of the usefulness of this workshop to freshmen in the College 101 orientation program was undertaken using pre- and posttests. The survey showed that although students had increased their awareness of the seriousness of plagiarizing they still found difficulty with citing Internet sources, with only 44 percent stating they were comfortable doing this, up only 13 percent from the pretest, indicating a need for more help in this area.

Concentrating primarily on citation, Liles and Rozalski (2004) developed a "Style Manual Workshop" at which students had the opportunity to identify examples of plagiarism and practice the correct way to cite. A website was set up to be used in conjunction with the workshop, giving opportunities to practice and reinforce the information given in person. The success of these workshops was attributed in part to the fact that students were able to practice citation using sources they had already identified for their research. Making the content relevant is always going to enhance the learning experience for overstretched freshman students.

Combining Collaboration with Technology

At Dickinson College, librarians found an innovative way to teach plagiarism to all first-year students (Bombaro, 2007). Although the first-year seminar program required a mandatory library visit for all freshmen, this provided only limited opportunity to touch on plagiarism. After being approached by the college's associate provost with a concern that the college freshman orientation program was not fully addressing the issue of academic honesty, the library director agreed to work with librarians to integrate plagiarism instruction into the first-year information literacy program. Armed with the support of administration and other teaching faculty, librarians set about devising a separate workshop to teach plagiarism avoidance, which they titled "The Seven Deadly Sins of Plagiarism." Recognizing that using technology to find information is often an unintentional cause of plagiarism or at least a cause of much confusion, the librarians decided to make use of technology "as a tool to ward off the mistakes, misunderstandings and abuses brought about partially by its own advantages" (Bombaro, 2007: 297). They decided to use an anonymous audience response system to ask questions at the beginning, during, and at the end of the session. Students indicated their level of understanding by clicking on the answer that they thought was correct without exposing themselves to possible ridicule or censure. By this method librarians were able to assess the level of understanding of the new students before and after the class and adjust future classes to meet needs expressed by the audience. An assessment of the program suggested that an increased number of students grasped the concept of academic integrity more fully, but many still had trouble with paraphrasing.

Providing Virtual Experiences

The opportunity to personally reach and teach new students about academic integrity varies not only with the composition of and support given to the First-Year Experience program but also with the size of the freshman class and the budget and staffing resources at hand. Therefore, many academic libraries use supplementary or stand-alone online tutorials and other virtual ways to reach their freshmen. Web-based instruction in the library began to be developed during the 1990s as a way to reach the increasing number of students admitted to colleges. As previously discussed, our technologically advanced students prefer to "go to the library" without leaving their home or dorm room, so why not deliver library instruction to the students via the website?

The Texas Information Literacy Tutorial (TILT) developed at the University of Texas–Austin was one of the first virtual instruction tools (University of Texas System Digital Library, 2004). Created in 1997 to fill a need to reach over 50,000 students with limited resources of time and manpower, it quickly became the basis of many tutorials developed by academic libraries nationwide. Although it was discontinued in August 2009, the Open Public License version remained available until May 2010. While covering many aspects of the research process, typical web tutorials usually have at least one section on citing and avoiding plagiarism. For example, Empower at Wichita State University (Wichita State University Libraries Information System, 2008) and the newly developed RIOT at Rutgers University (Rutgers University, 2009) are typical of many similar online tools available on library websites. Although not specifically formulated for a first-year program, this would be the optimum time for students to use this tool as part of the orientation to their new environment.

In a study of TILT, as an example of web-based instruction to first-year students, Orme (2004) suggested that this type of interactive virtual instruction was found to be at least as effective as in-person instruction for providing basic research skills. Recognizing that they may never have the time and resources to reach every new student personally, many libraries are now developing tutorials focused more specifically on plagiarism and academic integrity.

At Vaughan Memorial Library of Acadia University, the "You Quote It, You Note It!" tutorial is available on the library's website (Vaughan Memorial Library, 2008). Rutgers' Paul Robeson Library (2009) has a three-part video also available online. Although easily accessible, interactive, and engaging, these resources may not reach much of the audience who really need to use them. With all the demands on their time, taking an antiplagiarism tutorial may not reach a first-year student's "to-do" list. A tutorial named "Plagiarism: The Crime of Intellectual Kidnapping" (Jackson, 2006) was introduced during the required technical writing course for computer science majors at San Diego State University. Completing this interactive tutorial was a compulsory part of the class and therefore mandatory for graduation in computer science. In 2004, there were plans to include the tutorial, again as a required element, in a freshman experience program. Analysis of tutorial posttest quiz results showed that although most students scored well for questions concerning the definition and penalties of plagiarism and elements to include in a citation, they did less well for the more complex issues of paraphrasing and assessing what actually needs to be cited.

At Georgetown University a collaborative initiative took place in 2003 among students, faculty, and staff of many departments, including the libraries and the Honor Council, leading to the production of the mandatory online tutorial "Joining the Conversation: Scholarly Research and Academic Integrity" (Jacobs and Hussey, 2008). As a vehicle to address both the needs of the library to provide information literacy and the needs of the university administration to decrease honor violations, it exemplified a new perspective in addressing both research instruction and research ethics. This tutorial is a requirement of all first-year and transfer students to preregister for spring semester classes and is advertised on their student portal by a pop-up window. More important, students who do not complete this mandatory instruction are issued an individual reminder by their dean.

At the University of Scranton a mandatory online academic integrity tutorial based on the model from Georgetown was developed for all first-year students.

Recognizing the need for collaboration, the Weinberg Library worked with the Center for Teaching and Learning Excellence on this project (Oldham, 2009). The 95 percent completion rate for 2007 increased to 97 percent in 2008, and during that year a version was adapted and made available to new graduate students. Placing a link to the tutorial on a student's portal fulfilled the requirement of all busy first-year students for accessibility and ease of use. Once the tutorial is completed the link disappears.

Production of a plagiarism tutorial to be used as a required part of the First-Year Experience involves collaboration and creative use of technology plus "a heavy investment in development, both in cost and time" (Jacobs and Hussey, 2008: 128). Is this effort worthwhile in the battle against plagiarism? It is early yet to assess the efficacy of these mandatory online tools. However, ensuring the topic of academic honesty is a required part of freshman orientation activities focuses much-needed attention on an issue that seriously impacts all aspects of scholarship during the following four years.

Teaching the Professor

Another approach adopted by some libraries is to work directly with faculty on behalf of the students, teaching faculty to realize that the library, with its information access and skilled staff, is an intelligent place to start in their quest for plagiarism detection. They expect that librarians will know where to find that strange disjointed text in the middle of a paper or that passage which sounds far too sophisticated to be the work of this particular student. With their expert knowledge of databases and search engines, librarians may quickly assume the role of plagiarism detectives. According to Badke (2007), faculty may expose the plagiarist by using common search engines to discover copied and pasted websites or full-text databases and popular vehicles like Google Scholar to look for uncited articles. In a small study he found the latter to have a 50 percent chance of detecting a plagiarized scholarly article that was more than two years old. Many colleges do still invest in antiplagiarism services like Turnitin.com or iParadigms, but teaching professors still need to be aware of these services and prepared to use them consistently in order to catch the perpetrators (Embleton and Heifer, 2007).

Rather than being the plagiarism police, librarians may instead use their expertise to assist educators in developing strategies to increase confidence and pride in their students' research and writing. At Hanover College a pilot program took place to develop and deliver workshops espousing the principles of information literacy directly to teaching faculty (Loehr and Gibson, 2006). Workshops were offered on subjects ranging from "research skills and academic honesty" to "creating effective research assignments" (Loehr and Gibson, 2006: 35). Feedback from faculty was very positive, and many incorporated the material from the workshops almost immediately.

Time is precious and teaching faculty may not be able to squeeze in a library workshop unless its contents coincide with their own concerns. Realizing this, Cox and VanderPol (2004: 69) took what they labeled a "strategic approach" in the design of a workshop for instructors in the Introductory Communications program who had expressed concerns over the issues of plagiarism and the quality of research assignments completed by students in their classes. As well as covering these topics, the librarians were able to exhibit their skills not only in information location but also in its critical evaluation and ethical use. One rewarding outcome of these sessions was that librarians had the opportunity to demonstrate their expertise far beyond finding books and articles to encompass information literacy principles of critical evaluation and ethical use of information. As a result more teaching faculty asked for librarians to cover plagiarism and evaluation of information, whereas previously many just asked for a library tour.

Conclusion

This chapter has reviewed the history, evolution, and convergence of first-year programming and library instruction, with particular emphasis on academic integrity. With their unique characteristics, today's freshmen need and expect special treatment to orient them in the ways of scholarship. As information literacy goals and standards have evolved, the role of the academic library in the first-year student experience has expanded. Many librarians have moved beyond the quick library tour to working collaboratively with teaching faculty on behalf of students, developing credit courses, workshops, and online tools to educate new students in academic integrity. In some cases collaboration at the institutional level has led to the development of sophisticated tutorials dealing with the ethical use of information. In other cases the issue is explored between a confused new student and a librarian at the reference desk.

Developments in the next several years will no doubt be influenced by the state of the economy and its effect on college budgets. Whether first-year programs will flourish or falter and whether funding will allow for administrations to continue to reach out and collaborate is uncertain. In either situation librarians should be encouraged to look to creative ways to reach new students whether by the innovative use of technology or by seeking alternative funding opportunities. One thing is certain: a discussion must take place; the mere existence of an academic integrity policy is not sufficient. Perhaps Bill Gillis (2009) phrased it best when he wrote: "If students do not understand what we are talking about, not to mention what relevance it has for them, then what we say (even if we're laying out ultimatums) ultimately has no meaning." The dialogue must continue, in the library, in the classroom, between the students and the faculty, and among the students themselves. Starting the discussion during the students' first year gives the best chance of producing scholars who understand not only the how of attribution but also the concept of academic integrity.

References

Association of College and Research Libraries. 2000. *Information Literacy Competency Standards for Higher Education.* Chicago: Association of College and Research Libraries. Available: www.ala.org/ala/mgrps/divs/acrl/ standards/informationliteracycompetency.cfm (accessed May 27, 2010).

Badke, William. 2007. "Training Plagiarism Detectives: The Law and Order Approach." *Online* 31, no. 6 (November/December): 50–52.

Baker, Linda. 2006. "Library Instruction in the Rearview Mirror: A Reflective Look at the Evolution of a First-Year Library Program Using Evidence-Based Practice." *College and Undergraduate Libraries* 13, no. 2: 1–20.

Barefoot, Betsy. 2000. "The First-Year Experience: Are We Making It Any Better?" *About Campus* 4, no. 6: 12–18.

———. 2006. "Bridging the Chasm: First-Year Students and the Library." *Chronicle of Higher Education* 52, no. 20 (January 20): B16.

Bauman, M. Garrett. 2009. "CSI: Plagiarism." *Chronicle of Higher Education* 56 (October 5): B20.

Behr, Michele D., Maira Bundza, and Barbara J. Cockrell. 2007. "Going for the Gold: Recruiting Students and Engaging Administrators through Education and Entertainment in the Library." *College and Undergraduate Libraries* 14, no. 1: 1–13.

Boff, Colleen, Cheryl Albrecht, and Alison Armstrong. 2007. "Librarians with a First-Year Focus: Exploring an Emerging Position." In *The Role of the Library in the First College Year* (pp. 99–107), edited by Larry L. Hardesty. Columbia: University of South Carolina, National Resource Center for the First-Year Experience and Students in Transition, Monograph no. 45.

Bombaro, Christine. 2007. "Using Audience Response Technology to Teach Academic Integrity." *Reference Services Review* 35, no. 2: 296–309.

Bronshteyn, Karen, and Rita Baladad. 2006. "Perspectives on Librarians as Writing Instructors: Using Paraphrasing Exercises to Teach Beginning Information Literacy Students." *Journal of Academic Librarianship* 32, no. 5: 533–536.

Buranen, Lise. 2009. "A Safe Place: The Role of Librarians and Writing Centers in Addressing Citation Practices and Plagiarism." *Knowledge Quest* 37, no. 3 (January/February): 24–33.

Burtle, Laura G., and Tammy S. Sugarman. 2002 "The Citizen in the Information Age: Georgia State University's Creation of a Librarian-Led Freshman Learning Community." *College & Research Libraries News* 63, no. 4 (April): 276–279.

Cahoy, Ellysa Stern, and Rebecca Merritt Bichel. 2004. "A Luau in the Library? A New Model of Library Orientation." *College and Undergraduate Libraries* 11, no. 1: 49–60.

Cox, Jennifer L., and Diane VanderPol. 2004. "Promoting Information Literacy: A Strategic Approach." *Research Strategies* 20, no. 1–2: 69–76.

Davis, Philip M. 2003. "Effect of the Web on Undergraduate Citation Behavior Guiding Student Scholarship in a Networked Age." *portal: Libraries and the Academy* 3, no. 1: 41–51.

Denise, M. Sister. 1936. "Librarian's Contribution to Freshman Orientation." *Catholic Library World* 8 (September): 3–6.

Devlin, Eleanor. 1957. "Thoughts on Freshman Orientation." *Catholic Library World* 29, (October): 23–27.

Embleton, Kimberley, and Doris Small Heifer. 2007. "The Plague of Plagiarism and Academic Dishonesty." *Searcher* 15, no. 6 (June): 23–26.

English, Ada Jeannette. 1926. "How Shall We Instruct the College Freshman in the Use of the Library?" *School and Society* 24, no. 626: 779–785.

Erickson, E. Walfred. 1949. "Library Instruction in the Freshman Orientation Program." *College & Research Libraries* 10 (October): 445–448.

Gardner, John N., and Andrew K. Koch. 2007. "Drawing on the Past, in the Present, to Shape the Future of the First-Year Experience in American Higher Education." In *The Role of the Library in the First College Year* (pp. xv–xxvi), edited by Larry L. Hardesty. Columbia: University of South Carolina, National Resource Center for the First-Year Experience and Students in Transition, Monograph no. 45.

Gillis, Bill. 2009. "22nd International Conference on the First-Year Experience." Washington, DC: The George Washington University. Available: www.gelman.gwu.edu/about/organization/publications/renaissance-times/22nd-international-conference-on-the-first-year-experience (accessed May 27, 2010).

Gordon, Virgina P. 1989. "Origins and Purpose of the Freshman Seminar." In *The Freshman Year Experience: Helping Students Survive and Succeed in College* (pp. 183–197), edited by M. Lee Upcraft et al. San Francisco: Jossey-Bass.

Hall, Russell A. 2008. "The 'Embedded' Librarian in a Freshman Speech Class: Information Literacy Instruction in Action." *College & Research Libraries News* 6, no. 1 (January): 28–30.

Hardesty, Larry L. 2007a. "The Convergence of Information Literacy and the First-Year Experience: Looking to the Future." In *The Role of the Library in the First College Year* (pp. 169–174), edited by Larry L. Hardesty. Columbia: University of South Carolina, National Resource Center for the First-Year Experience and Students in Transition, Monograph no. 45.

Hardesty, Larry L., ed. 2007b. *The Role of the Library in the First College Year.* Columbia: University of South Carolina. National Resource Center for the First-Year Experience and Students in Transition, Monograph no. 45.

Harley, Bruce, Megan Dreger, and Patricia Knobloch. 2001. "The Postmodern Condition: Students, the Web and Academic Library Services." *Reference Services Review* 29, no. 1: 23–32.

Harris, Benjamin R. 2005. "Credit where Credit Is Due: Considering Ethics, Ethos, and Process in Library Instruction on Attribution." *Education Libraries* 28, no. 1: 4–11.

Hartz, Frederic R. 1965. "Freshman Library Orientation." *College & Research Libraries* 26 (May): 227–231.

Hurlbert, Janet McNeil, Cathleen R. Savidge, and Georgia R. Laudenslager. 2003. "Process-Based Assignments: How Promoting Information Literacy Prevents Plagiarism." *College & Undergraduate Libraries* 10, no. 1: 39–51.

Jackson, Pamela A. 2006. "Plagiarism Instruction Online: Assessing Undergraduate Students' Ability to Avoid Plagiarism." *College & Research Libraries* 67, no. 5 (September): 418–428.

Jacobs, Mark D., and Sandra R. Hussey. 2008. "A Tutorial with a Twist: How Plagiarism Advances Library Instruction." In *Moving Targets: Understanding Our Changing Landscapes* (pp. 127–129), edited by Theresa Valko and Bruce T. Halle. Ypsilanti, MI: LOEX Press.

James, Alan Edwin. 1941. "Freshmen and the Library." *Wilson Library Bulletin (R)* 15 (January): 403–407.

Jewler, A. Jerome. 1989. "Elements of an Effective Seminar: The University 101 Program." In *The Freshman Year Experience: Helping Students Survive and Succeed in College* (pp. 198–215), edited by. M. Lee Upcraft et al. San Francisco: Jossey-Bass.

Kuh, George D., Polly D. Boruff-Jones, and Amy E. Mark. 2007. "Engaging Students in the First College Year: Why Academic Librarians Matter." In *The Role of the Library in the First College Year* (pp. 17–27), edited by Larry L. Hardesty. Columbia: University of South Carolina, National Resource Center for the First-Year Experience and Students in Transition, Monograph no. 45.

Liles, Jeffrey A., and Michael E. Rozalski. 2004. "It's a Matter of Style: A Style Manual Workshop for Preventing Plagiarism." *College and Undergraduate Libraries* 11, no. 2: 91–99.

Loehr, Heather B., and Kenneth E. Gibson. 2006. "Promoting Librarian–Faculty Collaboration to Advance Information Literacy: Hanover College's Pilot Program." *Indiana Libraries* 25, no. 4: 33–36.

Madray, Amrita. 2007. "Developing Students' Awareness of Plagiarism: Crisis and Opportunities." *Library Philosophy and Practice* (June): 1–16.

Marcus, Sandra, and Sheila Beck. 2003. "A Library Adventure: Comparing a Treasure Hunt with a Traditional Freshman Orientation Tour." *College & Research Libraries* 64, no. 1 (January): 23–44.

McBride, Tom, and Ron Nief. 2009. "Beloit College Mindset List for the Class of 2013." Beloit, WI: Beloit College. Available: www.beloit.edu/mindset/2013.php (accessed May 27, 2010).

McCabe, Donald L., Linda Klebe Trevino, and Kenneth D. Butterfield. 2001. "Cheating in Academic Institutions: A Decade of Research." *Ethics & Behavior* 11, no. 3: 219–232.

Mellon, Constance A. 1989. "Library Anxiety and the Non-traditional Student." In *Reaching and Teaching Diverse Library User Groups* (pp. 77–81), edited by Teresa Mensching. Ann Arbor, MI: Pierian Press.

Moniz, Richard, Joyce Fine, and Leonard Bliss. 2008. "The Effectiveness of Direct-Instruction and Student-Centered Teaching Methods on Students' Functional Understanding of Plagiarism." *College and Undergraduate Libraries* 15, no. 3: 255–279.

Mounce, Michael. 2006. "Teaching Information Literacy at Delta State University." *Southeastern Librarian* 54, no. 3: 35–41.

National Center for Education Statistics, United States Department of Education, and Institute of Education Sciences. 2008. "Total First-Time Freshmen Fall Enrollment in Degree-Granting Institutions, by Attendance Status, Sex of Student, and Type and Control of Institution: 1955 through 2007." Available: nces.ed.gov/programs/digest/d08/tables/dt08_198.asp (accessed May 27, 2010).

Newsome, Mary Esther. 1940. "Library Course for Freshmen." *Wilson Library Bulletin (R)* 15 (December): 338.

Oldham, Bonnie. 2009. "Academic Integrity Tutorials." *PLA Bulletin* 64 no. 2: 9–10.

Olsen, Florence. 2000. "Campus Newcomers Arrive with More Skill, Better Gear." *Chronicle of Higher Education* 47, no. 10 (November 3): A39.

Orme, William A. 2004. "A Study of the Residual Impact of the Texas Information Literacy Tutorial on the Information Seeking Ability of First Year College Students." *College & Research Libraries* 65, no. 3 (May): 205–215.

Oseguera, Leticia. 2007. "How First-Year College Students Use Their Time: Implications for Library and Information Literacy Instruction." In *The Role of the Library in the First College Year* (pp. 29–47), edited by Larry L. Hardesty. Columbia: University of South Carolina, National Resource Center for the First-Year Experience and Students in Transition, Monograph no. 45.

Paul Robeson Library. 2009. "How to Avoid Plagiarism." Camden, NJ: Rutgers University. Available: library.camden.rutgers.edu/EducationalModule/Plagiarism (accessed November 11, 2009).

Ramsey, Karen M., and Jim Kinnie. 2006. "The Embedded Librarian." *Library Journal* 4, no. 131: 34–35.

Ranstead, Donald D., and Sherman H. Spencer. 1959. "Freshman Library Orientation Program." *Library Journal (1876)* 84 (January 15): 152–154.

Roach, Ronald. 1998. "Freshman-Year Experience." *Black Issues in Higher Education* 14, no. 26: 30–32.

Rutgers University. 2009. "Rutgers RIOT." New Brunswick, NJ: Rutgers University. Available: www.libraries.rutgers.edu/rul/lib_instruct/lib_instruct .shtml (accessed May 27, 2010).

Ryan, Michael R., and Patricia A. Glenn. 2004. "What Do First-Year Students Need Most: Learning Strategies Instruction or Academic Socialization?" *Journal of College Reading and Learning* 34, no. 2: 4–28.

St. Clair, Linda. 2002. "The LEAPing Librarian's Role in a Campus Learning Community." *College & Research Libraries News* 63, no. 1 (January): 24–29.

Stanford, Edward B. 1939. "Freshman Library Orientation." *Library Journal (1876)* 64 (January 15): 47–49.

Stephens, Jason M., Michael F. Young, and Thomas Calabrese. 2007. "Does Moral Judgment Go Offline when Students Are Online? A Comparative Analysis of Undergraduates' Beliefs and Behaviors Relating to Conventional and Digital Cheating." *Ethics & Behavior* 17, no. 3: 233–254.

Thompson, Christen. 2003. "Information Illiterate or Lazy: How College Students Use the Web for Research." *portal: Libraries and the Academy* 3, no. 2: 259–268.

University of Texas System Digital Library. 2004. "TILT." Austin: University of Texas. Available: tilt.lib.utsystem.edu/resources/index.html (accessed May 27, 2010).

Vaughan Memorial Library. 2008. "You Quote It, You Note It!" Wolfville, Nova Scotia: Acadia University. Available: library.acadiau.ca/tutorials/plagiarism (accessed May 27, 2010).

Wasielewski, Alice. 2009. "The Huge Hubbub: Freshman Orientation Fun at the Library." *College & Research Libraries News* 70, no. 7 (July/August): 394–396.

Watts, Margit Misangyi. 2005. "The Place of the Library versus the Library as Place." In *Challenging and Supporting the First-Year Student* (pp. 339–355), edited by M. Lee Upcraft et al. San Francisco: Jossey-Bass.

Wichita State University Libraries Information System. 2008. "Empower." Wichita, KS: Wichita State University. Available: library.wichita.edu/empower (accessed May 27, 2010).

Writing Center and Mantor Library. "Avoiding Plagiarism." Farmington: University of Maine. Available: library.umf.maine.edu/research_tools/plagiarism/plagiarism.php (accessed May 27, 2010).

8

Plagiarism: University Reaction and Subsequent Action

Dolores Pfeuffer-Scherer

Introduction

To prevent student plagiarism, universities have implemented policies that couple punitive consequences with both greater educational efforts and an emphasis on instructor assignment design. The punitive consequences for the students range in severity from reprimands, to failing grades, to expulsion. As technology expanded and transformed the process of student learning, so too have academic efforts to help students avoid plagiarism. Currently, universities employ a variety of tactics to educate students as to what constitutes plagiarism and instruct them on ways to avoid it. Armed with the knowledge that more students have access to sources via the Internet, and thus have the opportunity to engage in acts of plagiarism more easily, colleges and universities have had to reexamine their policies and punishments on the subject. Training for both students and instructors on the topic of intellectual honesty has become an academic norm. Students and teaching faculty are engaged as active participants in the process of avoiding plagiarism.

In high schools, colleges, and universities, the process of addressing plagiarism often begins with prevention. At student orientations the topic is often addressed in freshman orientation and courses, and instructors are offered workshops on designing assignments that help to avoid plagiarism. Syllabi are often required to include statements on the educational institution's policy regarding plagiarism and use of detection software such as Turnitin.com. Many instructors now require electronic submission of written work so they can check the papers through plagiarism detection sites. Even if universities do not pay for the use of such sites, it is as easy for instructors to search the web by typing in suspect phrases or sentences into a search engine.

The detection of a case of suspected plagiarism can involve a number of administrative levels. This process can entail a variety of rules and sanctions defined by the academic institution and can include such actions as transcript notations of academic dishonesty, suspension from school for one or more terms, and even official hearings presided over by students and faculty. Normally, the school is the first and last link in the entire process—from describing what constituted the violation to prescribing the sanction. Instructors are frequently required to incorporate antiplagiarism measures into their teaching and curriculum. As noted, departments may subscribe to plagiarism detection websites and include materials about plagiarism on the class syllabus or website. Making students aware of what specifically constitutes plagiarism as well as providing an understanding of the institution's rules and punishments for acts of intellectual dishonesty has become a standard administrative practice in higher education. This process, from administrative level to faculty to student, then back to the administration, is a multifaceted, continually evolving cycle that rests on continually evolving societal principles of academic honesty and truth.

This chapter examines university policies that deal with plagiarism. A wide sampling of schools was utilized. The sample included universities that were geographically, economically, and racially diverse. In this chapter, the differences and similarities between policies and process will be analyzed with the purpose of offering a comprehensive overview of how students and faculty have become an integral part of the entire procedure. The plague of plagiarism has created a new culture within the academic community and led to a new way of teaching—instructors give it great weight when designing assignments, creating syllabi, and grading papers. This comparison and analysis is intended to help readers understand some of the structures of this new culture and its impact on the community.

Common Ground: Normative Policy and Procedures

As a sign that the issue of plagiarism has crept into daily academic life, it is interesting to note that all schools examined for this chapter post on their websites established policies that prescribe specific ramifications for those suspected of plagiarism. However, there was no commonality among the universities examined as to where such information was posted. Some schools house their policy within the code of academic conduct; others have theirs available through the websites for student affairs offices. Regardless of its placement, the information provided by all the schools examined carefully outlines the specific procedures that the university will follow when investigating a suspected charge of plagiarism. Variations occur not only in the prescribed chain of action but also on how some universities offer students specific examples of what constitutes plagiarism and how to avoid it. There seems to be a distinct line between viewing the offense in terms of an occasion to teach students what their precise error was, working with them so they learn from the mistake, versus a focus primarily on punishment for failure to adhere to university standards. Many schools strongly suggest that by engaging in academic dishonesty, intentionally or not, the student sullies the reputation of the school and must come under harsh sanction to maintain its integrity.

Swarthmore College offers a good example of a university that has increased its outreach to students with greater information and an expanded plagiarism website. Not only does the site list procedures followed by instructors, but it also goes into depth about how to deter, avoid, and detect plagiarism. Instructors are encouraged to carefully design their assignments, to ask for rough drafts, and to include peer review sessions as part of the class, all in an effort to curb plagiarism. Recycling assignments is discouraged, and instructors are even told to make their assignments "obscure" (Swarthmore College, accessed 2010). Examples of syllabi are available to professors, including those that explicitly include the College Judicial Committee (CJC) procedures as well as those that mention plagiarism, but they do not outline the CJC consequences. Specific departments have links, including biology, English, and history, and instructors can simply click the links to see what their peers include in their syllabi. In creating such a site, the college is educating instructors on the best methods to avoid plagiarism as a means to combat the issue.

If a case of plagiarism is detected, Swarthmore College, like other schools, docs not allow faculty to handle the issues themselves. Instructors must turn over the case to the CJC so that students receive an impartial hearing and to ensure that sanctions are even. The group is composed of two students, two faculty members, the Dean and the Assistant Dean of Student Life. As a further deterrent, the college CJC publishes its verdict, posting it in the hallway of one building on campus, so that students are made aware that penalties exist, they will be applied, and students will experience consequences should they take the risk. First offenses typically result in the failure of the course, although this depends on the severity of the offense. The second offense normally will result in expulsion from the school. The college states that the CJC hears "surprisingly few" cases, perhaps because of its focus on assignment design and avoidance (Swarthmore College, *Plagiarism Resources*, accessed 2010).

Rutgers, The State University of New Jersey, offers only formal means to investigate accusations of plagiarism. Much like Swarthmore College's, Rutgers' policy states that once an instructor suspects a student of committing plagiarism, that instructor is not to meet in an informal manner with the student, but instead must submit the complaint to the Dean of Students of the student's school or to the Office of Compliance, Student Policy, and Judicial Affairs (Rutgers University, Department of Sociology, Anthropology, and Criminal Justice, accessed 2010). These offices individually review the material submitted by the instructor, and the Dean of Students determines the severity of the offense and whether the matter is grievous enough to warrant a university hearing. The university classifies offenses into four separate levels, offering students punishments based on the level of violation, with levels one and two being least severe and normally adjudicated in the school where the incident occurred. The Dean of Students or equivalent member of the staff notifies the student of the charges and then meets with the student, without the instructor present. The sanctions can include failure of the assignment, a failing grade in the course, suspension with a notation on the student's transcript for the duration of the suspension, and expulsion.

If a university hearing is warranted, the student is advised to select an on-campus advisor and is given a list of trained advisors who can aid in the student's defense. Students can select any member of the university community, however, even if they have not been trained. The advisor attends the closed hearing with the student, which is presided over by a hearing officer with a board composed of two professors and three students. Students may elect to consult with an attorney; however, attorneys cannot speak on behalf of students during the proceedings. The hearing board then makes a recommendation to the Vice President of Student Affair as to the sanction but does not determine or impose the actual punishment.

To help combat plagiarism, Rutgers University (*Paul Robeson Library: Video on Plagiarism,* accessed 2010) created video and slide productions to help educate students about what constitutes plagiarism and how to avoid it, hoping to arm students with the knowledge that it is a serious offense that is avoidable. This appears to be a trend as university libraries lead the way toward educating students about what plagiarism is, how to avoid it, and how to recognize it through website information. The library at Rutgers offers online video quizzes to students as way for them to actively learn what constitutes plagiarism and how to prevent it. At Rutgers University, Camden Campus, the department of Sociology, Anthropology, and Criminal Justice offers faculty and students links to sites, such as the New Brunswick Writing Program's Plagiarism Page and guidelines for students in the department. As with other university departments across the nation, plagiarism guidelines and information is now easily accessible online.

Other state universities follow a statewide code; issues of honesty in California State–sponsored universities are defined under Title 5, California Administrative Code, Section 41301, which states, "The SSU Cheating and Plagiarism Policy and Procedures is established under the authority of Executive Order 790, Student Disciplinary Procedures for The California State University, issued by the Chancellor on February 2, 2006 code of conduct for which students may be sanctioned" (Sonoma State University, accessed 2010). This regulation also outlines possible outcomes for those who break the discipline code: "Students who engage in cheating or plagiarism will be subject to academic sanctions, including a lowered or failing grade in a course; and the possibility of an additional administrative sanction, including probation, suspension, or expulsion" (Sonoma State University, accessed 2010). The specific policies for disciplinary measures, however, are given to the university's chancellor, to be followed by all campuses. In establishing a state code that outlines what offenses are punishable, California appears to have taken the lead away from the universities in creating the parameters of what constitutes misconduct. A state policy establishing a code of conduct leaves less opportunity for the universities to face charges of favoritism or unfairness.

The establishment of this state code, however, does not mean that California State schools are the most stringent in their policies toward plagiarism. This is not to say that they do not take the offense seriously; they do. The guidelines at Sonoma State University give the faculty discretion to determine if the accusation should be dealt with formally or informally. The policy instructs:

> Faculty members are encouraged to discuss with students academic ethics and the formulation of one's own intellectual material. It is also the policy of Sonoma State University to impose sanctions on students who cheat or plagiarize. Students are expected to be honest in meeting the requirements of courses in which they are enrolled. Cheating or plagiarism is dishonest, undermines the necessary trust upon which relations between students and faculty are based, and is unacceptable conduct. Students who engage in cheating or plagiarism will be subject to academic sanctions, including a lowered or failing grade in a course; and the possibility of an additional administrative sanction, including probation, suspension, or expulsion. (Sonoma State University, accessed 2010)

The instructor and student may also opt to include a third party such as the department chair to help facilitate the process.

At Sonoma State, the option to initiate formal proceedings also lies in the hands of the instructor. When faculty members feel the situation demands it, they can file a formal complaint that will ask that the case come up for consideration of academic and administrative sanctions (Sonoma State University, accessed 2010). Options of formal punishments include redoing the assignment, receiving a failing grade on the paper or project, having the course grade reduced, or receiving a failing grade in the course; it is also possible for multiple sanctions that incorporate more than one of these to be imposed. Serious violations fall under the purview of the Coordinator of University Student Discipline, and they can result in probation, suspension, or expulsion from the university. The hearing process is meticulously outlined, with the jury consisting of both faculty and students. Time specifications are also included, with the hearing jury being mandated to convene within five days after the instructor files the complaint. Pending the outcome, the jury must file its report within ten days. Members of the panel serve for one year, and participation is restricted to tenured faculty and students selected by the President of the Associated Students.

Even in a formal proceeding, faculty and student participation extends to the hearing process, with both being afforded the chance to "each reject one voting member of the Cheating and Plagiarism Jury; the Cheating and Plagiarism Jury Chair shall fill any such vacancies" (Sonoma State University, accessed 2010). Both may also request the hearing be closed, and each is entitled to receive a copy of the audio transcript of the proceedings at their own expense. Perhaps recognizing the antagonism that can arise from such accusations, it appears that Sonoma State University includes the student and instructor as part of the whole process rather than leaving the matter entirely in the hands of an administrative body. While the formal complaint is judged by a jury, the fact that the student and professor can participate in jury selection and dictate the openness of the proceedings indicates that the university is trying to incorporate them as active participants in the process from beginning to end.

The Role of the Faculty

While sanctions appear consistent at most state schools, the one issue where the greatest variation occurs is in terms of faculty involvement. Many schools like Sonoma State encourage faculty–student interaction throughout the process: this represents an attempt to facilitate an instructor–student resolution to the dispute. Instead of employing intermediary offices in the adjudication process, like Rutgers, some schools encourage professors to play a pivotal role in adjudicating the suspected plagiarism incident. Examples include the University at Albany, Florida State University, and the University of Illinois, which all allow instructors to informally meet with the student; they may even instruct faculty in ways to personally resolve the problem. The University at Albany policy states that: "When a faculty member has information that a student has violated academic integrity in a course or program for which he or she is responsible and determines that a violation has occurred, he or she will inform the student and impose and appropriate sanction" (University at Albany, accessed 2010).

Instructors must then file a written report to the Offices of Graduate or Undergraduate Studies, describing the violation and what penalties they imposed. Professors may also refer a case to the University Judicial System if they cannot reach an agreement with the student, and a hearing will be held to determine how the case will be adjudicated. Like Albany's policy, Florida State specifies that the professor must attempt to resolve the issue with the student directly:

> Each instructor is responsible for detecting and punishing academic fraud in his or her courses. An instructor who suspects academic fraud will first discuss the questionable assignment with the student; this discussion may clear up the instructor's questions. . . . In minor or borderline cases of this kind, the student may simply be required to redo all or part of the assignment. If an informal discussion does not resolve the problem, the instructor will withhold the student's grade for the assignment in question until the matter can be further investigated and more formally resolved. . . . If necessary, the student will be given a grade of "Incomplete" for the course while this investigation is carried out. (Florida State University, accessed 2010)

If the professor and student cannot agree, the case is sent to a hearing with a panel of five members, including two students. The decision of the panel is final, and it determines the appropriate sanction.

The University of Illinois at Urbana-Champaign takes the idea of faculty involvement in determining the validity of an accusation even further. Faculty are described as "fact-finders":

In the role of fact-finder, the instructor has broad powers to determine whether an infraction has occurred (through collecting relevant evidence, questioning other students, etc.). As the determiner of penalty, the faculty member should feel certain that the student has committed an infraction before determining the penalty. This decision may be based not only on the facts revealed by the investigation, but other factors that are relevant in the best judgment of the faculty member. (University of Illinois, accessed 2010)

What is striking about this particular policy is the ability of the faculty member to question other students regarding a pending accusation. This policy raises several questions: How far are faculty allowed to delve? Does such investigation trespass on the rights of the student? Or, does this allow for greater fairness, as the professor investigating the matter is the one directly involved with the situation and thus is perhaps best familiar with the student's work?

Policy Statements at Private Universities

Private universities, much like state schools, have had to include policies regarding academic integrity as part of their handbooks. Like public institutions, they vary in their approach to determining the validity of a case and in terms of faculty involvement in the development and adjudication of the incident. A random sampling of private colleges and universities indicates varying degrees of explanation and codification of policies regarding plagiarism. At Southern Methodist University in Texas efforts to prevent plagiarism have led to a rule that all new students must participate in an online tutorial and quiz on academic integrity. The responsibility for enforcing intellectual honesty, however, is shared by students, faculty, and the university's Honor Council. Faculty members are reminded that "confronting academic dishonesty is the shared responsibility of both faculty and students, although faculty members are called upon to play a greater role in the process" (Southern Methodist University, *The Role of Faculty in Confronting Academic Dishonesty at Southern Methodist University*, accessed 2010). As such, faculty are instructed that "every effort should be made to preserve the teacher–student relationship. The student should be given the opportunity to respond to the allegations and to present evidence in his or her defense." Faculty participation appears to be a vital component of the academic integrity policy versus sole reliance on administration. If the student is suspected of violating the code, the case then can proceed to the Honor Council, which then determines appropriate sanctions, or, if the student waives this right, the faculty member will complete a "Faculty Disposition Form" signed by both student and faculty member specifying prescribed penalties. The student is aware of his rights; the university places emphasis on the student's role in the process. As noted, "[if] the professor determines that a violation is likely, the student must be informed of his or her right to a hearing before the SMU Honor Council and the right to appeal any penalty decision the Honor Council may assess. This is an essential step" (Southern Methodist University, *The Honor Council of Southern Methodist University*, accessed 2010). Even if a student agrees to the faculty member handling the case, the student understands his or her rights and the Honor Council is aware of the violation.

Similar to Southern Methodist University, the University of Denver does not mandate faculty members to report serious incidents to its Office of Citizenship and Community Standards. Faculty members may consult unofficially with the office to seek assistance on how to pursue a violation of academic integrity. According to the honor code: "The faculty member may have the student redo the assignment, may fail the student for the assignment, may fail the student for the course, and/or take some other action as deemed appropriate by the instructor or academic unit. Then the faculty member will turn the documents over to the Office of Community and Citizenship Standards (CCS) for further action" (University of Denver, accessed 2010). Instructors may also meet with the student to determine whether or not the incident was deliberate, and they can assign penalties. Additionally, "faculty member may turn the student work into CCS for purposes of maintaining a data base. Faculty member may request 'no further action' on the part of the CCS [or] faculty member may request 'action' on the part of the CCS" (University of Denver, accessed 2010).

Intent is key. Whether or not a student had serious intent to deceive makes quite a difference in penalties ascribed. For serious plagiarism (with intent to deceive) the first offense results in academic probation; the second offense in suspension, and the third is expulsion from the university. For those who may or may not have "intent to deceive," for the first two offenses the sanction is academic probation, and beyond that it is suspension (University of Denver, accessed 2010). Despite the variations in requirements regarding the role of faculty in handling the case, at the University of Denver students are an integral part of the judiciary process, as are faculty and staff.

Student participation on the Conduct Review Board (CRB) is mandated: "If the accused is an undergraduate student, at least one voting member of the CRB shall be an undergraduate student. If the accused is a graduate student, at least one voting member of the CRB shall be a graduate student" (University of Denver, accessed 2010). Eligibility for participation on the board is also clearly defined: "Students must be registered as a full-time student in good academic and disciplinary standing after completing at least one quarter of coursework at the University. . . . Faculty must have been employed by and taught courses at the University for a minimum of one academic quarter. Faculty must also have taught at least one course within the most recent two academic quarters" (University of Denver, accessed 2010).

Bowdoin College in Maine takes a more traditional approach that is similar to the policies at other institutions where administrative of punitive and judiciary measures rest in the hands of an administrative body rather than with a faculty member's discretion:

> The Office of the Dean of Student Affairs will review all claims of alleged violations by Bowdoin students of both the Academic Honor and the Social Code. After reviewing the claims, cases will either be referred to a Student Affairs staff member to be handled admin-

istratively or to the Judicial Board for a formal hearing. Typically, minor violations will be resolved administratively and allegations of major violations will be referred to the Judicial Board, but the Dean of Student Affairs reserves the right to act administratively in appropriate cases without a Judicial Board hearing. (Bowdoin College, accessed 2010)

The student's voice, however, is heard if he or she disagrees with the sanctions imposed: "If a student believes that a disciplinary sanction issued by a member of the Student Affairs Staff is unfair, the student may elect to have the case adjudicated by the Judicial Board. In such cases, the Judicial Board will come to its own determination of responsibility and recommended sanction, without regard to the original administratively issued sanction" (Bowdoin College, accessed 2010).

The accused are afforded an active role in the trial. "If respondents wish, they may have a Supporter present at the hearing to provide personal support. The name of this person must be provided to the Judicial Board Advisor at least forty-eight hours prior to the scheduled hearing" (Bowdoin College, accessed 2010). Interestingly, accused students have the right to have a character witness speak on their behalf and also have the right to "request the removal of a single Board member (names of members are available from the Office of the Dean of Student Affairs) believed incapable of rendering an impartial decision" (Bowdoin College, accessed 2010).

Ivy League schools also have carefully outlined their policies on academic integrity. Plagiarism, as would be expected, is treated as a serious offense. The University of Pennsylvania's Charter of Student Disciplinary System oversees the process on the campus, from the initial complaint through the imposition of a sanction. The university handbook outlines the role of the Office of Student Conduct (OSC):

> The duties of the OSC include determining whether complaints warrant action by the OSC, referring complaints for mediation or resolution by other University offices, investigating complaints, determining whether to charge a student with violations of University policies, resolving complaints by voluntary agreements to sanctions, bringing charges of violations to a disciplinary hearing, presenting evidence at hearings, monitoring and enforcing the fulfillment of sanctions imposed pursuant to voluntary agreements or after disciplinary hearings, maintaining records of all disciplinary matters, providing administrative support for all aspects of the disciplinary process (including hearings), and preparing reports and compiling statistics. (University of Pennsylvania, accessed 2010)

There is a University Mediation Program that is staffed by volunteers, which includes students, faculty, and staff who have received training in conflict resolution and who try to work with the student and professor to come up with an appropriate sanction. The University Honor Council (UHC) oversees the disciplinary hearing process. What is interesting about this group is the student participation; Penn incorporates a large number of students, perhaps viewing them as an integral link in the process of enforcing the university's policy:

> The UHC consists of a minimum of 20 undergraduate students, recommended by the Nominations and Elections Committee (NEC). . . . The NEC and UHC are encouraged to ensure that nominees represent a broad cross section of the undergraduate student body. . . . Faculty members and graduate students designated by the Faculty Senate or GAPSA to sit on Disciplinary Hearing Panels may participate in the work of the UHC at the mutual convenience of the UHC and the faculty member or graduate student. (University of Pennsylvania, accessed 2010)

The UHC is also active in trying to prevent plagiarism. Throughout the academic year, "The University Honor Council (UHC) educates students, faculty and staff regarding both the standards of academic integrity and of behavioral conduct of the University community" (University of Pennsylvania, accessed 2010). While many faculty members include a discussion or handout on plagiarism in the syllabi or course, Penn's use of a separate administrative body that includes a large population of diverse students bespeaks to the university's attempt to reach students by another, independent means. As such, the administration moves away from punitive duties to prevention.

Yale University utilizes a mixture of tenured and nontenured professors, students, the dean of the college, as well as three designated members of the Executive Committee to adjudicate cases of academic dishonesty in the classroom. Of the universities examined for this chapter, this is the first instance found where faculty members without tenure are included as part of the committee. Dubbed the "Executive Committee," this group is appointed by the dean of the college. The structure of the committee is as follows: "It has thirteen members: three tenured members of the Yale College Faculty; three untenured members of the Yale College Faculty; three undergraduates; the dean of Yale College or the dean's designated representative; and the three officers of the committee, the chairman, the secretary, and the factfinder" (Yale University, accessed 2010).

The fact-finder is normally a "tenured member of the Yale College Faculty or an assistant or associate dean of Yale College, but may also be a tenured member of one of the other faculties or schools in the University." The secretary is an assistant or associate dean, and the chair is either a tenured faculty member or assistant or associate dean of the college. As with other universities, Yale allows the accused to enlist the assistance of an advisor, and if the student finds difficulties in procuring such assistance, the college dean will provide a list from which the student can select an advisor.

Much like Rutgers, there are a number of campus advisors who have been trained in the process and are willing to assist students and help guide them through questioning witnesses, presenting their case, and preparing the student for the format of the hearing. While students at Yale are a part of the Executive Council, they form a minority of the judiciary, with the majority being composed of tenured and nontenured professors. Unlike the University of Pennsylvania, there is not a student body that reaches out to help instruct students on academic integrity.

Conclusion

Plagiarism has become an important part of the academic landscape. Regardless of the type of university or college, academic institutions are enlisting faculty, staff, administrators, and students alike to help investigate and pass sanctions regarding intellectual honesty. While penalties such as dismissal, suspension, probation, and warnings are standard across the majority of schools, some offer alternative sanctions such as community service to help foster the learning aspect of the incident. The greatest variations appear to be in the involvement of faculty and students. Whereas some faculty members are entitled to handle the complaint between themselves and the student, others are mandated to remove themselves from the process by turning the complaint in to an administrative unit designed to investigate the accusation. There are some schools that urge faculty to find an informal resolution, while others insist on a formal process, even if the end result is derived not by a hearing, but by mediation. Some universities insist on student-run hearings, with governance by faculty and/or staff, while others rely on the role of faculty in conjunction with administration and staff.

What appears to have changed over the past five years are efforts toward educating students about what specifically constitutes plagiarism. Some academic departments within universities have begun to include examples and definitions of academic integrity on their webpages as a means to reach out to students and to clarify academic integrity. Many departments have done an admirable job, and it would appear that this trend is on the rise as more professors realize that the information must be disseminated to students on multiple levels. School libraries have taken the lead in creating websites, guides, and online tutorials and quizzes, all designed to help inform students what constitutes plagiarism and methods to avoid it.

Another interesting trend is to include sessions about plagiarism as part of new-student orientations, as well as freshman writing and other first-year courses. Assignment design is also an area that is being scrutinized as faculty are encouraged to be creative in their assignments and redesign assignment rubrics for their courses. In many ways, the rise of the Internet has changed how universities are responding to plagiarism—posting tutorials, interactive quizzes, worksheets, and guides online to better educate students. Simultaneously, faculty are also responding by being involved in the process of suspected cases of plagiarism and by reconsidering assignment design.

References

Bowdoin College. *Student Handbook 2009–2010.* Brunswick, ME: Bowdoin College. Available: www.bowdoin.edu/studentaffairs/student-handbook/col lege-policies/student-disciplinary-process.shtml (accessed May 27, 2010).

Florida State University. Center for Teaching and Learning. *Plagiarism and the Intellectually Honest Student.* Tallahassee: Florida State University. Available: learningforlife.fsu.edu/ctl/explore/bestPractices/docs/plagiarismstudent .pdf (accessed May 27, 2010).

Rutgers University, Department of Sociology, Anthropology, and Criminal Justice. *Plagiarism Policy.* Camden, NJ: Rutgers University. Available: sociology .camden.rutgers.edu/curriculum/plagiarism.htm (accessed May 27, 2010).

———. *Paul Robeson Library: Video on Plagiarism.* Camden, NJ: Rutgers University. Available: library.camden.rutgers.edu/EducationalModule/Plagiarism (accessed May 27, 2010).

Sonoma State University. *Cheating and Plagiarism Policy.* Rohnert Park, CA: Sonoma State University. Available: www.sonoma.edu/UAffairs/Policies/ cheating_plagiarism.htm (accessed May 27, 2010).

Southern Methodist University. *The Honor Council of Southern Methodist University.* Dallas, TX: Southern Methodist University. Available: smu.edu/ honorcouncil/default.asp (accessed May 27, 2010).

———. *The Role of Faculty in Confronting Academic Dishonesty at Southern Methodist University.* Dallas, TX: Southern Methodist University. Available: smu .edu/honorcouncil/PDF/Brochure_Acad_Honesty_Faculty_Role.pdf (accessed May 27, 2010).

Swarthmore College. *Plagiarism Resources.* Swarthmore, PA: Available: www .swarthmore.edu/NatSci/cpurrin1/plagiarism/avoidance.htm (accessed May 27, 2010).

University at Albany. *Undergraduate Bulletin, 2009–2010.* Albany, NY: University at Albany. Available: www.albany.edu/undergraduate_bulletin/ regulations.html (accessed May 27, 2010).

University of Denver. *Citizenship and Community Standards.* Denver: University of Denver. Available: www.du.edu/studentlife/ccs/crb.html#composition (accessed May 27, 2010).

University of Illinois. *Academic Integrity and Plagiarism.* Urbana-Champagne: University of Illinois. Available: www.library.illinois.edu/learn/research/ academicintegrity.html (accessed May 27, 2010).

University of Pennsylvania. *Outline of the Charter of the Student Disciplinary System.* Philadelphia: University of Pennsylvania. Available: www.upenn .edu/osc/outline.htm (accessed May 27, 2010).

Yale University. *Undergraduate Regulations 2009–2010.* New Haven, CT: Yale University. Available: www.yale.edu/yalecollege/publications/uregs/general .html (accessed May 27, 2010).

Plagiarism and the Nontraditional Student: Challenges and Perspectives

Dawn Amsberry

Introduction

English as a Second Language (ESL) and international students face a number of challenges as they navigate their way through the American educational system. Not only are they expected to communicate in an unfamiliar language, they are also expected to adhere to educational practices that may differ from what they are used to. If schools in their home countries emphasized memorization and test-taking, writing an academic essay may be a new experience. They may find themselves working to acclimate to expected educational norms just as they acclimate to the expectations of social and cultural discourse. In worst-case scenarios, students may be confronted with charges of plagiarism and violation of academic integrity.

Stories about the plagiarizing behavior of international students may lead some educators to conclude that these students "cheat" (Buranen, 1999). However, "cheating" implies an intent to deceive, and these students may see their behavior as perfectly honest. There is no universal definition of plagiarism; how plagiarism is defined may depend greatly on the context in which it is used (Valentine, 2006). Many writers have attributed plagiarism by ESL and international students to cultural differences (Dryden, 1999; Lund, 2004; Pennycook, 1996; Shi, 2006). However, other researchers have argued that because overseas students many not have been taught essay writing, inexperience as writers, rather than cultural background, is the primary factor contributing to inappropriate textual borrowing practices (Buranen, 1999; Gu and Brooks, 2008; Hu, 2001; Pecorari, 2003).

Regardless of cultural background, ESL and international students may be struggling with developing a new identity in their new culture and language. In their academic lives, they are developing identities as writers as they learn to write not just in a new language but in what may be an entirely new discourse: the academic essay. This chapter will outline the challenges students may face in establishing an authorial identity and offer some classroom suggestions for helping students develop their voice.

Challenges

Problems with Definitions

Before looking at causes of plagiarism, it is necessary to consider what exactly is meant by the term "plagiarism." The term is often used in a very generic sense, referring to infractions ranging from submitting a paper purchased on the Internet to copying a few sentences without quotation marks. The act of buying, stealing, or borrowing a term paper surely indicates an intention to deceive; however, inappropriate paraphrasing or failure to use quotation marks for an exact quote could be the result of undeveloped writing skills. Some argue that the word "plagiarism" (which implies a moral transgression and carries negative connotations) should be done away with altogether, in favor of a more neutral term like "inappropriate textual borrowing" or "transgressive intertextuality" (Chandrasoma, Thompson, and Pennycook, 2004).

Howard (1995) parses the term "plagiarism" by dividing it into three categories: cheating (submitting an entire copied paper), nonattribution (including copied sentences or passages without quotation marks or sources), and patchwriting, which Howard defines as "writing passages that are not copied exactly but that have nevertheless been borrowed from another source, with some changes" (Howard, 1995: 799). While students, both American and international, know that the first category, cheating, is wrong (although they may indulge in it anyway), they may not fully understand the other types of plagiarism. Their inappropriate uses of sources, then, could be a result of inexperience with academic writing expectations rather than intentional deception.

The definition problem is further compounded for students who are nonnative speakers of English. In interviews conducted by Shi (2006), some international students indicated that they had not encountered the English word "plagiarism" and its definition before coming to North America. Some claimed that there was no equivalent word in their language, and two Japanese students each gave a different term. Wheeler (2009: 18) expands further on the issue of terminology in Japanese, indicating that there are two technical terms for plagiarism that carry "strongly negative connotations," as well as the term *ukeuri*, which conveys a "far less harsh connotation" than the term "plagiarism" in English.

Confusion about the nuances of meaning carried by the term "plagiarism" may lead some students to copy without realizing they are breaking any rules. However, the reasons for inappropriate textual borrowing by international and ESL students are more complex than lexical misunderstandings. Cultural influences, differing educational practices, inexperience with academic discourse, and language barriers may all contribute to problematic uses of source texts.

Cultural Attitudes toward Textual Ownership

Some researchers argue that whereas Western cultures emphasize the importance of individual ownership of both intellectual and physical property, some cultures may take a more collective view of ownership, perceiving knowledge as belonging to society as a whole. For example, Duff, Rogers, and Harris (2006: 675) cite an instance in which an author's knowledge is considered commonplace by Japanese students and therefore belongs to the "realm of collective ownership." Shi (2006: 265) notes a similar concept within the Asian tradition of Confucianism, which "advocates open and broad access to knowledge as common heritage." As Buranen (1999) indicates, in China a writer may assume that the knowledgeable reader is already familiar with sources quoted in the text, rendering citation unnecessary. Under these circumstances, the source credit is implied rather than explicit.

In addition to this collective attitude toward text, some researchers also tie plagiarism to a deep respect for text and authors in some cultures. Hayes and Introna (2005) note that for Chinese students, using another author's words is an indication of respect. In this scenario, imitation is flattery, not cheating. Similarly, Lund (2004: 95) indicates that students from Confucian-influenced societies may plagiarize because they have been taught "reverence for the text and its author." Lund believes that a student who copied a paragraph from another text nearly verbatim was showing respect for a "much-admired author in his field." Thompson and Williams (2000) also note that students in some Asian cultures copy well-known authors "to show intelligence and good judgment."

The Role of Culture

The attribution of plagiarism to cultural beliefs has come under scrutiny in the literature. Oullette (2008) notes that conclusions about the importance of culture in textual borrowing practices have not always been based on empirical evidence. Lund's assertions about reverence for text, for example, are not based on interviews or empirical data. Because the student in question was not interviewed, one can only guess at his motives for copying, which could stem from linguistic as well as cultural factors. Although some interview data do support the possibility of cultural influences (Shi, 2006), Gu and Brooks (2008) caution against overemphasizing cultural factors, which could lead to reductionist attitudes toward a culture and its educational practices. Wheeler (2009: 26) is concerned that attributing students' plagiarizing behavior to cultural differences is "rife with negative potential, albeit unintentional."

The reasons for plagiarizing behavior are complex and cannot necessarily be easily attributed to culture. Based on questionnaires from many nonnative English-speaking students from various backgrounds, Buranen (1999) found no evidence that cultural differences were factors in plagiarism. In a study of Japanese students, Wheeler (2009: 25) found that "lack of awareness of what constitutes plagiarism" rather than cultural difference was the main force contributing to inappropriate textual borrowing practices. Pecorari (2003) also notes that students interviewed in her study did not mention cultural influence as a factor in plagiarism, although she acknowledges that culture may play a role in some cases. Educators should also consider additional factors, such as students' inexperience with academic essay writing.

Lack of Experience with Essay Writing

In many countries the instructional emphasis is on memorization of facts, and little time is devoted to writing instruction. Memorization is seen not as rote busy work but as a way to deeply understand a text or subject, and the ability to quote extensively from the "masters" is a sign of accomplishment (Pennycook, 1996). Students are often provided with source texts by their teachers, so there is little need for outside research (Shi, 2006). Dryden (1999) notes that in Japan, once students reach junior high, their education focuses on preparation for entrance exams rather than on writing and self-expression.

Consequently, overseas students may be required to do very little essay writing in their secondary and undergraduate education. Upon their arrival at an American university, they are asked to write not only in a new language but also in an unfamiliar discourse. They are "outsiders" to the academy, lacking the insider's knowledge of the standards for language use within the community (Valentine, 2006). As inexperienced writers, they lack facility with the "language" of academic essays, such as summarizing, paraphrasing, and quoting; in short, they do not know how to present themselves as authors (Abasi, Akbari, and Graves, 2006).

Inexperienced writers see texts as sources of irrefutable facts; they do not see themselves as having the ability to offer an opinion or counterargument (Abasi, Akbari, and Graves, 2006). Their perceived role, then, is to compile and present information gathered from sources. For example, an international student at my university submitted an essay that was copied almost verbatim (without quotation marks) from three published sources, which were properly and dutifully cited at the end of the paper. Obviously she did not intend to pass off the writing as her own words, or she wouldn't have cited the appropriate sources. Rather, she seemed to perceive her role to be one of presenting authoritative information she had compiled, thus indicating she had read and understood the texts.

This student was correct in the sense that presenting oneself as an author involves in part referring to authoritative sources. What was missing in her essay was her own voice, creating her own argument. This dual act of being both original and referential in the same essay presents a contradiction for many beginning writers (Pennycook, 1996). If someone else has already written authoritatively on this topic, the student may reason, why rewrite their ideas in my own less adequate words? The sense of contradiction may again stem from the student's position as outsider to the realm of academic discourse. Many other forms of writing with which students may be more familiar from their previous education or their own interests, such as novels or personal essays, are solely creative and do not involve crafting arguments using outside sources.

Students in the United States are encouraged to be original and creative in their essays. While their ideas and arguments should certainly be original, much of the actual language in academic writing consists of stock phrases that are used repeatedly by native speakers as the expected mode of expression (Schmitt, 2005). A few examples drawn from Schmitt's article include "a second and related factor," "a major challenge," "with particular regard," and "in conclusion." Encouraging ESL students to "use their own voice," then, may further their sense of confusion. Language acquisition involves learning "the conventionalized language of the community in which one finds oneself" (Schmitt, 2005: 68), not developing entirely new modes of expression. For experienced academic writers, the "insiders" in the discourse community, the use of formulaic phrases becomes automatic, but ESL students will need to learn how and when to employ these linguistic devices as part of their own authorial voice.

Language as Borrowed Words

In addition to the peculiarities of academic discourse, ESL students may struggle with English vocabulary and grammar. In interviews, ESL students often express their frustration with their perceived lack of facility with language (Leki and Carson, 1997). They feel that the "best" words have already been used by the original author, and rewriting a passage in their own words would only make the text worse (Currie, 1998). Copying, then, is a survival strategy. According to Hu (2001), in essence all words in English for ESL students are "borrowed words." If students feel they have no appropriate words of their own, the only recourse is to use the words provided in the source text.

Discipline-specific technical vocabulary presents a particular problem for ESL students not familiar with the terminology used in their area of study. Barks and Watts (2001) note that technical vocabulary in academic essays should not be paraphrased; it should be used in its original form to preserve the precise meaning. However, students with developing vocabularies in English may have difficulty differentiating technical terms from more commonly used words and phrases and thus be tempted to copy entire phrases or paragraphs in order to maintain the original meaning.

The need to "borrow" extensive sections of a source text may stem not just from lack of vocabulary but also from minimal understanding of the subject itself. Howard (1995: 799) notes that patchwriting is used by students when they are "unfamiliar with the words and ideas about which they are writing." Without a solid grounding in a subject gained from much reading and discussion, students have no base from which to make their own statements as authors and thus rely once again on the words provided for them in source texts. As Schmitt (2005: 69) points out, "requiring first-year undergraduates to write about a new discipline *in their own words* is distinctly problematic when knowledge of the discipline is anything but their own."

Classroom Suggestions

There is evidence in the literature that instruction has a positive effect on help-ing students avoid plagiarism (Duff, Rogers, and Harris, 2006; Soto, Anand, and McGee, 2004). However, teaching international students the mechanics of quoting and citing is not enough to address the complexity of issues surrounding plagiarism; they still may not understand why citation is considered important and when it is appropriate within the American academic community. As Pen-nycook (1996: 227) notes, any discussion of citation, paraphrase, and textual borrowing must include discussion of "how and why these notions have been constructed."

Discussion of Plagiarism as a Cross-Cultural Concept

A step toward promoting a deeper understanding of the complexities of plagia-rism might be to initiate classroom discussion of the varying cultural notions of authorship, plagiarism, etc. (Currie 1998). Barks and Watts (2001) suggest "consciousness-raising" activities that allow students to see textual borrowing practices in their own cultures in comparison with practices in the United States. Thompson and Williams (2000) advocate similar "student-centered" activities that involve discussions of problems that may arise in regard to textual bor-rowing practices as a result of cultural differences.

Barks and Watts (2001) also recommend classroom discussions about why citations are considered important and why copying without citation is con-sidered wrong. To draw students' attention to the range of practices that may fall under plagiarism, they recommend a classroom activity in which students examine examples of various types of textual borrowing activities (such as copy-ing a paragraph without attribution) and determine which practices constitute plagiarism and which are legitimate uses of text.

Students as Ethnographers

Barks and Watts (2001) identify "ethnographic approaches" to learning as tex-tual borrowing practices that require students to examine models and draw conclusions about language use. For example, after reading an academic journal article, students identify instances in which the author has used direct quotes; they then try to determine why the author chose to use direct quotes rather than paraphrase in those instances. Students can also compare their article to one of the original sources cited and note differences in language. They can also try to identify instances in a text in which an author is stating his or her own opinion or argument as opposed to paraphrasing another source.

These activities allow students to see how writers inside the academic dis-course community write. In addition to the conventions of citing, paraphrasing, and quoting, academic essays include numerous key stock phrases that are used repeatedly to convey particular functions: introducing, hedging, contradicting, restating, concluding, etc. As a classroom activity, students can locate these stock phrases within texts and try to determine the language function of the phrase. Examining multiple models will help students understand that the use of these phrases is not copying or cheating but in fact standard practice by members of the academic community.

Reading and Understanding Texts

Students may plagiarize because of a lack of deep understanding of a text, both linguistically and conceptually. It is nearly impossible to appropriately paraphrase what one doesn't comprehend. In order to gain a deeper understanding of both the subject matter and related vocabulary, students need to engage in very close readings of multiple texts on similar topics, followed by class discussion, before they begin to incorporate the source texts into their own essays. They can also benefit from reading a newspaper or magazine article on a topic before tackling the difficult vocabulary and concepts in a scientific journal.

In addition to linguistic and conceptual misunderstandings, students may plagiarize because of a lack of understanding of a text's rhetorical aspects. Kantz (1990) argues that beginning writers often misread persuasive essays as narratives rather than arguments and thus see texts as sources of irrefutable facts rather than claims based on an interpretation of facts. Retelling a story lends itself to copying or restating someone else's words; creating an argument that addresses a specific and novel rhetorical problem requires original writing. Kantz (1990) advocates teaching students to read rhetorically so that they will learn to consider such factors as audience and purpose and to recognize when an author is creating an argument rather than telling a story. Because how students write about texts depends on how they read the texts, developing awareness of rhetorical practices will help students begin to incorporate source texts in a more sophisticated way into their own essays.

Repeated Practice in Context

Only after students have discussed plagiarism in a larger context and examined models of academic discourse can they begin to tackle the mechanics of quotation, paraphrasing, and citation in their own writing. Valentine (2006: 93) argues that learning to avoid plagiarism is achieved "not through rule-following but through repeatedly carrying out what counts as citation in a context similar to the context in which citation will be required." Thompson and Williams (2000) further emphasize the importance of context. When teaching paraphrasing, they found that the traditional decontextualized one- or two-line exercises provided in many writing textbooks were not sufficient and recommend using "authentic, discourse level materials" such as entire articles and actual ESL student papers. Thompson and Williams (2000: 128) also recommend having students write paraphrases in class without looking at the original source, "forcing them to digest and present information in their own voices." Students can also benefit from reading each others' essays, looking for instances of plagiarism, and providing feedback.

Conclusion

It is clear from the foregoing discussion that overseas and ESL students face a number of challenges as they adjust to the American educational system. They may bring differing cultural attitudes toward text ownership, making the assumption that their readers are already familiar with their sources and thus do not expect citations. However, researchers differ on the extent to which cultural background plays a role in textual borrowing practices, and some writers point out that traditional attitudes toward text ownership and usage may be changing as some cultures become more westernized (Bloch, 2001).

Regardless of their cultural background, many international students may find that their educational training in their home countries did not prepare them for writing argumentative academic essays according to the expected standards at American schools and universities. If much of their educational experience involved either using a text provided by their instructor or writing narratives that did not necessitate outside sources, then the notion of creating an argument that incorporates other textual sources may be entirely new. As outsiders to academic discourse, ESL and international students are not familiar with the norms and conventions used within the academy.

Essay writing in a new genre is an even greater challenge for students whose first language is not English. Lacking the vocabulary and linguistic structures to write an appropriate paraphrase, students may feel compelled to copy the original text as their only means of expression. Reading, a skill inseparable from writing, also presents a challenge, because students cannot effectively respond to text they do not fully understand linguistically, conceptually, or rhetorically.

This chapter has discussed a number of strategies for educators to use in addressing the complex issue of plagiarism as it pertains to international and ESL students. The presentation of mechanical rules for citation is only one step in the process and should come only after discussion about why referencing is considered important in the Western academic tradition. In addition, providing students with multiple models of academic discourse can help them learn the language and conventions used within the discourse community. Finally, students need plenty of opportunity for practicing creating arguments supported by paraphrasing, quoting, and citing within the context of academic discourse in order to establish their identity as writers.

References

Abasi, Ali R., Nahal Akbari, and Barbara Graves. 2006. "Discourse Appropriation, Construction of Identities, and the Complex Issue of Plagiarism: ESL Students Writing in Graduate School." *Journal of Second Language Writing* 15, no. 2: 102–117.

Barks, Debbie, and Patricia Watts. 2001. "Textual Borrowing Strategies for Graduate-Level ESL Writers." In *Linking Literacies: Perspectives on L2 Reading–Writing Connections* (pp. 246–267), edited by Diane Belcher and Alan Hirvela. Ann Arbor: University of Michigan Press.

Bloch, Joel. 2001. "Plagiarism and the ESL Student: From Printed to Electronic Text." In *Linking Literacies: Perspectives on L2 Reading–Writing Connections* (pp. 209–228), edited by Diane Belcher and Alan Hirvela. Ann Arbor: University of Michigan Press.

Buranen, Lise. 1999. "But I *Wasn't* Cheating: Plagiarism and Cross-Cultural Mythology." In *Perspectives on Plagiarism and Intellectual Property in a Postmodern World* (pp. 63–74), edited by Lise Buranen. Albany: State University of New York Press.

Chandrasoma, Ranamukalage, Celia Thompson, and Alastair Pennycook. 2004. "Beyond Plagiarism: Transgressive and Nontransgressive Intertextuality." *Journal of Language, Identity & Education* 3, no. 3: 171–193.

Currie, Pat. 1998. "Staying out of Trouble: Apparent Plagiarism and Academic Survival." *Journal of Second Language Writing* 7, no. 1: 1–18.

Dryden, L.M. 1999. "A Distant Mirror or Through the Looking Glass? Plagiarism and Intellectual Property in Japanese Education." In *Perspectives on Plagiarism and Intellectual Property in a Postmodern World* (pp. 75–85), edited by Lise Buranen. Albany: State University of New York Press.

Duff, Andrea H., Derek P. Rogers, and Michael B. Harris. 2006. "International Engineering Students—Avoiding Plagiarism through Understanding the Western Academic Context of Scholarship." *European Journal of Engineering Education* 31, no. 6: 673–681.

Gu, Qing, and Jane Brooks. 2008. "Beyond the Accusation of Plagiarism." *System: An International Journal of Educational Technology and Applied Linguistics* 36, no. 3: 337–352.

Hayes, Niall, and Lucas D. Introna. 2005. "Cultural Values, Plagiarism, and Fairness: When Plagiarism Gets in the Way of Learning." *Ethics & Behavior* 15, no. 3: 213–231.

Howard, Rebecca Moore. 1995. "Plagiarisms, Authorships, and the Academic Death Penalty." *College English* 57, no. 7: 788.

Hu, Jim. 2001. "An Alternative Perspective of Language Re-use: Insights from Textual and Learning Theories and L2 Academic Writing." *English Quarterly* 33, no. 1–2: 52–62.

Kantz, Margaret. 1990. "Helping Students Use Textual Sources Persuasively." *College English* 52, no. 1: 74–90.

Leki, Ilona, and Joan Carson. 1997. "Completely Different Worlds: EAP and the Writing Experiences of ESL Students in University Courses." *TESOL Quarterly* 31, no. 1: 39–69.

Lund, James R. 2004. "Plagiarism: A Cultural Perspective." *Journal of Religious & Theological Information* 6, no. 3: 93–101.

Ouellette, Mark A. 2008. "Weaving Strands of Writer Identity: Self as Author and the NNES 'Plagiarist.'" *Journal of Second Language Writing* 17, no. 4: 255–273.

Pecorari, Diane. 2003. "Good and Original: Plagiarism and Patchwriting in Academic Second-Language Writing." *Journal of Second Language Writing* 12, no. 4: 317–345.

Pennycook, Alastair. 1996. "Borrowing Others' Words: Text, Ownership, Memory, and Plagiarism." *TESOL Quarterly* 30, no. 2: 201–230.

Schmitt, Diane. 2005. "Writing in the International Classroom." In *Teaching International Students: Improving Learning for All* (pp. 63–74), edited by Jude Carroll and Janette Ryan. New York: Routledge.

Shi, Ling. 2006. "Cultural Backgrounds and Textual Appropriation." *Language Awareness* 15, no. 4: 264–282.

Soto, Julio G., Sulekha Anand, and Elizabeth McGee. 2004. "Plagiarism Avoidance." *Journal of College Science Teaching* 33, no. 7: 42–48.

Thompson, Lenora C., and Portia G. Williams. 2000. "But I Changed Three Words! Plagiarism in the ESL Classroom." In *Student Cheating and Plagiarism in the Internet Era: A Wake-Up Call* (pp. 127–128), edited by Ann Lathrop and Kathleen Foss. Englewood, CO: Libraries Unlimited.

Valentine, Kathryn. 2006. "Plagiarism as Literacy Practice: Recognizing and Rethinking Ethical Binaries." *College Composition and Communication* 58, no. 1: 89–109.

Wheeler, Greg. 2009. "Plagiarism in the Japanese Universities: Truly a Cultural Matter?" *Journal of Second Language Writing* 18, no. 1: 17–29.

Part III

A Practitioner's Toolkit

10

Plagiarism: The Legal Landscape

Robert Berry

Introduction

Colleges and universities with plagiarism policies that are fundamentally fair—and that are applied consistently—enjoy three significant advantages over those that do not. First, these schools enjoy greater legitimacy in the eyes of the people who must live with their decisions. They exercise genuine moral authority in their decision making, which is much more consistent with the goals of education, and they avoid the exercise of raw power that often accompanies ad hoc decision making. Second, educational institutions with fair policies are less likely to be sued and, if sued, are less likely to lose. Third, the same procedures that ensure fairness also promote the effectiveness of university prohibitions against plagiarism by creating an educational milieu where a school's response to plagiarism is predictable and reliable.

A fair university plagiarism policy is one that (1) accords students or faculty accused of plagiarism basic procedural protections, such as notice and an opportunity to be heard; (2) ensures that decisions to impose discipline, as well as determinations of the severity of discipline to be imposed, are reasonably consistent and are not rooted in a motive to retaliate or engage in invidious discrimination; (3) ensures that decisions to impose discipline are supported by reliable evidence of plagiarism; (4) protects the privacy and reputational interests of persons accused of plagiarism by refraining from publicizing accusations; and (5) clarifies precisely what conduct is prohibited. If these qualities seem to resonate strongly with common sense, it is most likely because common sense draws from political traditions in which procedural fairness is of paramount importance and accusations are expected to be accompanied by reliable evidence. Examining the legal landscape of plagiarism will, of course, ensure that common sense judgments are appropriately connected to the law.

This chapter will examine some of the major types of legal challenges that can be brought against schools that impose discipline for plagiarism. These are challenges to the procedures an institution relies on in imposing academic discipline, challenges based on claims of illegal discrimination, and challenges based on claims of defamation. The claims are not mutually exclusive, of course, and all three categories of allegations can be brought in the same lawsuit. This chapter also explores some of the defenses and justifications students, and instructors, have relied on when they are accused of plagiarism. The definition of plagiarism will also be considered with reference to both court cases and state statutes prohibiting the sale of term papers to see how best to draw the line between plagiarism and conduct that is permissible, such as receiving tutorial or research assistance.

Claims against Educational Institutions Alleging Procedural Deficiencies: Due Process and Breach of Contract Claims

As a general proposition, courts will accord deference to the internal procedures employed by a college, university, law school, or other educational institution. Courts will review the procedures a school has employed for fundamental fairness but will not usurp a school's authority to administer discipline, even where the court may disagree with a particular outcome. One court, which clearly believed the discipline a university imposed, withholding the student's degree for one year, was too harsh under the circumstances and lacked consistency with prior impositions of discipline for plagiarism—expressed this concept as follows:

> As this court has noted in prior hearings and conferences, Princeton might have viewed the matter of the penalty with a greater measure of humanity and magnanimity, with a greater recognition of the human frailties of students under stress, as the university apparently has done in many cases in the past. This court cannot mandate compassion, however, and will not, nor should not, engraft its own views on Princeton's disciplinary processes, so long as the standard of good faith and fair dealing has been met and the contract between the student and the university has not otherwise been breached. (*Napolitano v. Trustees of Princeton University (Napolitano I)*, 1982: 584–85; 283)

Greater judicial deference is accorded private institutions than public institutions (*Rom v. Fairfield University*, 2006), greater judicial deference is accorded academic decisions than disciplinary decisions (*Napolitano v. Trustees of Princeton University (Napolitano II)* 1982: 569; 274), and greater judicial deference is accorded disciplinary decisions by military academies than their civilian counterparts (*Tully v. Orr*, 1985: 1226). Notwithstanding this judicial deference, however, courts will occasionally review university procedures for violations of

Fourteenth Amendment Due Process protections, where tax-supported schools are concerned, and for breaches of contract—including the implied covenants of good faith and fair dealing—where private educational institutions are concerned.

Persons who have been found to have committed plagiarism often face substantial disciplinary sanctions that can include expulsion or dismissal as well as the loss of professional opportunities. In one case, for instance, a law student submitted a paper for an independent study that had been partially written by another person and that had included unattributed text taken from an article in a law journal. The law school suspended the student for three semesters. After graduation, the Connecticut Bar Examining Committee recommended that the student not be admitted to the Bar, based, in part, on the plagiarized paper (*Doe v. Connecticut Examining Committee*, 2003: 39; 14). Disciplinary sanctions imposed for plagiarism thus often create a powerful incentive to sue. Claims alleging deficiencies in disciplinary procedures are the most prevalent type of legal challenge to discipline imposed for plagiarism at educational institutions. In the case of private universities and colleges, these challenges to procedures will take the form of claims for breach of contract, breach of implied contract, and, occasionally, violation of "a common law duty to provide . . . due process" by failing to provide "appropriate notice and an opportunity to be heard" (*Edward Waters College v. Southern Association of Colleges and Schools, Inc.*, 2005).

The obligation of state universities to provide students fair procedures was recognized in the nineteenth century. As one Pennsylvania judge wrote:

> To those who have charge of the culture of our youth, is conceded the power of making needful rules and regulations for their government and control, and these may be enforced, if done in a due manner without external interference, even though at times hardships may seemingly be done and innocency suffer, but the reasonableness of such rules and regulations, as well as the regularity of the proceedings under them, have been decided, not infrequently, to be a proper subject for judicial inquiry. (*Commonwealth v. McCauley*, 1887: 459; 77)

At a minimum, Due Process requires notice and a hearing. A crucial case for expounding this principle was *Dixon v. Alabama State Board of Education*. Students from Alabama State College had organized a sit-in at a courthouse lunch grill to protest segregation. Twenty-nine student leaders of these protests were identified and either expelled or placed on probation. A federal court found that, whereas the "minimum procedural requirements" required by the Constitution would "depend upon the circumstances and the interests of the parties involved," students facing expulsion were entitled to notice and an opportunity to be heard (*Dixon v. Alabama State Board of Education*, 1961: 157, 158–59).

The relationship between private colleges, or universities, and their students is primarily contractual. Thus students at private educational institutions, "who are being disciplined are entitled only to those procedural safeguards which the school specifically provides," provided, however, that the "disciplinary procedures established by the institution must be fundamentally fair" (*Psi Up-silon of Philadelphia v. University of Pennsylvania*, 1991: 609–10; 758). A private university's decision to impose discipline must not be arbitrary or capricious. Courts have held that notice and a hearing are sufficient protections (*Morris v. Brandeis University*, 2001).

Students and instructors who have been disciplined for plagiarism have claimed a right to procedural protections in addition to notice and an opportunity to be heard. These claims have included, for instance, a right to a second hearing, a right to institutional review of a disciplinary finding (e.g., *Chandamuri v. Georgetown University*, 2003: 76), the right to have the assistance of an advisor from the university or college (*Morris v. Brandeis University*), and the right to counsel (*Tully v. Orr*).

Courts have refrained from imposing additional procedural burdens on colleges, or universities, beyond the basic protections of notice and an opportunity to be heard. Where a school has instituted additional procedural protections, however, courts will examine whether there has been compliance with these procedures. In *Cho v. University of Southern California*, a student was expelled after being found to have plagiarized portions of textbooks in a doctoral qualifying examination administrated in a take-home format. A California appellate court carefully reviewed the University of Southern California's procedures to evaluate, and ultimately reject, the plaintiff's contention that "she was entitled to have her case heard by a University Review Panel composed of two faculty members and one student." The court found that the university had complied with its procedures (*Cho v. University of Southern California*, 2006).

In determining what specific procedural protections should be afforded to students, or professors, who are accused of plagiarism, it is helpful to identify the underlying purposes of these protections. Notice and an opportunity to be heard protect against the arbitrary imposition of discipline by ensuring that the person responding to the charges has an opportunity to prepare, to present evidence, and to test the evidence presented against her or him. Notice should set forth the specific charges, identify the specific rules violated, identify the sanctions that might be imposed, and identify the procedures that will be followed. A hearing should afford a person responding to the charges an opportunity to present evidence, including witnesses, and an opportunity to cross-examine witnesses against her or him. These procedural protections ensure that discipline is imposed only where adequate evidence supports the charges. Consistency with established procedures protects against ad hoc decision making.

In *Dixon v. Alabama State Board of Education*, discussed earlier, a U.S. District Court provided its view "on the nature of the notice and hearing required by due process prior to expulsion from a state college or university":

> The notice should contain a statement of the specific charges and grounds which, if proven, would justify expulsion under the regulations of the Board of Education. . . . By its nature, a charge of misconduct, as opposed to a failure to meet the scholastic standards of the college, depends upon a collection of the facts concerning the

charged misconduct, easily colored by the point of view of the witnesses. In such circumstances, a hearing which gives the Board or the administrative authorities of the college an opportunity to hear both sides in considerable detail is best suited to protect the rights of all involved. . . . In the instant case, the student should be given the names of the witnesses against him and an oral or written report on the facts to which each witness testifies. He should also be given the opportunity to present to the Board, or at least to an administrative official of the college, his own defense against the charges and to produce either oral testimony or written affidavits of witnesses in his behalf. If the hearing is not before the Board directly, the results and findings of the hearing should be presented in a report open to the student's inspection. If these rudimentary elements of fair play are followed in a case of misconduct of this particular type, we feel that the requirements of due process of law will have been fulfilled. (*Dixon v. Alabama State Board of Education*)

It should be noted that where "at will" employees of an educational institution are involved, a university, or college, dismissing an employee for plagiarism might, in good faith, make the argument that, because the employee is "at will" and without the protection of an employment contract, she or he can be dismissed for any reason at all and is thus entitled to neither notice nor a hearing. Even in these situations, however, courts in some states have reviewed the dismissal of an employee under implied contract theories to determine if the dismissal was arbitrary and capricious. In these instances educational institutions that have afforded the discharged employee some type of hearing are in a better position to rebut allegations that the dismissal was arbitrary and capricious. (See, e.g., *Matikus v. University of Dayton*, 2003: 1114, for the view that at-will employees are not entitled to notice or a hearing.)

Claims against Educational Institutions Alleging Illegal Discrimination

Students and instructors who have been subjected to academic or professional discipline for plagiarism also frequently claim they were the victims of invidious discrimination. These claims may allege violations of the federal or state constitutional provisions, violations of federal civil rights statutes—such as the 1964 Civil Rights Act or Americans with Disabilities Act (ADA)—and violations of state civil rights statutes. Where a state educational institution is involved, claims may be brought pursuant to 42 U.S.C. § 1983, which codifies a right to sue where civil rights were violated by a state actor, acting under the color of law, that originated in the Civil Rights Act of 1871. Additionally, federal and state civil rights statutes often contain provisions that prohibit retaliation against an employee or student undertaken in response to complaints of discrimination or harassment.

Discrimination claims involve a wide range of situations. In one case involving plagiarism on a conference paper, and a consequent denial for tenure, for instance, an assistant professor sued alleging discrimination on the basis of race and national origin under Title VII of the 1964 Civil Rights Act, 42 U.S.C. § 2000e-2; the Civil Rights Act of 1866, 42 U.S.C. § 1981; and 42 U.S.C. § 1983. In that case the plaintiff, a Sunni Muslim from Jordan, claimed, ultimately unsuccessfully, that he was discriminated against by a dean who was a Shia Muslim from Iran (*Amr v. Virginia State University*, 2009). In another case, *Childress v. Cement*, the plaintiff alleged violations of the ADA and the Rehabilitation Act to challenge his expulsion from Virginia Commonwealth University for plagiarism and for cheating by submitting the paper in question in more than one course. Childress claimed the university failed to accommodate his learning disabilities, which included dysgraphia and other disorders of written expression (*Childress v. Cement*, 1998: 390).

One of the key issues in discrimination cases is whether the reasons discipline was imposed were proper or whether they were discriminatory. For instance, in *Gilbert v. Des Moines Area Community College* a college provost alleged violations of Title VII of the 1964 Civil Rights Act and the Iowa Civil Rights Act after he applied for the position of college president but was not selected for an interview. In investigating the complaint, filed with the Equal Opportunity Employment Commission and the Iowa Civil Rights Commission, it was discovered that the provost had committed plagiarism in preparing the essay portions of his application. He was then demoted. He claimed the demotion was done in retaliation for the civil rights complaints. In reviewing the case, a United States Court of Appeals found that whereas the college could "articulate a legitimate, nondiscriminatory reason" for each of the actions it took, the plaintiff was unable to produce evidence that the college's explanations for its decisions were merely a "pretext for unlawful discrimination" (*Gilbert v. Des Moines Area Community College*, 2007: 906).

Where the ADA is concerned, successful plaintiffs must show that they have a disability as defined by the ADA, that with or without reasonable accommodation they are able to meet an educational program's requirements, and that an adverse action was taken against them by the educational institutions based on their disability. In *Childress* the court found that the plaintiff could not show that the university did not provide reasonable accommodations where he had been encouraged by two different professors to visit the university's English Lab to get assistance with composing citations, but found the lab closed on his first visit there and never returned (*Childress v. Cement*, at 392).

In another case alleging discrimination based on a disability, *Dixon v. Pomeroy School District*, a high school senior had admitted committing plagiarism in preparing a term paper for an English class. As a consequence Dixon failed the class and, although he submitted a revised term paper, was unable to graduate with his cohort. Dixon's parents filed a complaint alleging that the school district "denied Justin an education by failing to identify a temporary disability due to stress related to his father's illness or provide adequate services" (*Dixon v. Pomeroy School District*, 2000 WL 155290 [Wash. App. Div. 3 2000]). The case, ultimately dismissed, illustrates the wide range of theories that have arisen in discrimination cases.

Federal and state statutes make it unlawful to retaliate against a person for exercising rights protected by law. For example, a student in a distance education program sued for retaliation in violation of the First Amendment when he was accused of plagiarism and expelled. The case was ultimately dismissed for lack of personal jurisdiction over the school (*Martin v. Godwin*, 2007: 299). The *Gilbert* court set forth the elements of a prima facie retaliation claim:

> To establish a prima facie case of retaliation, Gilbert must demonstrate (1) he engaged in statutorily protected activity, (2) he suffered an adverse employment action, and (3) a causal connection exists between the two. (*Gilbert v. Des Moines Area Community College*, 2007: 917)

Where a legitimate rationale exists for an adverse action retaliation claims will be dismissed.

Claims against Educational Institutions Alleging Defamation

Defamation claims also follow situations where students, or instructors, have been found by universities to have committed plagiarism. To prove that a communication is defamatory, a plaintiff must show that the nature of the communication would tend to cause injury to a person's reputation and that the communication was published.

Defamation traditionally has included both slander, involving oral communications, and libel, involving written communications. To prove that a communication is defamatory, a plaintiff must establish that the defendant published a defamatory communication to a third party, that the defendant asserted facts about the plaintiff, and that the communication was a proximate cause of injury to the plaintiff. Some communications are defamation per se, meaning that a plaintiff does not have to prove "special," or quantifiable, damages, such as lost earnings. As one New Mexico court wrote:

> A statement is deemed to be defamatory per se, if, without reference to extrinsic evidence and viewed in its plain and obvious meaning, the statement imputes to plaintiff: the commission of some criminal offense involving moral turpitude; affliction with some loathsome disease, which would tend to exclude the person from society; unfitness to perform duties of office or employment for profit, or the want of integrity in discharge of the duties of such office or employment; some falsity which prejudices plaintiff in his or her profession or trade; or unchastity of a woman. (*Newberry v. Allied Stores, Inc.*, 1989: 28; 1235)

Defendants can raise the truth of the communication as an affirmative defense.

Where a public figure, such as a university professor, is concerned, a plaintiff alleging defamation must also show there was actual malice by clear and convincing evidence. Thus, where one professor had formally accused another of plagiarizing his idea for a course, where a university investigation had concluded that there was in fact no plagiarism, and where the accusing professor refused to retract his allegations, a jury properly found that there was actual malice (*Abdelsayed v. Narumanchi*, 1995: 381).

Other theories related to defamation violations include claims that a liberty interest protected by the Due Process Clause was infringed and false light invasion of privacy claims. With regard to the former:

> In order to prevail on a claim for a violation of this type of liberty interest under the Due Process Clause of the Fourteenth Amendment, a plaintiff must prove that the charges against him: "(1) placed a stigma on his reputation; (2) were made public by the employer; (3) were made in conjunction with his termination or demotion; and (4) were false." (*Amr v. Virginia State University*, 2009; quoting *Sciolino v. City of Newport News*, 480 F.3d 642, 646 [4th Cir. 2007])

With regard to false light invasion of privacy:

> One who gives publicity to a matter concerning another that places the other before the public in a false light is subject to liability to the other for invasion of privacy, if (a) the false light in which the other was placed would be highly offensive to a reasonable person, and (b) the actor had knowledge of or acted in reckless disregard as to the falsity of the publicized matter and the false light in which the other would be placed. (*Grigorenko v. Pauls*, 2003: 446, 448)

Not surprisingly, two central concerns in resolving any defamation claim where plagiarism is concerned are whether the allegations of plagiarism were true and whether the allegations were disseminated to a sufficiently large audience to cause reputational damage. False light invasion of privacy claims require an injurious communication to be disseminated widely. Thus, in *Grigorenko*, where only "nine persons at Yale and three persons outside the Yale community" knew about allegations of plagiarism, the claim was dismissed (*Grigorenko v. Pauls*). On the other hand, this threshold was clearly met in *Gunasekera* where the plaintiff was suing for defamation, which requires less dissemination of the communication, and the university held a press conference to announce a report that was highly critical of him. The report concluded that rampant plagiarism existed "in mechanical-engineering graduate-student theses" and accused Gunasekera, a professor, of neglecting his responsibilities, contributing to an academic atmosphere where plagiarism was tolerated (*Gunasekera v. Irwin*, 2009: 464).

Defenses and Justifications Voiced in Response to Allegations of Plagiarism

Students, or instructors, who have been accused of committing plagiarism produce a wide assortment of defenses and justifications, beyond the challenges to procedure and other claims discussed earlier. These defenses and justifications include contentions that no plagiarism was committed, that the plagiarism was unintentional, or that the plagiarism was permitted.

Some persons accused of plagiarism contend that the university or college policy on academic integrity does not cover the situation in question. In *Cho v. University of Southern California*, for example, the plaintiff claimed that she did not need to provide attribution for passages from textbooks inserted verbatim into essays prepared for her doctoral qualifying examination because the information contained therein was "common knowledge" to the persons who would grade her essays. Cho also claimed that the university's prohibitions against plagiarism did not apply to take-home examinations. The court reviewing the university's policies and procedures found both arguments unavailing, inasmuch as the university plagiarism policy had no exception for common knowledge and the university's conduct code prohibiting "[i]mproper acknowledgement of sources in essays or papers" would indeed apply to take-home examinations (*Cho v. University of Southern California*, 2006).

Persons accused of plagiarism will often argue that the plagiarism was unintentional. As discussed later, some plagiarism policies require that the conduct prohibited be deliberate, and others do not. In either situation, however, the claim will fall flat where the plagiarism is blatant, as, for example, where text from the plagiarized source is copied verbatim. For example, in *Sanderson v. University of Tennessee* an undergraduate student plagiarized verbatim from several sources in preparing the first draft of a term paper. Pleased with the "84" he received on the draft, he submitted the paper in a campuswide writing competition where his breaches of academic integrity came to light. An administrative law judge, focusing narrowly on the definition of plagiarism in Black's law dictionary, found Sanderson had not intended to plagiarize and was therefore not guilty of it. This decision was reversed by the University Chancellor, and the Chancellor's findings were upheld on appeal. In light of the definition of plagiarism provided to the class Sanderson attended ("using an author's words or ideas without giving credit") and the numerous instances where Sanderson appropriated text verbatim from other sources without attribution, it was clear to the court that he was guilty of plagiarism (*Sanderson v. University of Tennessee*, 1997).

Perhaps the most bizarre justifications for plagiarism are those that attempt to shift the blame to a third party who, it is argued, actually prepared the paper and committed the plagiarism. These persons are saying, in other words, that they did not plagiarize, but the person they got to write their paper for them did. This was the argument in *Gilbert* where a provost applying for the position of president of Des Moines Area Community College (DMACC) was not interviewed and subsequently complained of discrimination. In investigating the complaint it was discovered that the essay accompanying his application plagiarized other sources. When asked about this, Gilbert attempted to shift blame to a consultant he had hired to write his essay for him:

> Gilbert acknowledged his application contained plagiarized materials, but Gilbert denied having knowledge of or being involved in the actual act of plagiarism. Gilbert stated (1) he had hired a consultant to assist him in completing his application, (2) the consultant prepared the essay answers for Gilbert and apparently committed the act of plagiarism, and (3) he was unaware any plagiarism had occurred.
>
> DMACC officials interviewed Gilbert again on December 22, 2004, and Gilbert again claimed the consultant, whom Gilbert stated he had paid about one thousand dollars in cash (with no receipt from the consultant), had prepared the essay answers. However, Gilbert could not recall the consultant's name, the number of times he met with the consultant, or the length of their meetings. Gilbert was unable to provide a description of the consultant. When asked whether the consultant was male or female, Gilbert replied, "Both." Gilbert then said, "I met with more than one sex." When asked how many people he consulted, Gilbert stated, "It would be one or two, because I think there was [*sic*] two, but I'm not sure." (*Gilbert v. Des Moines Area Community College*, 2007: 912)

Defining Plagiarism

Courts will occasionally look to university, or college, definitions of plagiarism in evaluating claims against colleges and universities. In *Chandamuri v. Georgetown University*, a U.S. District Court examined Georgetown University's definition to evaluate a claim that the Honor Code was improperly applied because Chandamuri "did not *intend* to pass off the work of others as his own." The argument was unavailing inasmuch as university's rules prohibited "plagiarism in any of its forms, whether it is intentional or unintentional" (*Chandamuri v. Georgetown University*, 2003: 78–79).

Similarly in *Napolitano II* a New Jersey Superior Court quoted at length from Princeton's "General Requirements for the Acknowledgment of Sources in Academic Work." The university's rules identified and clarified fundamental principles of academic integrity regarding the acknowledgment of sources relied on. In addition to requiring the "precise indication of the source—identifying the author, title, place and date of publication (where relevant), and page numbers" when sources are quoted from or paraphrased, the General Requirements specifically require attribution where a source was consulted long before the paper was prepared, where the source contains facts and ideas that the student then elaborates on, or where a student consults an essay or notes prepared by another student:

Occasionally, students maintain that they have read a source long before they wrote their papers and have unwittingly duplicated some of its phrases or ideas. This is not a valid excuse. The student is responsible for taking adequate notes so that debts of phrasing may be acknowledged where they are due.

Ideas and Facts. Any ideas or facts which are borrowed should be specifically acknowledged in a footnote or in the text, even if the idea or fact has been further elaborated by the student. Some ideas, facts, formulae, and other kinds of information which are widely known and considered to be in the "public domain" of common knowledge do not always require citation. . . .

Occasionally, a student in preparing an essay has consulted an essay or body of notes on a similar subject by another student. If the student has done so, he or she must state the fact and indicate clearly the nature and extent of his or her obligation. The name and class of the author of an essay or notes which are consulted should be given, and the student should be prepared to show the work consulted to the instructor, if requested to do so. (*Napolitano II*, 1982: 266–67)

A central consideration in defining plagiarism where students are concerned is whether the conduct prohibited must be deliberate and whether there must be some intention to represent the writing as one's own work. Prohibitions against plagiarism should, of course, state clearly whether the misconduct must be deliberate or not. Policies that impose discipline even where the conduct was not deliberate may be appealing insofar as they promise to streamline disciplinary hearings. There are, nonetheless, some advantages to requiring conduct warranting punishment to be deliberate and to reflect an intention to improperly pass work off as one's own. This approach is more consistent with a tradition where the imposition of punishment is associated with an intentional act. Defining plagiarism as a form of academic fraud requiring that intent to deceive be found also preserves flexibility in dealing with individual circumstances. Where sources have been used without attribution, but make up only a small portion of an academic writing and can be attributed to carelessness, a poor grade, warning, or effort to remediate a student's understanding of citation principles may better serve an institution's educational mission than a failing grade, a notation on a student's transcript, suspension, or expulsion.

A Florida state appellate court expressed criticism of one plagiarism policy that did not require a finding of intentional plagiarism on the grounds that it promoted unlimited university discretion and the possibility of disparate punishments for similar conduct. The case involved a student who had referred to the Posse Comitatus Act in her paper, included language directly from the act in quotation marks, but had failed to supply a citation to the Act. The court wrote:

An overbroad reading of the University's definition of plagiarism, coupled with the University's position that intent to plagiarize is not required to constitute a violation of the academic code, arguably results in almost unlimited discretion afforded to faculty to determine whether a student plagiarized a paper. . . . The hearing board upheld the professor's charge that A.K. had committed plagiarism but also concluded that she had no intent to do so. However, that concession is of little benefit to A.K. Neither this conclusion nor the University's definition of plagiarism will appear on A.K.'s transcript. It is this transcript which will be reviewed by postgraduate and professional schools to which A.K. may apply. . . .

Several procedural issues plagued the proceedings between A.K. and the University. Following the Academic Integrity Hearing Board's decision upholding the professor's finding of plagiarism, A.K. sought an appeal she believed was authorized by the University's rules. The University informed A.K. that the hearing board's decision was final and nonappealable, a position it maintained throughout most of the proceedings in the circuit court below. A.K. disagreed, citing a version of the University's Student Handbook. Eventually the trial court determined that the University's position was incorrect—an appeal from the hearing board was authorized and permitted. . . .

Finally, the record suggests that another student committed similar citation errors in his paper as A.K. committed in hers. Professor LaRose graded his paper with a "C" and made no accusation of plagiarism, while A.K. received the substantial punishments already described. If this reference is accurate, the academic treatment of the two students appears to be disparate. (*LaRose v. AK*, 2009)

Another challenge in defining plagiarism is determining how to explicitly prohibit some conduct—such as representing writing prepared by another as one's own work—while permitting conduct such as receiving the assistance of a writing tutor or a reference librarian. Some state legislatures that have drafted laws prohibiting term paper sales have wrestled with this problem, and the statutes they arrived at are instructive.

State governments have recognized the destructive potential of plagiarism in laws prohibiting the sale of term papers and other materials. Colorado's statute, for instance, declares that "practice of trafficking in academic materials, commonly referred to as ghostwriting, serves no legitimate purpose and tends to undermine the academic process to the detriment of students, the academic community, and the public . . ." (C.R.S.A. § 23-4-101).

Educators who examine state statutes designed to ban the sale of term papers, like those who survey relevant case law, are better prepared to draft plagiarism policies with precision than their colleagues who rely solely on experience and their knowledge of existing university policies. Some provisions in these statutes—such as, in some instances, criminal penalties and prohibitions on advertising—have little relevance to academic plagiarism policies. Other provisions, however, are highly relevant. These statutes were drafted by legislators who strove to define prohibited conduct carefully. They also worked to distinguish conduct that would be prohibited from permissible activities. These are the same issues that educators will confront in creating and using university plagiarism policies. The statutes were carefully drafted to reduce ambiguity and vagueness. These statutes are therefore useful aids to drafters of university policies who seek to clearly prohibit some conduct, clearly permit other conduct, and reduce to a reasonable minimum the types of conduct for which their policy provides no clear guidance.

California, Colorado, Connecticut, Florida, Illinois, Maine, Maryland, Massachusetts, Nevada, New Jersey, New York, North Carolina, Oregon, Pennsylvania, Texas, Virginia, and Washington all have enacted statutes banning the sale of term papers. Relevant sections of these statutes can be found in the following state codes:

California	West's Ann. Cal. Educ. Code §§ 66400-405 (*Prohibition concerning Preparation, Sale and Distribution of Term Papers, Theses, etc.*)
Colorado	C.R.S.A. §§ 23-4-101-105 (*Preparation, Sale, and Distribution of Academic Materials—Advertising*)
Connecticut	C.G.S.A. §§ 53-392a–e (*Preparation of Assignments for Students Attending Educational Institutions Prohibited*)
Florida	West's F.S.A. § 877.17 (*Works to Be Submitted by Students without Substantial Alteration*)
Illinois	110 IL. C.S. §§ 5/0.01-5/1 (*Academic Plagiarism Act*)
Maine	17-A M.R.S.A. § 705 (*Criminal Simulation*)
Maryland	MD Code, Education, §§ 26-201 (*Sales Prohibited*)
Massachusetts	M.G.L.A. 271 § 50 (*Sale of Research Papers, etc.; Taking of Examinations for Another at Educational Institutions*)
Nevada	N.R.S. 207.320 (*Preparation or Sale of Academic Writings*)
New Jersey	N.J.S.A. 18A:2-3 (*Sale of Term Papers or other Assignments; Penalties; Actions for Injunction*)
New York	McKinney's Education Law § 213-b (*Unlawful Sale of Dissertations, Theses and Term Papers*)
North Carolina	N.C.G.S.A. § 14-118.2 (*Assisting, etc., in Obtaining Academic Credit by Fraudulent Means*)
Oregon	O.R.S. § 164.114 (*Sale of Educational Assignments*)
Pennsylvania	18 Pa. C.S.A. § 7324 (*Unlawful Sale of Dissertations, Theses and Term Papers*)
Texas	V.T.C.A., Penal Code § 32.50 (*Deceptive Preparation and Marketing of Academic Product*)
Virginia	Va. Code Ann. §§ 18.2-505-508 (*Preparation, etc., of Papers to be Submitted for Academic Credit*)
Washington	West's RCWA 28B.10.580-584 (*Term Papers, Theses, Dissertations, Sale of Prohibited—Legislative Findings—Purpose*)

The basic approach these statutes take is to (1) prohibit the sale of term papers, theses, and other materials submitted for academic credit; (2) specifically exempt certain types of activities, such as providing tutorial and research assistance; and (3) provide for remedies and sanctions.

California, like most other states with statutes banning the sale of term papers, prohibits the sale of materials that will be submitted for academic credit:

> No person shall prepare, offer to prepare, cause to be prepared, sell, or otherwise distribute any term paper, thesis, dissertation, or other written material for another person, for a fee or other compensation, with the knowledge, or under circumstances in which he should reasonably have known, that such term paper, thesis, dissertation, or other written material is to be submitted by any other person for academic credit at any public or private college, university, or other institution of higher learning in this state. (*Prohibition concerning Preparation, Sale and Distribution of Term Papers, Theses, etc.*, West's Ann. Cal. Educ. Code § 66400)

Some states provide a broader definition of the types of materials covered. Connecticut, for instance, prohibits preparing or offering to prepare "any term paper, thesis, dissertation, essay, report or other written, recorded, pictorial, artistic or other assignment" in "return for pecuniary benefit" (*Preparation of Assignments for Students Attending Educational Institutions Prohibited*, C.G.S.A. §§ 53-392b[A]). Maine specifically prohibits taking "an examination for another person" in "return for pecuniary benefit" (*Criminal Simulation*, 17-A M.R.S.A. § 705). Some states, such as Florida, also slightly broaden their prohibitions beyond materials submitted for academic credit to include materials submitted "in fulfillment of the requirements for a degree, diploma, or course of study . . ." (*Works to Be Submitted by Students without Substantial Alteration*, West's F.S.A. § 877.17).

Academic writings that are not clearly covered by these acts would include essays written to accompany applications for admission, writings submitted for writing competitions, writings by student journalists, and other not-for-credit, nonrequired materials that nonetheless benefit students by helping them gain admission, win honors, and gain success at extracurricular activities. Accordingly, educators should consider whether university plagiarism policies should specifically prohibit plagiarism in connection with various types of not-for-credit writings. They should also consider whether it is desirable to specifically enumerate various types of noncredit writings or to instead include general language such as "submitted for academic credit or other academic benefit."

Many of the statutes explicitly recognize that some types of assistance given to students preparing academic writings are appropriate and desirable. These include typing or assembling term papers, furnishing research or information, and providing tutorial assistance, editing assistance, and so forth. Pennsylvania's statute, for instance, specifically authorizes these activities:

> Nothing herein contained shall prevent such educational institution or any member of its faculty or staff from offering courses,

instruction, counseling or tutoring for research or writing as part of a curriculum or other program conducted by such educational institution. Nor shall this section prevent any educational institution or any member of its faculty or staff from authorizing students to use statistical, computer, or any other services which may be required or permitted by such educational institution in the preparation, research or writing of a dissertation, thesis, term paper, essay, report or other written assignment. Nor shall this section prevent tutorial assistance rendered by other persons which does not include the preparation, research or writing of a dissertation, thesis, term paper, essay, report or other written assignment knowing, or under the circumstances having reason to know, that said assignment is intended for submission either in whole or substantial part under said student's name to such educational institution in fulfillment of the requirements for a degree, diploma, certificate or course of study. Nor shall any person be prevented by the provisions of this section from rendering services for a fee which shall be limited to the typing, transcription or reproduction of a manuscript. (*Unlawful Sale of Dissertations, Theses and Term Papers*, 18 Pa. C.S.A. § 7324e)

It is possible, of course, for tutorial, editorial, or research assistance to exceed reasonable bounds, such that an academic writing is no longer substantially the work of the person submitting it. One approach, taken by Oregon, to forestall this is to specify that the assistance cannot make up a substantial part of the assignment:

(3) Nothing in this section prohibits a person from rendering for a monetary fee:
(a) Tutorial assistance if the assistance is not intended to be submitted in whole or in substantial part as an assignment; or
(b) Service in the form of typing, transcribing, assembling, reproducing or editing an assignment if this service is not intended to make substantive changes in the assignment. (*Sale of Educational Assignments*, O.R.S. § 164.114)

In defining plagiarism it may be desirable to distinguish it from copyright infringement because the two concepts are often confused and conflated. Copyright refers to rights based in federal statutes enacted pursuant to Article I, Section 8 of the Constitution. Two key differences between copyright infringement and plagiarism are whether lack of permission or lack of attribution renders the use of another's work improper. In regard to plagiarism, using a source to quote small passages and to support contentions is fine, so long as accurate citations are employed to provide attribution on a use-by-use basis. No permission to use the material is required.

Copyright, on the other hand, refers to transferable statute-based rights to reproduce and distribute a creative work. Here uses of material must either be by permission from the copyright owner or pursuant to some statutory exception, such as works that have entered the domain or fall under fair use. University, or college, copyright policy typically works to facilitate (1) acquiring (and paying for) permissions; (2) educating people about fair use under 17 U.S.C. § 107; (3) imposing nonstatutory guidelines reflecting the university's understanding of the parameters of fair use; (4) ensuring the college, or university, complies with, and gets the full benefit of, statutory provisions under the TEACH Act and the Digital Millennial Copyrights, which provisions protect universities and colleges from liability if they comply with statutory procedures; and (5) ensuring that the provisions of 17 U.S.C. § 108, allowing limited copying for preservation purposes, are properly utilized.

Plagiarism, on the other hand, although it occasionally involves copying sections of a work without permission, is a breach of academic integrity. Prohibitions against it are enforced by university disciplinary proceedings. Some universities and colleges may, of course, want to prohibit copyright infringement and impose discipline in appropriate circumstances. Given the importance of clarity in university plagiarism policies, however, copyright infringement should be dealt with under separate provisions.

Conclusion

While reviewing the law of plagiarism will not always provide educators with specific answers, it should give them a basic set of questions to ask when reviewing and revising their plagiarism policy. These questions might be stated, for example, as follows:

1. How does the college or university define plagiarism?
2. Is the definition consistent across all divisions of the university?
3. Does the disciplinary policy provide persons accused of plagiarism with effective notice of the charges against them and an opportunity to be heard?
4. What additional procedural protections exist or would be desirable to institute?
5. Is the text of the policy clear, and is it published prominently?
6. Is the policy supported with adequate training and education to ensure it is enforced fairly and consistently?
7. What counts as evidence of plagiarism?
8. What evidence could be produced that would rebut a charge of plagiarism?
9. What type of record of the proceedings should be prepared and preserved?
10. When should failures to properly cite works be grounds for a poor grade, as opposed to grounds for academic discipline?
11. What are appropriate punishments for plagiarism?
12. What procedures will be in place to preserve the confidentiality of disciplinary proceedings?

References

Abdelsayed v. Narumanchi, 668 A.2d 378, 381 (1995).

Amr v. Virginia State University, 2009 WL 112829 (E.D. Va., 2009).

Chandamuri v. Georgetown University, 274 F. Supp. 2d 71, 76 (D.C. 2003).

Childress v. Cement, 5 F. Supp. 2d 384, 390, 392 (D.C. E.D. Va. 1998).

Cho v. University of Southern California, 2006 WL 1476911 (Cal. Ct. App. 2006) (unpublished opinion).

Commonwealth v. McCauley, 2 Pa. C. C. 459, 3 Pa. C. C. 77, 1887 WL 4879, 4 Lanc. L. R. 50 (Pa. Ct. Com. Pl. 1887).

Criminal Simulation, 17-A M.R.S.A. § 705 (Maine).

Dixon v. Alabama State Board of Education, 294 F.2d 150, 157, 158–59 (5th Cir. 1961).

Dixon v. Pomeroy School District, 2000 WL 155290 (Wash. Ct. App. 2000).

Doe v. Connecticut Examining Committee, 263 Conn. 39, 818 A.2d 14 (Conn. 2003).

Edward Waters College v. Southern Association of Colleges and Schools, Inc., 2005 WL 6218035 (M.D. Fla. 2005).

Gilbert v. Des Moines Area Community College, 495 F.3d 906, 907, 912, 917 (8th Cir. 2007).

Grigorenko v. Pauls, 297 F. Supp. 2d 446, 448 (2003).

Gunasekera v. Irwin, 551 F.3d 461, 464 (6th Cir. 2009).

LaRose v. AK, 2009 WL 2194509 (Fla. 2009) (unpublished opinion demarked as not yet released and subject to revision or withdrawal).

Martin v. Godwin, 499 F.3d 290, 299 (3d Cir. 2007).

Matikas v. University of Dayton, 788 N.E.2d 1108, 1114 (Ct. App. Ohio 2003).

Morris v. Brandeis University, 2001 WL 1470357 (Mass. Super. 2001).

Napolitano v. Trustees of Princeton University (Napolitano I), 186 N.J. Super. 576, 584–85, 453 A.2d 279, 283 (Super. Ct. N.J. Chanc. Div. 1982).

Napolitano v. Trustees of Princeton University (Napolitano II), 186 N.J. Super. 548, 569, 453 A.2d 263, 274 (Super. Ct. N.J. 1982).

Newberry v. Allied Stores, Inc., 108 N.M. 424, 428, 773 P.2d 1231, 1235 (Sup. Ct. N.M. 1989).

Preparation of Assignments for Students Attending Educational Institutions Prohibited C.G.S.A. §§ 53-392a–e (Connecticut).

Prohibition concerning Preparation, Sale and Distribution of Term Papers, Theses, etc., West's Ann. Cal. Educ. Code § 66400 (California).

Psi Upsilon of Philadelphia v. University of Pennsylvania, 404 Pa. Super. 604, 591 A.2d 755 (Pa. Super. 1991).

Rom v. Fairfield University, 2006 WL 390448 (Super. Ct. CT 2006) (unpublished opinion).

Sale of Educational Assignments, O.R.S. § 164.114 (Oregon).

Sanderson v. University of Tennessee, 1997 WL 18427 (Tenn. Ct. App. 1997) (unpublished opinion).

Tully v. Orr, 608 F. Supp. 1222, 1226 (E.D.N.Y. 1985).

Unlawful Sale of Dissertations, Theses and Term Papers, 18 Pa. C.S.A. § 7324e (Pennsylvania).

Works to Be Submitted by Students without Substantial Alteration, West's F.S.A. § 877.17 (Florida).

11

Professional Organizations' Recommendations Regarding Intellectual Honesty

Frances Kaufmann
Julie Still

> You who are on the road
> Must have a code that you can live by.
> —Graham Nash, "Teach Your Children"

Introduction

People like rules, and they like them to be fairly simple and straightforward. A big red signs mean stop. Tax forms are due April 15th. Cheat on a spouse and you risk divorce. Cheat in a class and you risk failure. The Ten Commandments and the Code of Hammurabi are historical examples that people in groups set up behavioral guidelines; the same thing happens in kindergarten classes all across America. The popularity of books with titles like *The 7 Habits of Highly Effective People* (Covey, 2004), *The Rules* (Schneider and Fein, 1995), and *The Man Code* (Wilhoit, 2006) demonstrate our continuing belief in having guidelines for work and play.

In the working world, professional societies, unions, and guilds often provide guidelines. In the academic world, professional societies play a large role, with each academic discipline having its own variation on the standards with some individual specifics thrown in. Those of us who face the daily rewards and challenges of working with students to teach them the ethics and methodology of scholarly research and writing are fortunate to be able to tap into resources and recommendations of professional associations for guidance. Numerous professional organizations have faced the issues of plagiarism and academic integrity. In response, they have published style manuals and formulated policy statements, codes of ethics, and standards of professional conduct. This chapter will examine resources from professional organizations in the humanities, social sciences, education, and the sciences. What do their policies have in common, and how do they differ? Are there some general guidelines that can be gleaned from among these diverse organizations? How can we use these resources to make our students aware of what constitutes plagiarism and teach them the importance of academic integrity and honesty in their research and writing?

The Humanities

Founded in 1883, the Modern Language Association (MLA) is an organization with more than 30,000 members. The mission of MLA is to promote and "strengthen the study and teaching of language and literature" (Modern Language Association, "About the MLA," accessed 2010). The organization's *MLA Handbook for Writers of Research Papers* (Gibaldi, 2009) has long been considered the standard guide for college students writing research papers in the humanities. Now in its seventh edition, the book features an excellent chapter on plagiarism. It is interesting to note that in the fifth edition, published in 1999, plagiarism was covered as a subsection of the chapter titled "Research and Writing." In the sixth edition, the guide expanded coverage on the topic of plagiarism by devoting an entire chapter to the subject; the seventh edition updates and changes some of the introductory material. Interestingly, the seventh edition focuses more on the professional consequences of plagiarism in lieu of the sixth's on personal shame. The seventh edition also adds a paragraph on human subjects research, but the general guidelines remain essentially unchanged. With this expansion, MLA has certainly indicated the importance of clearly explaining all aspects of plagiarism to today's generation of students. The text acknowledges that students may be very aware of charges of plagiarism in the publishing and recording industries. It discusses the existence of guidelines and honor codes at their schools and in their classrooms on the topic. Separate sections cover the definition of plagiarism, its consequences, and how the Internet has transformed the exchange of information.

Section 2.3, "Information Sharing Today," discusses the ease of finding, modifying, and sending information over the Internet. It stresses that authorship of materials available electronically must be properly acknowledged. Section 2.5, "Forms of Plagiarism," shows exactly what constitutes plagiarism and recommends careful note keeping during research. The section includes excellent examples of plagiarism, presenting the original source material and then illustrating how plagiarism is committed by paraphrasing, borrowing specific terms, or presenting another's line of thinking without giving credit or documentation. It explains how to avoid plagiarism by inserting parenthetical documentation in the narrative and giving proper credit in the list of works cited. Students ought not to be confused about what constitutes plagiarism once they consider this clearly stated guideline: "If you have any doubt about whether or not you are committing plagiarism, cite your source or sources" (Gibaldi, 2009). The chapter ends with a point-by-point summary of what constitutes plagiarism and how plagiarism can be avoided. The seventh edition of the *MLA Handbook* is an excellent resource guide for anyone teaching students research and writing in the humanities.

Another source of guidance from MLA is their "Statement of Professional Ethics," intended to "embody reasonable norms for ethical conduct" (Modern Language Association, "Statement of Professional Ethics," accessed 2010). The third point in the statement's preamble includes plagiarism in the list of unethical behavior, with reference to this explanatory note: "In this statement we adopt the definition of plagiarism given in Joseph Gibaldi's *MLA Style Manual*: 'Using another person's ideas or expressions in your writing without acknowledging the source constitutes plagiarism'" (Modern Language Association, "Statement of Professional Ethics," accessed 2010). The MLA statement goes on to note "that this definition does not distinguish between published and unpublished sources, between ideas derived from colleagues and those offered by students, or between written and oral presentations."

Another excellent resource for faculty, graduate students, and administrators who direct writing programs and writing centers or teach freshman composition and writing is the Council of Writing Program Administrators (WPA) (www.wpacouncil.org). The WPA has produced an outstanding document on plagiarism, *"Defining and Avoiding Plagiarism: The WPA Statement on Best Practices,"* adopted January 2003. The statement defines plagiarism and examines its causes. It explains the responsibilities of students, faculty, and administrators. The most practical and helpful section is the list of five best practices that merit integration into teaching and guiding students through the research and writing process. Recommendations include how to explain plagiarism, the need for clear policies, and how to design and sequence assignments that promote inquiry. Concise and well written, the WPA strategies support "students throughout their research process" making "plagiarism both difficult and unnecessary" (Council of Writing Program Administrators, 2003). This document is a must have for any librarian or instructor.

Many scholarly organizations publish codes of ethics and standards of professional conduct that include statements on plagiarism. For example, the American Historical Association's (AHA) Professional Division has responsibility for ethical concerns. The Division developed and published the *Statement on Standards of Professional Conduct* in May 2003, with revisions adopted in January 2005. The introduction to the online version urges members "to share this document with your students and colleagues, whether by ordering additional copies or photocopying this publication" (American Historical Association, 2005). The document includes a separate section, "Statement on Plagiarism," that clearly explains and defines plagiarism:

> The clearest abuse is the use of another's language without quotation marks and citation. More subtle abuses include the appropriation of concepts, data, or notes all disguised in newly crafted sentences, or reference to a borrowed work in an early note and then extensive further use without attribution. (American Historical Association, 2005)

Careful research habits, including detailed note taking, distinction between exact quotations and paraphrasing, and the importance of checking manuscripts against cited sources, are obligations of the ethical historian. The importance of having procedures in place to handle suspected cases of plagiarism is discussed, but the responsibility for investigating and sanctioning such misconduct is placed with the employing agency. Shortly after this policy was published, an article in the *Chronicle of Higher Education* reported on the AHA announcement that it would no longer investigate complaints of suspected plagiarism. William J. Cronon, head of the Professional Division, noted that of 50 to 100 inquires annually, fewer than 10 cases required formal investigation. In addition, the organization has no power to impose sanctions (Bartlett, 2003: A12). This has opened up debate as to the effectiveness of statements of professional conduct and ethical codes without the power of enforcement. Even in light of this debate, historians are well served by having these guidelines in place and being able to use them to guide the work of their students and their own research.

In the 2005 professional standards document, the American Historical Association shifts the burden of investigating plagiarism to the individual historian's employer:

> Usually, it is the employing institution that is expected to investigate charges of plagiarism promptly and impartially and to invoke appropriate sanctions when the charges are sustained. Penalties for scholarly misconduct should vary according to the seriousness of the offense, and the protections of due process should always apply. A persistent pattern of deception may justify public disclosure or even termination of a career; some scattered misappropriations may warrant a formal reprimand. (American Historical Association, 2005)

Social Sciences

The American Psychological Association (APA) has published style manuals for more than 70 years. The *Publication Manual of the American Psychological Association,* better known as the *APA Style Manual*, is the recognized authority in the field of psychology. According to APA's website, "*APA Style* originated in 1929 . . . to establish . . . *style rules* that would codify the many components of scientific writing to increase the ease of reading comprehension" (American Psychological Association, "What Is APA," accessed 2010). The sixth edition, released in 2009 (copyrighted for 2010), includes improved and revised guidelines for avoiding plagiarism. A section on ethics explains when to use quotation marks, gives examples of how to appropriately paraphrase sources, and refers to exact section locations that include detailed information on quotations, paraphrasing, and referencing the work of others. The section on plagiarism and self-plagiarism provides more assistance to students on how to avoid plagiarizing the work of others. The Association also maintains a webpage (www. apasytle.org) to provide information on changes between editions.

The APA, like other professional organizations, is governed by a code of ethics. Their newest code, the 2002 APA Code of Ethics, went into effect on June 1, 2003. Its formal title is *Ethical Principles of Psychologists and Code of Conduct.* Section Eight of the code, titled "Research and Publication," clearly defines the organization's stand on plagiarism: "Psychologists do not present portions of another's work or data as their own, even if the other work or data source is cited occasionally" (American Psychological Association. *Ethical Principles*, accessed 2010). This information is also included in the *APA Manual*'s initial chapter, "Writing for the Behavioral and Social Sciences," in the section "Ethical and Legal Standards in Publishing" (American Psychological Association, 2010). Social scientists, who use APA's varied sources to keep informed about ethical standards in the profession, will be well prepared to teach their students about properly acknowledging sources and avoiding plagiarism.

Likewise the American Sociological Association has a set of "Ethical Standards" that it follows. This document also spells out ways to avoid plagiarism:

> In publications, presentations, teaching, practice, and service, sociologists explicitly identify, credit, and reference the author when they take data or material verbatim from another person's written work, whether it is published, unpublished, or electronically available. (American Sociological Association, 1999)

Anthropologists follow the *Code of Ethics of the American Anthropological Association* (American Anthropological Association, 2009). In the extensive section addressing research, plagiarism is addressed in "Section III. Research, Subsection B. Responsibility to Scholarship and Science":

> [A]nthropological researchers are subject to the general moral rules of scientific and scholarly conduct: they should not deceive or knowingly misrepresent (i.e., fabricate evidence, falsify, plagiarize), or attempt to prevent reporting of misconduct, or obstruct the scientific/scholarly research of others. (American Anthropological Association, accessed 2010)

While social science organizations do not present methods for teaching students how to avoid plagiarism, they do offer definitions of what constitutes plagiarism. With these guidelines in hand, social scientists should have the beginnings of a foundation upon which to begin to address the best ways to instruct their students about ethical research practices. In fact, fields without a code of ethics sometimes feel the lack of one. The American Economics Association does not have a code of ethics, or at least none is listed on their website (www.aeaweb.org). Two economists surveyed journal editors in the field and found that nearly 66 percent of them wanted the profession to have a code of ethics that provided guidelines on plagiarism (Enders and Hoover, 2004).

Education and Libraries

Founded in 1857 as the National Teachers Association (NTA) by educator Robert Campbell, The National Education Association (NEA) has worked to advocate for public education from preschool through graduate school. Membership is open to teachers on all levels at public institutions. Retired educators and college students studying to become teachers may also join the organization. While there seems to be no official policy statements on plagiarism, the NEA does provide resources for teachers on the topic. NEA Higher Education's *Advocate*

Online, published online eight times a year, examines hot topics in the field. The December 2000 issue includes a discussion of "cyber-cheating" and presents helpful information on how honor codes can help to discourage plagiarism. It also provides a list of excellent publications about academic cheating and preventing and detecting plagiarism (Crawley, 2000). A search for "plagiarism" on the NEA's website (www.nea.org) will lead to many helpful links to information about technology and student cheating, including a discussion group with suggestions on how to prevent plagiarism.

The National Association of Secondary School Principals (NASSP) in December 1998 issued a legal memorandum, *The Internet, Students' Rights, and Today's Principal* (Permuth, Mawdsley, and Westberry, 1998). It explores legal implications associated with student Internet use. Separate sections cover copyright law and the Internet, authors' rights, and fair use. A sample acceptable use policy, including a statement on plagiarism, will help high school administrators and professionals who provide computer and systems support in secondary schools to formulate such a policy for their own school districts.

Some professional organizations that focus on higher education have issued their own statements on academic integrity and fraud and misconduct in research. The Association of American Universities, founded in 1900, is composed of 62 major research universities ranging from Ivy League schools to land grant institutions. In 1988, the organization published *Framework for Institutional Policies and Procedures to Deal with Fraud in Research* (Association of American Universities, 1988). Although it was formulated to have policy in place to deal mainly with scientific research sponsored by outside agencies, it can serve as a model for what should be included in policies that deal with academic dishonesty. The document defines research fraud in detail and outlines the processes for handling allegations and proceeding with an inquiry.

The Association of American Colleges and Universities (AACU) represents institutions engaged in the process of undergraduate liberal education. More than 900 accredited institutions ranging from research universities to liberal arts colleges to community colleges work together through the organization to promote quality liberal education. In the AACU *Statement on Liberal Learning* (Association of American Colleges and Universities, 1998) its members assert, "we cultivate a respect for *truth*" and "we experience the benefits of liberal learning by pursuing intellectual work that is *honest*, challenging, and significant." While no official policy on academic integrity seems to exist, the Association's position was put forward in *CQ Researcher's* excellent issue, "Combating Plagiarism." Debra Humphreys, the association's vice president of communications and public affairs, commented on the importance of integrity in a liberal education:

> Academic honesty is the cornerstone of college learning and liberal education and, indeed, is a continuing problem that colleges face.
> . . . Problems related to plagiarism on campus paralleled problems in the larger society, such as newspaper plagiarism scandals and illegal file sharing of music and movies. (Hansen, 2003: 775)

One of the AACU's most outstanding resources for educators is The Center for Academic Integrity, a consortium of 320 institutions whose students, faculty, and administrators share information about academic integrity and promote its importance. Affiliated with the Robert J. Rutland Institute for Ethics at Clemson University, the Center sponsors an annual conference, a newsletter, a listserv, and an excellent website (www.academicintegrity.org) with links to helpful how-to resources for starting a program at your own institution, member institution honor codes, an assessment guide, and information about the Center's Fundamental Values Program. This program is described in the Center's publication *The Fundamental Values of Academic Integrity*. The publication defines five elements of academic integrity and discusses why it is an essential component of higher education. Plagiarism is addressed specifically through this directive: "All must show respect for the work of others by acknowledging their intellectual debts by proper identification of sources" (Center for Academic Integrity, 1999). At its publication in 1999, this statement was distributed to colleges and universities. A copy is available free for download from the Center's website (www.academicintegrity.org/fundamental_values_project/index.php).

The American Library Association is the oldest and largest library association in the world. With more than 60,000 members, the organization "promotes the highest quality library and information services and protects public access to information" (American Library Association, 2003a: vii). Two divisions, the American Association of School Librarians (AASL) and the Association of College and Research Libraries (ACRL), have resources concerning honesty in research. The AASL advocates for library media services for children and has issued a guide for school library media specialists. The *AASL Resource Guides for School Media Program Development* (American Library Association, accessed 2010) includes a bibliographic section on copyright with citations to articles especially relevant to use in elementary and high school libraries.

The ACRL, with more than 12,000 members, "enhances the effectiveness of academic and research librarians to advance learning, teaching, and research in higher education (American Library Association, 2003a: 83). The ACRL has developed *Standards for Libraries in Higher Education* that aid in assessing the effectiveness of academic libraries and librarians. Plagiarism is addressed under "Instruction": "Information literacy skills and bibliographic instruction should be integrated into appropriate courses with special attention given to intellectual property, copyright, and plagiarism" (American Library Association, 2004.) In addition, the organization has long been concerned with information literacy and developing lifelong learners. As a result of this responsibility, the ACRL produced *Information Literacy Competency Standards for Higher Education* (American Library Association, 2003b) and promotes use of these standards in higher education. Its recommendations are very clear. Standard Five states: "The information literate student understands many of the economic, legal, and social issues surrounding the use of information and accesses and uses information ethically and legally." Furthermore, Outcome 2F of the standard asserts: "Demonstrates an understanding of what constitutes plagiarism and does not represent work attributable to others as his/her own" (American Library Association, 2003b). In 2007, the ACRL published a collection of library plagiarism policies as part of its CLIP Note series, *Library Plagiarism Policies: CLIP Note 37*, compiled by Vera Stepchyshyn and Robert S. Nelson. Any library wishing to develop a plagiarism policy would find this collection very useful. Thus, it is apparent that educators, administrators, and librarians on all educational levels, from primary through graduate school, have a wide range of excellent policy statements and tools available from professional organizations in their field to guide them through the process of creating ethics codes and training students about academic integrity.

Science and Engineering

Scientific and technical organizations have long been concerned with the ethics of research because of the use of animal and human subjects and because the falsification or misappropriation of information could have dire consequences not only for the research subjects themselves but also for the advancement of science and for society in general. This section will cover only official statements and policy on plagiarism in the scientific and engineering community. It does not attempt to be all-inclusive but concentrates on major government organizations concerned with scientific research and with a selection of professional societies that govern individual fields in science and engineering.

The National Science Foundation (NSF), an agency of the federal government founded in 1950, has as its mission the initiation and support of scientific and engineering research through grants and contracts, as well as to strengthen research and education programs. NSF's Office of the Inspector General (OIG) investigates allegations of misconduct in science, including research misconduct. The NSF defines research misconduct as "fabrication, falsification, plagiarism, or other serious deviation from accepted practices" (National Science Foundation, "Regulation of Research," accessed 2010). Plagiarism is defined as "the appropriation of another person's ideas, processes, results, or word without giving appropriate credit" (National Science Foundation, "Research Misconduct Regulation," accessed 2010). An OIG outreach program directed at administrators, researchers, and students involved in federally supported research sponsors seminars that use actual cases to encourage discussion of ethical choices and makes presentations at professional society conferences to inform the community it serves. The NSF may conduct its own investigation or refer the matter to the institution receiving the grant. Sometimes, however, the NSF acts quickly and with purpose. In October 2009, a Michigan university was asked to return over $600,000 in NSF grant money when an accusation of plagiarism was substantiated against one or more lead researchers (Ecker, 2009)

The National Institutes of Health (NIH) comprises 27 centers and institutes in the areas of medical and behavioral research ranging from the National Cancer Institute, established in 1937, to one of the newest, the National Center on Minority Health and Health Disparities, begun in 1993. The NIH has a detailed policy that governs their Intramural Research Program that includes a definition of plagiarism (National Institutes of Health, 1991). The Department of Health and Human Services Office of Research Integrity handles research misconduct cases for the NIH.

The National Academy of Sciences was created by an act of incorporation signed by President Abraham Lincoln on in March 1863. Today experts in all areas of science, medicine, technology, and engineering give their time to study critical issues in these areas and to advise the government and the general public. Its publishing arm, the National Academies Press, makes more than 3,000 books available free online, including *Integrity in Scientific Research: Creating an Environment that Promotes Responsible Conduct* (National Academy of Sciences, 2002). The document spells out what is expected: Researchers will not report the work of others as if it were their own. This is plagiarism. Furthermore, they should be honest with respect to the contributions of colleagues and collaborators (National Academy of Sciences, 2002). It also recommends that instruction for future researchers include professional ethics training and topics such as "plagiarism, honorary authorship, data selection, and graphic design" (National Academy of Sciences, 2002). In 2009, the Academy published the third edition of *On Being a Scientist: A Guide to Responsible Conduct in Research*, which "offers researchers—particularly early-career scientists and their mentors—guidance on how to conduct research responsibly and avoid misconduct such as fabrication and plagiarism" (National Academy of Sciences, 2009).

Professional organizations in the sciences also have professional codes of conduct. For example, the American Chemical Society expects its members to follow *The Chemical Professional's Code of Conduct* approved and adopted in 1994. It states: "Conflicts of interest and scientific misconduct, such as fabrication, falsification and plagiarism, are incompatible with this code (American Chemical Society, 2007). The American Chemical Society (accessed 2010) also produced a document titled *Plagiarism: Intellectual Property Rights*. However, it is not so much a guide to avoiding plagiarism as it is information on intellectual property rights and how to protect them.

Another professional organization committed to fostering intellectual honesty is Sigma Xi. This organization is the international honor society for science and engineering, and it actively promotes integrity in science and sponsors educational programs on scientific integrity. Two excellent publications are available for purchase from the society, *Honor in Science* for graduate students and *The Responsible Researcher: Paths and Pitfalls* for faculty and administrators and covers expectations and issues for undergraduate through faculty, deans, and department chairs. More information about the society and its policies are available at its website (www.sigmaxi.org).

An exceptional source for ethics information in engineering is The Online Ethics Center for Engineering and Science at Case Western Reserve University (www.onlineethics.org). The Center was established in 1995 under an NSF grant and in 2007 became an activity of the National Academy of Engineering. A distinguished roster of experts from academia, professional societies, corporations, and the government serve as advisors to the Center. The website section titled "Responsible Research" (www.onlineethics.org/CMS/2963.aspx) contains links to essays on research ethics, scenarios, and cases to use in student faculty discussions, educational resources including materials that can be used in courses, and an extensive list of reference materials on research integrity. The Online Ethics Center is required surfing and studying for anyone involved in teaching science and engineering students.

Other Disciplines

The Association for Computing Machinery produced *ACM Policy and Procedures on Plagiarism* in October, 2006, but it focuses primarily on the Association as a publisher and procedures on dealing with plagiarism in ACM-copyrighted materials. However, the *Ten Commandments of Computer Ethics* is a farsighted and useful document that has relevance for anyone who uses computers. Since it was presented by Ramon C. Barquin at the Computer Ethics Conference in 1992, countless schools have used it. Commandment 8 is clear and to the point, "Thou Shalt Not Appropriate Other People's Intellectual Output" (Computer Ethics Institute, *Ten Commandments*, accessed 2010). The Computer Ethics Institute began as a project of the Brookings Institution but is now a 501c3 organization devoted to interface of advances in information technologies within ethical frameworks (Brookings Institution, accessed 2010; Computer Ethics Institute, *What Is CEI*, accessed 2010).

Conclusion

It is clear that most professional associations whose members engage in research have prepared ethical guidelines that include information on plagiarism, providing educators, librarians, researchers, and students with a wealth of essential and useful information to guide them in properly crediting the work and ideas of others. Professional organizations in the humanities, social sciences, education, and the sciences have created excellent style manuals, websites, guidelines, ethics codes, and policy statements that clearly define academic honesty and present practical, easy to use tools for teaching and learning about the ethical use of information. While it is true that a horse can be led to water but not made to drink, those engaging in research and writing have little room to claim ignorance of those rules. As the song says, they have a code that they can live by.

References

American Anthropological Association. 2009. *Code of Ethics of the American Anthropological Association*. Arlington, VA: AAA. Available: www.aaanet .org/_cs_upload/issues/policy-advocacy/27668_1.pdf (accessed May 27, 2010).

American Chemical Society. *Plagiarism: Intellectual Property Rights*. Washington, DC: ACS. Available: portal.acs.org/portal/fileFetch/C/CTP_006637/pdf/ CTP_006637.pdf (accessed May 27, 2010).

———. 2007. *The Chemical Professional's Code of Conduct*. Washington, DC: ACS. Available: portal.acs.org/portal/acs/corg/content?_nfpb=true

&_pageLabel=PP_ARTICLEMAIN&node_id=1095&content_id=
CTP_004007&use_sec=true&sec_url_var=region1&__uuid= (accessed May
27, 2010).

American Historical Association. 2005. *Statement on Standards of Professional
Conduct*. Washington, DC: AHA. Available: www.historians.org/pubs/
Free/ProfessionalStandards.cfm (accessed May 27, 2010).

American Library Association. *AASL Resource Guides for School Library Media
Program Development*. Chicago: ALA. Available: www.ala.org/Printer
Template.cfm?Section=resourceguides&Template=/ContentManagement/
HTMLDisplay.cfm&ContentID=15782 (accessed May 27, 2010).

———. 2003a. *ALA Handbook of Organization 2003–2004*. Chicago: ALA.

———. 2003b. *Information Literacy Competency Standards for Higher Education*.
Chicago: ALA. Available: www.ala.org/ala/mgrps/divs/acrl/standards/
standards.pdf (accessed May 27, 2010).

———. 2004. *Standards for Libraries in Higher Education*. Chicago: ALA. Available: www.ala.org/ala/mgrps/divs/acrl/standards/standardslibraries
.cfm (accessed May 27, 2010).

American Psychological Association. "What Is APA Style?" APA Style.org. Available: www.apastyle.org/learn/faqs/what-is-apa-style.aspx (accessed July
12, 2010).

———. *Ethical Principles of Psychologists and Code of Conduct*. Washington, DC:
APA. Available: www.apa.org/ethics/code/index.aspx#8_11 (accessed
May 27, 2010).

———. 2010. *Publication Manual of the American Psychological Association*. Washington, DC: APA.

American Sociological Association. 1999. *Code of Ethics and Policies and Procedures
of the ASA Committee on Professional Ethics*. Washington, DC: American
Sociological Association. Available: www.asanet.org/images/asa/docs/
pdf/Ethics Code.pdf (accessed May 27, 2010).

Association for Computing Machinery. 2006. *ACM Policy and Procedures on Plagiarism*. New York: Association for Computing Machinery. Available: www
.acm.org/publications/policies/plagiarism_policy (accessed May 27, 2010).

Association of American Colleges and Universities. 1998. *Statement on Liberal
Learning*. Washington, DC: Association of American Colleges and Universities. Available: www.aacu.org/about/statements/liberal_learning
.cfm (accessed May 27, 2010).

Association of American Universities. 1988. *Framework for Institutional Policies and
Procedures to Deal with Fraud in Research*. Washington, DC: Association of
American Universities. Available: www.aau.edu/reports/FrwkRschFraud
.html (accessed May 27, 2010).

Bartlett, Thomas. 2003. "Historical Association Will No Longer Investigate Allegations of Wrongdoing." *Chronicle of Higher Education* 49, no. 37: A12.

Brookings Institution. *About the Brookings Institution*. Washington, DC: Brookings Institution. Available: www.brookings.edu/about.aspx (accessed July
12, 2010).

Center for Academic Integrity. 1999. *The Fundamental Values of Academic Integrity*.

Clemson, SC: Clemson University. Available: www.academicintegrity.org/fundamental_values_project/index.php (accessed May 27, 2010).

Computer Ethics Institute. *What Is CEI?* Washington, DC: Computer Ethics Institute. Available: computerethicsinstitute.org/aboutcei/whatiscei.html (accessed May 27, 2010).

––––––. *Ten Commandments of Computer Ethics.* Washington, DC: Computer Ethics Institute. Available: computerethicsinstitute.org/publications/tencommandments.html (accessed May 27, 2010).

Covey, Stephen R. 2004. *The 7 Habits of Highly Effective People.* New York: Free Press.

Council of Writing Program Administrators. 2003. *Defining and Avoiding Plagiarism: The WPA Statement on Best Practices.* Available: www.wpacouncil.org/positions/WPAplagiarism.pdf (accessed May 27, 2010).

Crawley, Arthur. 2000. "How Do We Keep Students Honest?" *Advocate Online* 18, no. 2: 6.

Ecker, Patricia. 2009. "CMU to Return $619K in Grants." *Morning Sun* (Central Michigan) (October 30). Available: www.themorningsun.com/articles/2009/10/30/news/srv0000006719655.txt (accessed May 27, 2010).

Enders, Walter and Gary A. Hoover. 2004. "Whose Line Is It? A Survey of Plagiarism in the Economic Profession." *Journal of Economic Literature* 42, no. 3: 487–493.

Gibaldi, Joseph, ed. 2009. "Chapter 2: Plagiarism." In *MLA Handbook for Writers of Research Papers.* New York: Modern Language Association.

Hansen, Brian. 2003. "Combating Plagiarism." *CQ Researcher* 13, no. 32 (September 19): 773–796.

Modern Language Association. "About the MLA." New York: MLA. Available: www.mla.org/about (accessed May 27, 2010).

––––––. "Statement of Professional Ethics." New York: MLA. Available: www.mla.org/repview_profethics (accessed May 27, 2010).

National Academy of Sciences. 2002. *Integrity in Scientific Research: Creating an Environment that Promotes Responsible Conduct.* Washington, DC: National Academies Press. Available: www.nap.edu/openbook.php?isbn=0309084792 (accessed May 27, 2010).

––––––. 2009. *On Being a Scientist: A Guide to Responsible Conduct in Research.* Washington, DC: National Academies Press. Available: www.nap.edu/catalog.php?record_id=12192 (accessed May 27, 2010).

National Institutes of Health. 1991. "Policies and Procedures Relating to Possible Scientific Misconduct in the IPR at NIH." In *NIH Policy Manual.* Bethesda, MC: NIH. Available: www1.od.nih.gov/oma/manualchapters/intramural/3006/main.html (accessed May 27, 2010).

National Science Foundation. "Regulation of Research: Research Misconduct." Arlington, VA: NSF. Available: www.nsf.gov/od/ogc/regulation.jsp (accessed July 12, 2010).

––––––. "Research Misconduct Regulation." Arlington, VA: NSF. Available: www.nsf.gov/oig/resmisreg.pdf (accessed July 12, 2010).

Permuth, S., R. Mawdsley, and R. Westberry. 1998. "The Internet, Students'

Rights, and Today's Principal." In *Legal Memorandum* (December): 1–6. Reston, VA: National Association for Secondary School Principals.

Schneider, Sherrie and Ellen Fein. 1995. *The Rules: Time-Tested Secrets for Capturing the Heart of Mr. Right*. New York: Grand Central Publishing.

Stepchyshyn, Vera and Robert S. Nelson. 2007. *Library Plagiarism Policies: CLIP Note 37*. Chicago: Association of College and Research Libraries.

Wilhoit, Skip. 2006. *The Man Code: An In-Depth Look at the Rules of Engagement for Today's American Man*. Frederick, MD: PublishAmerica.

Inoculating against Plagiarism: Resources for Teaching and Learning

Leslie Murtha

Introduction

The eminent musicologist Charles Seeger is reported to have said that "plagiarism is basic to all culture" (quoted by Seeger and Guthrie, 1975). Ideas and practices regarding intellectual property vary not only across time and cultures but also according to context within a culture. In Western society, the academy places a high value on acknowledging the work of other scholars, not only because ideas represent intellectual capital, but because the basis of the scholarly enterprise rests on the ability to trace connections among ideas. The literature on plagiarism routinely invokes such terms as "theft" and "kidnapping" to describe the act of presenting the ideas of others without attribution. Teachers at all levels of the educational enterprise have a responsibility to instill in their students an understanding of the ethics of scholarship and the habit of routinely acknowledging their sources and marking the boundaries between their own words and ideas and those of others.

Inherent in the promulgation of any set of rules or standards is the necessity to uphold and enforce them. Thus, teachers inevitably find themselves not only in the role of the mentor or the sage, but also the detective, police person, and judge. As in other law enforcement situations, those who recklessly accuse others may find themselves unexpectedly in the role of defendant. The purpose of this chapter is to help educators to identify and select information resources and teaching materials that can help them in the task of teaching academic integrity and good writing practices and in developing policies and programs in support of ethical scholarship.

In reviewing the literature relating to teachers and teaching and plagiarism, three major perspectives emerge. Writers may approach teaching about plagiarism and academic integrity as an ethical or legal issue, as an issue of epistemological development or communication skills, or as an issue of cultural difference. It seems reasonable to assume that all three of these factors come into play in determining whether or not students engage in plagiarism, and that they should all be taken into account when developing both curriculum and policy.

Experts generally agree that having a unified and well-articulated institutional policy on academic integrity is important from both a pedagogical and a legal standpoint. It makes all parties aware of institutional expectations and provides a transparent and defensible structure within which to enforce them. Decoo (2007) writes eloquently of the importance of coming to a common understanding of what is meant by plagiarism and offers suggestions for a framework within which to develop a fair and nuanced policy. A number of educators have written about their experiences in developing an institutional response to plagiarism (Cogdell and Aidulis, 2007; Devlin, 2006; Park, 2004; Thomas, 2007). Abilock discusses the hazards of lack of consensus within an organization (Abilock, 2006) and offers suggestions for strategies for developing a community of understanding (Abilock, 2009). The importance of including libraries and academic support systems in both policy development and program planning has also received considerable attention. Madray (2008) and Sciammarella (2009) discuss their respective libraries' involvement in campuswide antiplagiarism initiatives, and Fox (2008) and Wilson and Ippolito (2007) explore the advantages of involving a broad range of student service organizations.

Many have raised their voices, on either side, to argue that plagiarism, particularly by undergraduates, is the result of laziness or dishonesty or, conversely, that it results from an ignorance of customs or from poor writing skills. Some researchers, however, would contend that instructors themselves may frequently diverge from established norms in their understanding of issues and concepts, and that they often fail to model good practices. Reporting on a study of attitudes toward plagiarism among lecturers at a Swedish university, Eriksson and Sullivan (2008) found wide variation in how instructors defined plagiarism and in how they communicated with their students on the subject. In two interrelated studies, Roig (2001) examined the paraphrasing practices of college professors and found that many did not recognize divergences from traditional practice either in student writing or in their own. Additionally, Buranen (2009: 25) states that "faculty . . . routinely draw from a variety of sources when they prepare lectures or printed materials for classes, sources that often remain anonymous and may appear to be a teacher's 'original' ideas and arguments." It seems clear that teachers require ongoing access to learning opportunities and information resources in order to develop and maintain a solid understanding of current thought on the subject of academic integrity.

If college professors sometimes struggle with adhering to academic writing standards, it is hardly surprising that students encounter difficulties with the finer points of attribution. Despite cries of alarm regarding paper mills and an alleged increase in cheating, few researchers would suggest that students are unaware when they commit blatant acts of academic dishonesty. Careless or inadvertent acts of plagiarism, however, are extremely common and require a more considered reaction. According to Madray (2007), substantial numbers of high school students report having had little or no instruction regarding plagiarism in secondary school, and many first-year undergraduates believe that unattributed copying of source material is acceptable. Studies by Roig (1997) confirm that undergraduates have difficulty recognizing inappropriate paraphrasing. Research conducted by Williamson and McGregor (2006) with Australian secondary school students offers insights into the way students think and learn about research and academic writing. From this, it seems reasonable to conclude that there is a strong need to rethink the ways in which we teach scholarly writing practices at both the secondary and tertiary levels.

For students studying in a foreign culture, and/or not in their native language, understanding quotation and paraphrase practices is an even greater problem. Many international students report a lack of confidence in their academic writing skills (Zimitat, 2007). Cultural differences in educational practices, particularly in Asian nations, but also across Europe, are suggested to contribute to international students' misunderstandings about copying and documentation (Abasi, Akbari, and Graves, 2006; Hayes and Introna, 2005; Introna and Hayes, 2007; Sowden, 2005), though some of those contentions may be disputed (Liu, 2005). Any instructor or institution dealing with international students and nonnative speakers should take these factors into account.

It has been suggested by some researchers that most students, regardless of background, face similar challenges in making the transition to writing in the scholarly tradition. Noting the importance of imitation as a learning strategy, Howard (1993: 233) has coined the term "patchwriting" to describe material too lightly paraphrased. Howard (1995) suggests that patchwriting is a transitional form that helps a student move toward understanding the source. Salmons (2007) suggests that students' writing be viewed as falling into a continuum between plagiarism and original work and offers strategies for designing learning activities that encourage original work. McGowan (2007: 102) proposes four phases that students pass through as entry-level college students on their way to becoming "competent researchers" and suggests that students in the intermediary stages make use of the language of others as part of the learning process. Chandrasoma, Thompson, and Pennycook (2004: 171) also suggest that students employ patchwriting as a learning strategy and suggest replacing the idea of plagiarism with an understanding of "transgressive or nontransgressive intertextuality." In a slightly different vein, Zwagerman (2008) considers the hazards to the community of criminalizing plagiarism and questions the legitimacy of a value system that prizes grades over learning. These ideas, which problematize mainstream concepts of plagiarism, should be given thoughtful consideration when developing policies regarding academic integrity.

These theoretical perspectives provide ample fodder for beginning a conversation about institutional and personal responses to plagiarism. The resources reviewed later offer more practical assistance in developing policy, implementing programs, and constructing curricula and pedagogy in regard to plagiarism and academic integrity. These resources were gathered through extensive searching of educational databases, WorldCat, Amazon, and the Internet.

Resources for Teachers and Administrators

Materials in this section contain practical advice, models, professional development tools, and classroom resources for teachers and administrators.

Recent Books

DeSena, Laura Hennessey. 2007. *Preventing Plagiarism: Tips and Techniques*. Urbana, IL: National Council of Teachers of English.

This work is directed primarily at secondary school teachers and makes a strong philosophical statement about the teaching of writing. DeSena believes that, in order to develop their own voice, students should work first and foremost with primary sources; the use of secondary sources should be introduced much later in the learning process, after students have written extensively of their own thoughts and reactions. A holistic strategy for teaching authentic writing is presented, with specific suggestions for ways to create assignments that discourage plagiarism. Issues relating to the challenges facing non-English speakers and students from non-Western cultures are briefly addressed, as is detection and response to plagiarism. DeSena is a playwright and teaches English and humanities at both the secondary and tertiary levels. She offers a full and rich conception of teaching writing in the realms of literature, history, and the arts, but her thesis is less well developed and less plausible when she considers teaching writing in the sciences and social sciences. Her approach also demands a high level of engagement from teachers of writing, not only with their students and their teaching, but also with a broad, multidisciplinary knowledge base that supports a creative approach to writing assignments.

Gilmore, Barry. 2008. *Plagiarism: Why It Happens, How to Prevent It*. Portsmouth, NH: Heinemann.

Gilmore teaches English and social studies to middle and high school students and this book is intended for teachers of these grades, but it also has value for educators working above and below these levels. Primary school teachers will find it useful in preparing their students for the expectations of secondary education, and instructors working with college students in lower division and developmental courses will gain insight into the continuum along which students acquire their understanding of plagiarism and documentation. Many of the ideas presented are useful to any educator who requires students to write. In seven well-written, accessible chapters, Gilmore discusses the problem of plagiarism, outlines causes and types of plagiarism, provides suggestions for detection and response to cheating behaviors, makes suggestions for designing assignments and assessments that discourage plagiarism and encourage good writing practices, and concludes with a discussion of building a school culture that values academic integrity. The book contains many practical tips, suggestions, and samples of useful forms and assignments. Although it starts from a pejorative position, the author strongly favors a developmental approach to teaching about plagiarism. He recommends that policies be nuanced and flexible and that individual teacher responses take into account both the intent and the developmental stage of the student. Gilmore also takes issue with some of the common suggestions for plagiarism-proofing assignments, pointing out that they can rob students of the opportunity to learn valuable writing skills and to practice documentation. Gilmore does not explicitly address issues of patchwriting but does provide valuable suggestions for constructing writing assignments. A weakness in an otherwise admirable work is that, in discussing the purposes of citation, Gilmore never deals with the important concepts of situating one's work in the context of existing discourse or drawing on the authority of established experts.

Lampert, Lynn D. 2008. *Combating Student Plagiarism: An Academic Librarian's Guide.* Oxford, England: Chandos.
   This work provides a theoretical framework for defining the role of librarians in combating plagiarism and for incorporating teaching about plagiarism and citation into an information literacy program. Although the stated audience for the book includes administrators, academic support staff, faculty, and public librarians, its greatest value is for academic librarians seeking to design an information literacy curriculum that includes information ethics. In eight short chapters, Lambert frames contemporary student plagiarism as a social problem derived from the rapid advance of technology, reviews the role of librarians in the fight against plagiarism through the professional literature, and discusses approaches to combating plagiarism through the framework of information literacy, using discipline-based pedagogies, and through collaboration. She presents some practical ideas for teaching citation and utilizing detection services.

Lathrop, Ann. 2005. *Guiding Students from Cheating and Plagiarism to Honesty and Integrity: Strategies for Change.* Westport, CT: Libraries Unlimited.
   Containing writings by noted researchers and theorists and by rank-and-file practitioners, this edited book focuses on ways in which schools and families can cooperate to foster an institutional culture that values and promotes academic integrity. The theme is the discouragement of all types of cheating and dishonest behavior; the discussion of plagiarism is not extensive and addresses only tangentially the process of teaching writing and issues of unintentional plagiarism. However, the multidimensional approach to changing attitudes and behavior make this a valuable resource for educators working at any level. Liberally scattered throughout the book are information resources, ideas for lessons, handouts, boilerplate policies, and other teaching materials. Clearly marked "copy me," these items may be reproduced in print, for clearly defined educational purposes, with suitable acknowledgment.

Online Resources

General

Abilock, Debbie. 2006. *Ethical Researcher*. Palo Alto, CA: NoodleTools. www .noodletools.com/debbie/ethical.

Debbie Abilock, a prominent teacher–librarian and the editor of *Knowledge Quest*, offers a selection of resources on teaching research, academic integrity, and citation in the K–12 environment. Abilock is also the cofounder of Noodle-Tools, a subscription-based online citation tool. NoodleTools is designed to teach novice researchers the process of creating bibliographic citations while facilitating the mechanical aspects of producing and formatting a bibliography.

Bailey, Jonathan. 2005. Plagiarism Today Blog. New Orleans, LA. www. plagiarismtoday.com.

This weblog posts information on copyright and intellectual property issues. Primarily intended as a resource for creators of online content, this site is a good source for news and opinions about intellectual property in an online environment. Information found on this site should not be construed as legal advice.

Center for Academic Integrity. Clemson, SC: Rutland Institute for Ethics, Clemson University. www.academicintegrity.org/index.php.

Founded in 1992, the Center for Academic Integrity is a consortium of institutions of secondary and higher education, with the purpose of providing leadership, support, and resources to promote academic integrity (Center for Academic Integrity, accessed 2010). The Center's website provides access to a brief bibliography of articles on plagiarism and cheating, links to institutions with exemplary programs, online tutorials, and models and samples of educational materials. Sample policies, syllabus statements, forms, and marketing resources are of practical value for instructors and administrators seeking to develop policies and programs around academic integrity. Additional benefits are available to member institutions.

Center for Youth Ethics. Los Angeles: Josephson Institute. charactercounts.org/ index.html.

The Josephson Institute, founded in 1987, is a nonsectarian, nonpartisan organization devoted to the promotion of ethics in society (Josephson Institute, accessed 2010). The Center for Youth Ethics offers training and tools to help teachers and administrators embed ethics in the curriculum. In addition to fee-based training and teaching materials, the Center offers a free collection of lesson plans and classroom administration tools. The current relevant lesson plans concentrate on cheating and are appropriate for the middle-school cohort.

International Journal for Educational Integrity. www.ojs.unisa.edu.au/index.php/ IJEI.

This open access journal from the University of South Australia (Adelaide) is published semiannually. It includes articles on research, theory, and pedagogy relating to academic integrity.

Oliphant, T. *Faculty Guide to Cyber Plagiarism.* Edmonton: University of Alberta Libraries. www.library.ualberta.ca/guides/plagiarism/index.cfm.

This site provides a brief but comprehensive overview of plagiarism issues from the instructors' perspective. By condensing a series of complex issues and problems to bulleted paragraphs, the site enables instructors to quickly familiarize themselves with the topic of plagiarism in higher education. A list of causes for student plagiarism is presented, and strategies for promoting academic integrity, designing assignments, detecting and reporting plagiarism are considered within the framework of the codes and policies of the University of Alberta. Links are provided to locally developed teaching resources as well as to other online sites dealing with academic integrity. Many colleges and universities now post similar guides on their websites; they may be found in such diverse places within the websites as locations devoted to the library, the office of academic or judiciary affairs, the teaching and learning center, or the writing center. This site is one of the better examples found; however, instructors seeking a more nuanced examination of the issues, or more structured suggestions regarding pedagogy or response to student misconduct, will need to address themselves to the book and journal literature.

Plagiarism.org. Oakland, CA: iParadigms. www.plagiarism.org.

A public service of iParadigms, the publishers of TurnItIn® and other plagiarism detection services, this site provides a superficial overview of the concept of plagiarism and offers a few suggestions on teaching about or detecting plagiarism. Several free webinars dealing with plagiarism in secondary and tertiary education are also available. nLearning, iParadigms' U.K. partner, manages the site PlagiarismAdvice.org (www.plagiarismadvice.org), a service founded by the Joint Information Systems Committee (a government-funded initiative to support IT in higher education in the United Kingdom). PlagiarismAdvice. org offers customized training for institutions, publishes guides for educators, and conducts research relating to plagiarism and academic integrity. They also sponsor an international conference on plagiarism. The free resources on this site tend to be more substantial than those found on the iParadigms site.

Plagiary: Cross-Disciplinary Studies in Plagiarism, Fabrication and Falsification. Ann Arbor: University of Michigan. www.plagiary.org.

Plagiary is an open access scholarly journal published by the University of Michigan. It is devoted to the study of plagiarism and related issues of textual fraud in scholarly, professional, and popular discourse. The publishers seek to bring a cross-disciplinary perspective to research into plagiarism. Articles dealing with derivative works, such as parody, are also considered appropriate subject matter for this journal. Papers are published online continuously, and an annual print volume is produced and is available by subscription (University of Michigan, 2006).

Assignment Guidelines

The following resources offer guidance in developing plagiarism-proof assignments and assignments that teach good writing practices:

- *Creating Effective Research Assignments*
  www.lib.umd.edu/guides/assignment.html
- *Defining and Avoiding Plagiarism: The WPA Statement on Best Practices*
  wpacouncil.org/node/9
- *Plagiarism: A Good Practice Guide*
  www.jisc.ac.uk/uploaded_documents/brookes.pdf
- *Tools for Teaching: Preventing Academic Dishonesty*
  teaching.berkeley.edu/bgd/prevent.html
- *Virtual Salt: Anti-Plagiarism Strategies for Research Papers*
  www.virtualsalt.com/antiplag.htm

Lesson Plans

Here are some sites that offer free lesson plans that include the subjects of academic integrity and/or plagiarism:

- Educator's Desk Reference
  www.eduref.org/Virtual/Lessons/index.shtml
- Gateway to Twenty-First Century Skills
  www.thegateway.org/
- LibraryInstruction.com
  www.libraryinstruction.com/lessons.html
- NY Times Lesson Archive
  www.nytimes.com/learning/teachers/lessons/archive.html
- Thinkfinity
  www.thinkfinity.org/home.aspx

Directories

These sites can lead you to additional online resources.

Beard, Carla. 2000. *Web English Teacher.* www.webenglishteacher.com/plagiarism.html.
   Collected by a highly experienced high school teacher, this directory of resources for English teachers includes a section on plagiarism. Though not extensive, the list of links is up-to-date and reflects a variety of perspectives.

Stoerger, Sharon. *Plagiarism.* www.web-miner.com/plagiarism.

Originally created for the Office of the Vice Chancellor for Research at the University of Illinois at Urbana-Champaign, this site is a selective directory of online resources on plagiarism and copyright. Links to a selection of news stories and some scholarly articles are included, along with a variety of tutorials, plagiarism detection tools, case studies, and other resources for instructors, primarily in higher education. The author is an instructor in the School of Library and Information Science at Bloomington University.

Resources for Students

The resources in this section have been written and developed for a student audience. These reviews are intended to help instructors to select texts and teaching tools for classroom use and to find models and inspiration for using technology in their teaching about academic integrity.

Recent Books

Fox, Tom, Julia Johns, and Sarah Keller. 2007. *Cite It Right: The SourceAid Guide to Citation, Research, and Avoiding Plagiarism,* 3rd ed. Osterville, MA: SourceAid.

The purpose of this book is to provide a quick guide to the construction of citations using the four most common style manuals. Three brief introductory chapters cover the ethics of academic writing, selection and evaluation of sources, and the process of composing a research paper. The four subsequent chapters contain a highly condensed version of each of the style manuals covered: Modern Language Association, American Psychological Association, *Chicago Manual of Style*, and Council of Science Editors. General rules and examples of common formats are included. This is a useful guide for students who are required to use a variety of different styles.

Francis, Barbara. 2005. *Other People's Words: What Plagiarism Is and How to Avoid It.* Berkeley Heights, NJ: Enslow.

Written for high school students, this short book does an excellent job of explaining and illustrating the ethical issues surrounding plagiarism. Francis situates plagiarism in an historical and cultural context while concentrating on the contemporary Western understanding of intellectual property and attribution practices. Her discussion extends beyond textual plagiarism to cover visual and audible media. "Real world" examples illuminate the consequences of plagiarism for students and for working professionals. The book is highly readable and filled with examples and illustrative anecdotes drawn from historical and contemporary sources. The title, however, is deceptive; the author concentrates on rules and ethics and has little in the way of practical advice about avoiding plagiarism. No attempt whatever is made to teach citation, and paraphrase and summary are touched on only in the most perfunctory manner. This work would be a suitable introductory text for students in high school and middle school, and for college students in developmental classes, as part of a systematic curriculum initiative on academic integrity and academic writing practices.

Gaines, Ann Graham. 2008. *Don't Steal Copyrighted Stuff! Avoiding Plagiarism and Illegal Internet Downloading.* Berkeley Heights, NJ: Enslow.
This work does an excellent job of introducing the idea of intellectual property and the rules surrounding its use. The concept of fair use is explained, with particular reference to use by students, and individual chapters cover the basics of using graphics, music and recorded sound, and various types of digital media. Several chapters address the issue of plagiarism and provide tips for conducting research and note taking and an introduction to citation. While the discussion of the writing and documentation process should be regarded as purely introductory, the fact that a variety of media resources are discussed and that presentations beyond the traditional research paper are given serious consideration makes this a valuable tool. Additional chapters provide guidelines for acquiring permission to reproduce or perform copyrighted works and suggestions for protecting one's own material. A good text for an introductory unit on intellectual property, the book is written at a level that is appropriate for high school students and contains much information that would be of value to college students.

Harris, Robert A. 2002. *Using Sources Effectively: Strengthening Your Writing and Avoiding Plagiarism*, 2nd ed. Glendale, CA: Pyrczak Publishing.
This well-designed text provides a comprehensive overview of the process of selecting, employing, and documenting external sources for a research paper. In the introductory chapter, Harris describes the role sources play in a research paper. The second chapter provides a clear explanation of how plagiarism is defined in academia, covering both ethical and practical issues. The next two chapters deal with the process of selecting and evaluating sources and using them. Quotation, paraphrase, and summary are covered, with well-constructed examples. The remaining chapters teach the process of weaving sources into the fabric of the whole paper, with advice about voice switching, boundary markers, and other valuable strategies for mastering the academic style of writing. Specific citation styles are not discussed in any depth, but the underlying principles are thoroughly explained. Review questions, exercises, and assessment tools designed to reinforce the learning process follow each chapter. This is an excellent resource for undergraduate writing students and is appropriate for high school students with advanced writing skills.

Lipson, Charles. 2004. *Doing Honest Work in College: How to Prepare Citations, Avoid Plagiarism, and Achieve Real Academic Success*, 2nd ed. Chicago: University of Chicago Press.
Adhering to the theme of academic honesty, this book focuses on the process of citation. The initial chapters offer advice on understanding and maintaining academic integrity, effective note taking, and understanding and recognizing plagiarism. A very brief chapter outlines the underlying principles of citation.

The remainder of the book provides examples of citations for common source formats in nine styles, representing a variety of academic disciplines. The book is a useful tool for undergraduates who are required to use multiple style manuals, although most are likely to have recourse to using the official manuals to complete a substantial paper.

Stern, Linda. 2007. *What Every Student Should Know about Avoiding Plagiarism.* New York: Pearson/Longman.

This extraordinarily compact and comprehensive guide provides college students with an accessible and sophisticated overview of the practice of documentation in academic writing. Succinct definitions and explanations are provided to explain concepts and issues relating to plagiarism. Well-drawn examples illustrate the difference between proper and inappropriate practices and model the use of language in constructing clean, free-flowing text. The exercises at the end of the book demand active learning and critical thinking. The book is an appropriate supplementary text for a research or writing course for students who are competent writers of non-academic prose, but it is potentially over the heads of novice writers and students with limited English proficiency.

Online Resources

Digital technology has altered forever the way we think about teaching and learning, but we are still in the beginning stages of learning how to use technology to effectively facilitate learning. Digital teaching tools can extend the classroom across time and distance, but they carry their own limitations and challenges. None of the tools reviewed here can be considered sufficient to address an institutional need to teach academic integrity principles or documentation practices. Their value lies in the way in which they reinforce what is taught elsewhere and in their ability to engage students outside the classroom and address the needs of students with a variety of learning styles. Most of the resources reviewed here are institution specific and are best used as models or sources of inspiration, but a few are intended for general use. All are intended for an undergraduate audience; unfortunately, the only items found that were intended for secondary school students were discovered, upon close examination, to be unsuitable for inclusion.

Badke, William 2001. *Writing Research Essays in North American Academic Institutions: A Guide for Students of All Nations.* Langley, British Columbia: Norma Marion Alloway Library, Associated Canadian Theological Seminaries of Trinity Western University. www.acts.twu.ca/Library/research_essays.htm.

Intended for international students, this short guide outlines the basic process of writing a research paper. The first section is devoted to topic selection, question development, and the structure of a paper. The second section is concerned with the concept of documentation. Badke, a librarian at Trinity Western University, offers simple explanations of the idea of intellectual property in Western academic culture, with basic guidelines for quotation and paraphrase. Information about style manuals is presented, with links to additional resources. A sample paper is also linked. The guide is supplemented by a short narrated presentation that expands on the definition of plagiarism and provides additional examples of paraphrase, interpretation ,and quotation. The guide is a plain-text HTML document, and the presentation was constructed using Quarbon's ViewletBuilder™ screen capture program.

Bazzoni, Jana O'Keefe, Louise Klusek, and Diane DiMartino. 2007. *Guide to Research for Oral Presentations: Finding, Evaluating and Using Online Sources.* New York: William and Anita Newman Library, Baruch College. www.baruch.cuny .edu/tutorials/weissman/oral_presentations/launch.html.

This highly polished interactive multimedia video presents a comprehensive overview of the process of conducting research for the preparation of oral presentations. In nine sections, the tutorial introduces a variety of research resources and tools and discusses finding, selecting, and evaluating research materials and crediting sources in oral presentations. Two assignments embedded in the tutorial provide a template for students to explore their own research projects. Section Six of the tutorial covers the basics of collecting citation information and constructing a reference. Section Seven deals with strategies for giving credit and avoiding plagiarism when presenting material orally. Embedded video clips show noted speakers modeling good practices, and additional videos are available to students seeking more examples. The tutorial is crisply and clearly narrated, with key points appearing as text; the animations and graphics are highly professional. Viewing the text of the narration is an option that enhances the accessibility of the tutorial, and navigation and player controls permit students to select chapters, review sections, and control the sound. Links to research tools and additional resources are available from all pages. The tutorial is Flash based and was developed for the Newman Library by Kognito.com.

Bowman, Vibiana, and John B. Gibson. 2004. *How to Avoid Plagiarism.* Camden, NJ: Paul Robeson Library, Rutgers University. library.camden.rutgers .edu/EducationalModule/Plagiarism.

Considerably revised since it was originally created, this Flash-based tutorial has been reconceived as vintage cinema and television. Incorporating elements from anime, classic comics, and graphic novels, Bowman and Gibson parody a grade school classroom from hell to present a brief overview of the concept of plagiarism and the practice of documentation. Divided into two features, the tutorial is quite short—more of a cautionary tale than a lesson in good writing practices. The third section, "The Cite Is Right," follows a game show format. Students complete a five-question quiz (with immediate feedback) in which correct answers are rewarded with imaginary "guacamoles." With its irreverent humor and ironic cultural elusions, this resource is designed to appeal to contemporary undergraduates, and it makes a good primer for a more in-depth classroom discussion of academic ethics and good documentation practices.

Crowe, Edith, Pamela Jackson, Marci Hunsaker, Bridget Kowalczyk, Jessie Cai, Wan Si Wan, and Andrea Lam. 2003. *Plagiarism: The Crime of Intellectual Kidnapping*. San Diego, CA: San Diego State University. tutorials.sjlibrary.org/tutorial/plagiarism/index.htm.

As one might expect from the title, this tutorial frames the concept of plagiarism as an intellectual crime. An initial quiz is provided to assess students' awareness of plagiarism issues; oddly, though, no feedback is provided. The tutorial introduces and defines the idea of plagiarism and provides an explanation of common knowledge. Most of the content is given over to explaining paraphrase, with examples of proper construction and citation, as well as samples of inappropriate intertextuality. Citation style is covered briefly, and detection services are mentioned. The tone of the tutorial is conversational, and the explanations are clear and concise. A 13-question quiz completes the tutorial, echoing the initial assessment. It is primarily constructed of multiple choice and true/false questions, but the final question requires students to construct a properly cited paraphrase of a passage of text. With the exception of this item, students are given immediate feedback for each question, and a final score is provided as a printable page and also via e-mail. Scores are also saved for future reference. In addition to the quiz, two questions are appended to assess students' perceptions of the learning experience.

Since its original publication in 2003, this tutorial has been considerably revised and updated, and the original illustrations have been replaced by Flash-based animated cartoons (a non-Flash version is still available). The cartoons are charming and the sound effects striking, though the meaning of some of the sequences is somewhat elusive. Unfortunately, the engaging nature of the multimedia additions works against pedagogical effectiveness; the cartoons tend to distract attention from the text that carries the more important message. Some simple tweaks in the design could solve this problem while retaining features calculated to appeal to the undergraduate audience. In addition to the Flash animations, the tutorial employs HTML, CSS, and JavaScript. Available to other institutions via an open publications license, this work has been widely adopted or adapted by colleges and universities across the United States.

Dorn, Sherman. 1997. *Lemonade Tutorials: Plagiarism*. Tampa: College of Education, University of South Florida. www.coedu.usf.edu/~dorn/Tutorials/Plagiarism/plagiarism.htm.

Even though it has grown some whiskers, this witty but pertinent tutorial deserves an honorable mention. The author is a professor at the School of Education at the University of South Florida, and the tutorial is a conversation directed at his students. Dorn is primarily concerned here with addressing the ethics of documentation and articulating the expectations of the academic community to a flock of novice researchers. Using a format of FAQ and FPE (Frequently Proffered Excuses), the tutorial addresses the common concerns, attitudes, and questions of students with thoughtful, concise explanations of the principles and mechanics of submitting work that meets academic standards. Issues covered include intellectual piracy, fraud, cultural differences, verbatim regurgitation, paraphrase and quotation, and defense against unjustified suspicions. Tips on documentation, paraphrasing, and note taking are included, but writing styles and strategies are not addressed in any detail. Unfortunately, because of the age of the tutorial, many of the links to external resources no longer function. In appearance, the *Lemonade Tutorial* is very plain vanilla, without illustration or technological bells and whistles, but Dorn's idiosyncratic and sardonic voice lend great charm to this work. A bonus is an outrageously funny satiric song, written and performed by the author, accessible from the opening page of the tutorial.

Gardner, David. 2002. *Plagiarism and How to Avoid It*. Hong Kong: English Center, University of Hong Kong. ec.hku.hk/plagiarism.

This tutorial, developed for students at the University of Hong Kong, has been around for a while, but the information contained is still valid and the explanations are simple and easily read, without being simplistic. Gardner introduces the concept of plagiarism and covers the basics of quotation, paraphrase, and citation. Strategies for transitioning from source to analysis are illustrated, and examples of common citations are provided. The most remarkable thing about this tutorial is that it remains one of the few online learning objects dealing with plagiarism that attempts to make an authentic assessment of students' ability to put what they have learned into practice. Students are asked to examine five examples of essays based on two related source texts and decide whether or not they are plagiarized. This exercise is fairly common, but what makes it unusual is that the students are asked to justify their judgment and to rewrite the passage to eliminate plagiarism. When the answer is submitted, the student can then view the author's comments on the passage of text. Because the feedback is immediate and preconstructed, the student's corrections are not critiqued; this weakness could be overcome without great difficulty, although doing so would certainly impose a burden on the instructor and would work best in a more closed environment. The tutorial is written in plain text, and the exercise is driven by JavaScript.

Harrison, Tanja, Erin Patterson, Jamie Chang, Kaur Singh, and Scott Olszowiec. 2004. *You Quote It, You Note It!* Wolfville, Nova Scotia: Acadia University. library .acadiau.ca/tutorials/plagiarism.

This short interactive tutorial, employing Flash and JavaScript, provides a brief but well-designed introduction to issues of plagiarism in academic writing. Attractive cartoon graphics and clever animations and sound effects lend interest to the lessons. Students select one of four student characters, each representing an area of study, to follow throughout the tutorial. The examples presented change according to the discipline the student has selected. Interactive questions are dispersed throughout the tutorial, and links to definitions and explanations of unfamiliar vocabulary open in a separate window. Topics addressed include the meaning and consequences of plagiarism, project management, common knowledge, quotation, and paraphrase. A small fault in the design is that the size of the display does make some of the text examples difficult to read. This tutorial is too short and superficial to facilitate any in-depth learning, but it would make a good introduction to a unit on documentation in academic writing.

Harvey, Michael. 2003. *Nuts and Bolts of College Writing: Plagiarism*. Indianapolis, IN: Hackett Publishing and Chestertown, MD: Washington College. nutsand bolts.washcoll.edu/plagiarism.html.

Nuts and Bolts of College Writing remains one of the best free resources on the process of essay writing available online. The site has not been changed or updated in some time, so some sections, particularly those that deal with Internet resources, have become quite dated. Overall, however, the quality, quantity, and presentation of these lessons on academic writing make this resource a perennial favorite. The chapter on evidence contains sections on plagiarism, quotation and paraphrase, and documentation using the four style manuals most commonly used by undergraduates. Harvey provides cogent explanations of the concepts of plagiarism, citation, and common knowledge. The section on quotation (which also covers paraphrase, though obliquely) is exceptional because it explicitly deals with issues of voice and transitions, and it attempts to teach good academic writing practices. The sections on style provide condensed versions of the basic rules most applicable to student essays and include extensive examples of in-text citations and references. A cautionary note here: because the site has not been updated recently, the examples for online materials are limited and do not reflect the changes detailed in the latest editions of the manuals. *Nuts and Bolts* is colorful and well laid out, with a few illustrations to break up the text. Built in basic HTML, with a few simple JavaScript effects, it contains no interactive elements.

Islam, Ramona. 2002. *Plagiarism Court: You Be the Judge*. Fairfield, CT: DiMenna Nyselius Library, Fairfield University. www.fairfield.edu/lib_plagiarismcourt .html.

This Flash-based tutorial is another classic among multimedia resources on plagiarism. Playing off the popularity of the television melodrama "People's Court," the graphical interface of the tutorial evokes a courtroom. This analogy, however, has largely vanished from the content as it has been revised over time. The tutorial provides a definition of plagiarism, outlines potential consequences, discusses the purposes of documentation, provides tips for note taking, quotation, and paraphrase, and introduces the idea of citation styles. A ten-question multiple-choice quiz, originally embedded in the Flash presentation, is now presented as a separate document driven by JavaScript. Immediate feedback has been replaced by answers provided at the end of the quiz, and results can be printed out or e-mailed to an instructor. Problems with the sound, navigation, and selected animations have been resolved in the revisions, and questions have been rewritten and clarified. These are important improvements, but unfortunately some of the original vision has been sacrificed along the way. Other online learning tools offer considerably more substance, and quite a few can now match the smoothly professional graphics of the *Plagiarism*

Court. However, the spirit of creativity and experimentation is alive and well at Fairfield University, as evidenced by a recent companion video linked from this site. The *Dr. Dhil Show*, spoofing television's Dr. Phil, is intended to raise students' awareness of plagiarism issues through humor. The video was written and directed by former Fairfield student Jared Mezzocchi.

Lewis-Clark State College Library. 2003. *Avoiding Plagiarism*. Lewiston, ID: Lewis-Clark State College. www.lcsc.edu/library/ILI/Module_2A/Welcome.htm.

This tutorial is part of a suite of online learning resources developed by the Information Literacy Institute at Lewis-Clark State College. Other selections deal with the basics of library research and with more advanced research techniques for selected disciplines. It is divided into four sections, and the Level Two module deals with academic integrity, citation formats, and construction of references in the APA and MLA styles. The chapter on avoiding plagiarism begins with a definition of plagiarism and a brief discussion of academic integrity in general, framed by the Lewis-Clark College's *Code of Student Conduct*. A short multiple-choice exercise allows students to assess their understanding of the basic categories of offense, and subsequent sections deal with the concepts of citation, paraphrase, and copyright. The section on paraphrase is particularly well designed, with examples that progress from blatant copying to properly cited and constructed paraphrase. A final quiz is available only to registered students. Employing only HTML and a few animated GIF files, this tutorial is visually attractive, with nice graphics and good navigation tools. The conversational tone and clear language are well geared to novice researchers, and the examples reflect typical student writing behaviors.

Price, Margaret. 2003. *St. Martin's Tutorial on Avoiding Plagiarism*. New York: Bedford/St. Martin's. bcs.bedfordstmartins.com/plagiarismtutorial/default.asp.

Since the earlier version of this book was published, a new category of plagiarism tutorials has emerged: sites developed and published by commercial textbook publishers. Unlike Harvey's *Nuts and Bolts of College Writing*, which began life on the web and subsequently was expanded into a published text (Harvey, 2003), these new tutorials have been commissioned by publishers either as companions to a published text or as independent projects. Much of the content of these sites may be available without charge; access to some features or functions may be restricted to users of the print textbook or may require free or fee-based registration. *St. Martin's Tutorial on Avoiding Plagiarism*, published by Bedford/St. Martins, is one of the better examples of a publisher-developed free resource. Authored by an academic currently on the faculty of Spelman College, the site offers a comprehensive introduction to plagiarism and the rules of documentation. Project management and writing strategies are suggested, and paraphrase, summary, quotation, and common knowledge are intelligently addressed. The language of the tutorial is formal but easy to read, and the explanations are more finely nuanced and sophisticated than those found in most online tutorials. Although some references reveal that the tutorial is somewhat dated, the quality of the material makes up for this small disadvantage. Access to the exercises requires (free) registration but is worth the trouble; true/false and multiple-choice questions are augmented by short writing exercises in which students practice integrating sources and citing them, and results can be e-mailed to an instructor on request.

Visually, this tutorial is less interesting than many. Entirely text based, it is sometimes dense and difficult to read on screen, and poor use of white space contributes to this difficulty; also, the navigation system leaves something to be desired. These considerations, however, are still outweighed by the intelligent discussion and sophisticated active learning exercises. Technologically, the tutorial is created in plain HTML text and formatted with frames and CSS. The exercises are driven by an assessment management system from Question*mark*™. Links are provided to a variety of additional resources, including a proprietary citation manager and another suite of tutorials associated with a textbook published by Bedford/St. Martin's. This suite also contains some material on avoiding plagiarism.

Regan, Caroline, Jacki Haas, Philippa Stevens, Rebecca Goldsworthy, David Wood, and Southnary Tan. 2003. *iResearch: Information Skills for Life: Plagiarism and Academic Integrity*. Sydney, Australia: University of Sydney Library. elearning.library.usyd.edu.au/index.php.

This self-paced screencast tutorial deals with plagiarism and academic integrity. Brief explanations and interactive exercises help students to recognize quotations, paraphrases, and differing degrees of common knowledge. The slippery ethics of cut and paste and collaboration and collusion are briefly but effectively addressed. A companion piece, "How to Reference," provides practice in recognizing and formatting the elements of citations to common information styles. "Plagiarism and Academic Integrity" makes good use of the features of the Adobe's Captivate program. Introduction and commentary by Professor Gareth Denyer, of the Biosciences Department, University of Sydney, puts a human face on the more didactic elements of the tutorial and makes it more accessible for aural learners. The background graphics are designed to resemble sketchy doodles but are actually highly professional. The use of sound is generally effective; best practices suggest that the narration of text that also appears on screen in problematic, but in this case the brevity of the passages and the use of comic-style dialogue balloons reduces the potential for distraction. The interactive exercises are dispersed throughout the tutorial, and the feedback is immediate and thoughtful. Some of the animations appear to lack professional smoothness, but that may be a feature of the transmission rather than a fault in the tutorial.

Stec, Eileen, Anthony Joachim, Scott Hines, and the faculty and staff of the Mabel Smith Douglass Library. 2001. *Plagiarism & Academic Integrity*. New Brunswick, NJ: Rutgers University Libraries. www.scc.rutgers.edu/douglass/sal/plagiarism/intro.html.

Developed in 2001 for use with a first-year mission course at Douglass College, this Flash-based multimedia tutorial remains the most extensive example of role-playing drama as a vehicle for teaching academic integrity. In eight short skits centered on a single plot line, characters enact scenarios illustrating the typical dilemmas and uncertainties about academic integrity that students face while in the process of researching and writing a paper. Stock cartoon graphics represent the voice of the academic establishment to point out errors and pitfalls. Interspersed throughout the skits are interactive exercises asking students to address a particular ethical dilemma. Issues examined include basic note-taking and documentation practices, the shifting boundaries of common knowledge, selling or purchasing papers, and collusion. The colorful graphics make this an attractive piece, and a small but diverse cast presents situations with which students may readily identify. Although the interactive quizzes are in multiple-choice format, they require some reflection, and the feedback is thoughtful. The cast is drawn from the faculty and staff of the library, and the acting is adequate, but not polished.

Web 2.0 Resources

Although Web 2.0 applications are a hot topic in educational circles, not very many have yet been put to use in teaching about plagiarism. Here are a few innovative examples.

Dangler, Doug, Ben McCorkle, and Time, Barrow. 2006. *Plagiarism Blues*. Columbus: Center for the Study and Teaching of Writing, College of Humanities, Ohio State University. cstw.osu.edu/podcasts/mp3/PlagiarismBlues.mp3.

This three-minute podcast is basically a marketing piece for the Writing Center. The narrator defines plagiarism, briefly describes common forms of student plagiarism, encourages students to seek help through the Center's tutoring services or online resources.

Hensley, Merinda Kaye, and Melissa Bowles-Terry. 2008. *Cite a Source: How and Why You Should Do It*. Urbana: University Library, University of Illinois at Urbana Champaign. www.library.uiuc.edu/learn/videos/cite_source/cite_source .html, www.youtube.com/watch?v=A_F1ZYYiAYs

This three-minute video is essentially a narrated PowerPoint presentation. It provides a very brief overview of the process of documentation. Well-timed and clearly narrated, it is an excellent example of this approach to streaming video.

Alberti, John. 2009. *Credit Where Credit Is Due*. University Heights: W. Frank Steely Library, Northern Kentucky University. www.youtube.com/ watch?v=qTCkO7Tpdqg.

Narrated by Professor John Alberti, of the English department at Northern Kentucky University, this video discusses the social aspects of citation. The quality of the image and Dr. Alberti's thoughtful commentary keep this presentation interesting despite the simple lecture format.

Baker, Robert. 2008. *Info Literacy 11: Plagiarism & Citation Styles*. Tucson, AZ: Library, Pima Community College. www.youtube.com/watch?v=gbAcQcDTxdo.
This seven-minute video combines narration by Dr. Robert Baker, director of the libraries at Pima Community College, with text and illustrations. Plagiarism is defined, and note-taking tips, citation elements, citations styles, and citation managers are discussed. The alternation of a talking head with text and graphics adds interest to this streaming video production.

Center, Business Writing Center and Technology. 2008. Plagiarism: *Your Writing, Not Someone Else's*. Seattle: Michael G. Foster School of Business, University of Washington. www.youtube.com/watch?v=sQGBhZ0ov6o.
This nine-minute video is a good example of an elaborate theatrical production as a video learning object. The video follows one undergraduate and his highly annoying academic coach through the process of writing a research paper.

Conclusion

The resources reviewed here represent a wide range of theoretical perspectives, pedagogical approaches, and technological applications to teaching about plagiarism. There are tools for policy makers, instructional materials for teaching ethics and writing, and resources for classroom management, policy enforcement, and professional learning. It is hoped that readers will find tools here to meet their needs and those of their students.

References

Abasi, Ali R., Nahal Akbari, and Barbara Graves. 2006. "Discourse Appropriation, Construction of Identities, and the Complex Issue of Plagiarism: ESL Students Writing in Graduate School." *Journal of Second Language Writing* 15, no. 2: 102–117.
Abilock, Debbie. 2006. "Is Your Ethics Policy a Quick Fix or a Civic Outcome?" *Knowledge Quest* 34, no. 4: 7–9.
———. 2009. "Guiding the Gifted to Honest Work." *Knowledge Quest* 37, no. 3: 12–15.
Buranen, Lise. 2009. "A Safe Place: The Role of Librarians and Writing Centers in Addressing Citation Practices and Plagiarism." *Knowledge Quest* 37, no. 3: 24–33.
Center for Academic Integrity. "Welcome to the Center for Academic Integrity." Clemson, SC: Rutland Institute for Ethics, Clemson University. Available: www.academicintegrity.org/index.php (accessed January 12, 2010).
Chandrasoma, Ranamukalage, Celia Thomson, and Alastair Pennycook. 2004. "Beyond Plagiarism: Transgressive and Nontransgressive Intertextuality." *Journal of Language, Identity & Education* 3, no. 3: 171–193.
Cogdell, Barbara, and Dorothy Aidulis. 2007. "Dealing with Plagiarism as an Ethical Issue." In *Student Plagiarism in an Online World: Problems and Solu-*

tions (pp. 38–59), edited by T.S. Roberts. Hershey, PA: Information Science Reference.

Decoo, Wilfried. 2007. "Substantial, Verbatim, Unattributed, Misleading: Applying Criteria to Assess Textual Plagiarism." In *Student Plagiarism in an Online World: Problems and Solutions* (pp. 228–243), edited by T.S. Roberts. Hershey, PA: Information Science Reference.

Devlin, Marcia. 2006. "Policy, Preparation, and Prevention: Proactive Minimization of Student Plagiarism." *Journal of Higher Education Policy & Management* 28, no. 1: 45–58.

Eriksson, Erik J., and Kirk P.H. Sullivan. 2008. "Controlling Plagiarism: A Study of Lecturer Attitudes." In *Student Plagiarism in an Online World: Problems and Solutions* (pp. 23–36), edited by T.S. Roberts. Hershey, PA: Information Science Reference.

Fox, Brian F. 2008. "Supporting and Facilitating Academic Integrity in Distance Education through Student Services." In *Online and Distance Learning: Concepts, Methodologies, Tools, and Applications* (pp. 2049–2060), edited by L. Tomei. Hershey, PA: Information Science Reference.

Harvey, Michael. 2003. *Nuts and Bolts of College Writing: Background*. Chestertown, MD: Washington College. Available: nutsandbolts.washcoll.edu/nb-home .html (accessed January 18, 2010).

Hayes, Niall, and Lucas D. Introna. 2005. "Cultural Values, Plagiarism, and Fairness: When Plagiarism Gets in the Way of Learning." *Ethics & Behavior* 15, no. 3: 213–231.

Howard, Rebecca Moore. 1993. "Plagiarism Pentimento." *Journal of Teaching Writing* 11, no. 3: 233–246.

———. 1995. "Plagiarisms, Authorships, and the Academic Death Penalty." *College English* 57, no. 7: 788–806.

Introna, Lucas D., and Niall Hayes. 2007. "International Students and Plagiarism Detection Systems: Detecting Plagiarism, Copying or Learning?" In *Student Plagiarism in an Online World: Problems and Solutions* (pp. 108–122), edited by T.S. Roberts. Hershey, PA: Information Science Reference.

Josephson Institute. "About the Josephson Institute." Los Angeles: Josephson Institute. Available: josephsoninstitute.org/about.html (accessed January 18, 2010).

Liu, Dilin. 2005. "Plagiarism in ESOL Students: Is Cultural Conditioning Truly the Major Culprit?" *ELT Journal* 59, no. 3: 234–241.

Madray, Amrita. 2007. "Developing Students' Awareness of Plagiarism: Crisis and Opportunities." *Library Philosophy and Practice*. Available: www .webpages.uidaho.edu/~mbolin/madray.htm (accessed March 27, 2010).

———. 2008. "The Anatomy of a Plagiarism Initiative: One Library's Campus Collaboration." *Public Services Quarterly* 4, no. 2: 111–125.

McGowan, Ursula. 2007. "International Students: A Conceptual Framework for Dealing with Unintentional Plagiarism." In *Student Plagiarism in an Online World: Problems and Solutions* (pp. 92–107), edited by T.S. Roberts. Hershey, PA: Information Science Reference.

Park, Chris. 2004. "Rebels without a Clause: Towards an Institutional Framework for Dealing with Plagiarism by Students." *Journal of Further and Higher Education* 28, no. 3: 291–306.

Roig, Miguel. 1997. "Can Undergraduate Students Determine Whether Text Has Been Plagiarized?" *Psychological Record* 47, no. 1: 113.

———. 2001. "Plagiarism and Paraphrasing Criteria of College and University Professors." *Ethics & Behavior* 11, no. 3: 307–323.

Salmons, Janet. 2007. "Expect Originality! Using Taxonomies to Structure Assignments that Support Original Work." In *Student Plagiarism in an Online World: Problems and Solutions* (pp. 208–226), edited by T.S. Roberts. Hershey, PA: Information Science Reference.

Sciammarella, Susan. 2009. "Making a Difference: Library and Teaching Faculty Working Together to Develop Strategies in Dealing with Student Plagiarism." *Community & Junior College Libraries* 15, no. 1: 23–34.

Seeger, Pete, and Arlo Guthrie. 1975. *Pete and Arlo Together in Concert.* Burbank, CA: Reprise. Sound recording.

Sowden, Colin. 2005. "Plagiarism and the Culture of Multilingual Students in Higher Education Abroad." *ELT Journal* 59, no. 3: 226–233.

Thomas, P.L. 2007. "Of Flattery and Thievery: Reconsidering Plagiarism in a Time of Virtual Information." *English Journal* 96, no. 5: 81–84.

University of Michigan. *Plagiary: Cross-Disciplinary Studies in Plagiarism, Fabrication and Falsification.* 2006. Ann Arbor: University of Michigan. Available: www.plagiary.org (accessed January 12, 2010).

Williamson, K., and J.H. McGregor. 2006. "Information Use and Secondary School Students: A Model for Understanding Plagiarism." *Information Research* 12, no. 1: 288.

Wilson, Frankie, and Kate Ippolito. 2007. "Working Together to Educate Students." In *Student Plagiarism in an Online World: Problems and Solutions* (pp. 60–75), edited by T.S. Roberts. Hershey, PA: Information Science Reference.

Zimitat, Craig. 2007. "A Student Perspective of Plagiarism." In *Student Plagiarism in an Online World: Problems and Solutions* (pp. 10–22), edited by T.S. Roberts. Hershey, PA: Information Science Reference.

Zwagerman, Sean. 2008. "Scarlet 'P': Plagiarism, Panopticism, and the Rhetoric of Academic Integrity?" *College Composition and Communication* 59, no. 4: 676–710.

13

Write It, Then Cite It: Guiding Students toward Reliable Techniques and Resources for Effective Scholarly Writing

Robert J. Lackie

Introduction: Web Resources for Citing, Research, and Writing

Although magazines and websites feature a plethora of articles about preventing academic dishonesty in writing and combating plagiarism, in general, within our high schools and colleges, many articles do not effectively distinguish among the different types of plagiarism that teachers and professors find in academic writing. True, downloading an entire paper from the web is wholesale, intentional cheating. However, many students—even above-average high school and college students—make mistakes while summarizing, paraphrasing, and quoting source materials and integrating these into their research papers. Some experts on plagiarism feel that by focusing on the skills needed for proper writing and scholarly citation, plagiarism would be far less prevalent (Abilock, 2008; Howard, 2009; Howard and Davies, 2009). Donald L. McCabe, Professor of Management & Global Business and founder of the Center for Academic Integrity at Rutgers University, is known for his widely cited studies and expertise concerning ethical decision making and cheating by secondary and higher education students. He and his coauthors believe that "what is really needed [regarding academic dishonesty] in their view, and ours, are 'broader programmatic efforts based upon notions of ethical community building,' an approach which involves creating a 'culture of integrity and responsibility . . .'" (McCabe, Feghali, and Abdallah, 2008: 465).

Many students, especially in college freshmen English composition courses, do not seem to have a lot of experience with generating, revising, and editing academic papers, much less actually researching ideas and attributing sources used. That is why Debbie Abilock, Editor-in-Chief of the American Association of School Librarians' journal *Knowledge Quest*, developed the NoodleBib software (discussed later in this chapter), which coaches and supports students, teaching faculty, and librarians throughout the research, writing, and attribution processes. She agrees with Howard, McCabe, and many other experts on plagiarism prevention, stating that "some educators are as confused as their students about the role of imitation in learning, what constitutes common knowledge and need not be cited, and whether careless work without attribution should be treated as deliberate plagiarism" (Abilock, 2008: under "Introduction").

Fortunately, for today's educators and students, there are many free or inexpensive, interactive, and user-friendly resource and tutorial sites available on the web that can greatly assist educators in teaching proper research and academic writing skills to high school and college students. However, as the coverage and content of the web summarily advances and transforms, it is becoming increasingly difficult and time consuming for many teachers and librarians to efficiently find those accurate and reliable education sites—sites that make teaching and learning about research and academic writing easier and more enjoyable. This chapter will serve as a specific resource guide to those quality sites for the intended audience of high school and higher education English faculty, instruction librarians, and their students. The topics to be covered here will include web-based style guides and online tools, concentrating on the Modern Language Association's (MLA) but also providing guides to other frequently used citation and documentation styles. In addition, this chapter will introduce free quality research and writing websites that provide guidelines for researching and constructing exemplary papers and address the quandaries of how, when, and why to cite sources.

Giving Proper Credit: Key Web Resources for Scholarly Citation

Figuring out how to cite the various types of sources integrated into a research paper is not what most students describe as a *fun* activity. In fact, some of the most frequently asked questions from anxious and/or frustrated students to their instructors (whether teaching an English class, leading a library instruction research session, or conducting a reference interview at the library reference desk) deal with how to properly cite and document a source for a paper or speech. Obviously, students struggle with generating works cited pages and in-text parenthetical citations, trying to formulate correct formatting, punctuation, and so forth, for all of their attributions. All of this certainly can be time consuming and even overwhelming for many new scholars as they attempt to read and interpret the most common current style handbooks and manuals, such as the *Modern Language Association Handbook* (7th edition, 2009) and the *Publication Manual of the American Psychological Association* (APA) (6th edition, 2009) guidebooks. Several of these style handbooks have very recently been updated, significantly improving upon previous editions by adding many more web-based items. However, one cannot deny that the free web *is* specifically advantageous because it provides web-based frequently asked questions (FAQs), interactive tools and tutorials, additional citation examples, and general assistance with the published style manuals after the print publications have been published (Harris, 2009; Lackie, 2004).

The MLA (www.mla.org/style), APA (www.apastyle.org), and the University of Chicago Press/*The Chicago Manual of Style* (CMS) (www.chicagomanualof style.org) all supply excellent accompanying websites to the latest published editions of their handbooks/manuals, containing especially useful online FAQ sections. However, although all of them can be of value, they still do not answer many of the questions teachers, professors, and librarians frequently enter- tain from students regarding proper documentation. Conducting a search on a major web search engine will yield an overabundance of help sheets, guides, and explanations. However, examples found on some sites contradict those on other sites, or the examples and explanations are now incorrect as they follow outdated versions of the published style guides. This is especially true for sites detailing MLA and APA guidelines; both of these organizations published new editions in mid-2009.

Because students must learn when and how to properly cite borrowed words and ideas from others' works, the goal for this section of the chapter is to high- light websites (other than the official organizations' sites already mentioned) that now provide librarians and other educators with the best online assistance to help students (and other interested parties) with proper documentation of sources. Following are brief abstracts to a few of the best free, quality documen- tation sites on the web that provide abundant examples, explanations, tools, and handouts concerning the proper use of a variety of documentation styles, especially MLA.

Research and Citation
owl.english.purdue.edu/owl

Created by Purdue University and their Writing Lab staff, the Online Writing Lab (OWL) is a free, comprehensive writing assistance and teacher resource site highly recommended by many experts and evalu- ative web directories. The "Research and Citation" section of their site not only provides clearly written instructions and extensive explanations for citing sources using MLA and APA styles, but it also lists several other discipline-related resources for documenting sources. This section also links to official and explanatory sites for each source when avail- able and much more. Because Purdue staff are updating and revising the entire OWL site, including some major section headings, you may want to check back often and view this and other sections via their use- ful Site Map (owl.english.purdue.edu/sitemap). The OWL at Purdue is discussed further later in this chapter.

Citing Sources and Avoiding Plagiarism
library.duke.edu/research/citing

Duke University provides citation assistance with various styles, includ- ing MLA, APA, Council of Science Editors (CSE), Chicago, and Tur- bian. The fantastic team at Duke University Libraries and the Univers

Writing Program has included the 2009 updates to the MLA and APA guides, as well as a special section on avoiding plagiarism. Original site creators Kelly A. Lawton, Laura Cousineau, and Van E. Hilliard examine plagiarism via improper citation, but more complex concepts of plagiarism, such as quoting out of context or disregarding an author's intent, are also clearly explained. A new scholar's awareness of the differences and similarities among the styles can provide a broader understanding of the core values of all of them, making the student aware of the sometimes microscopic differences between the styles, such as in-text citation methods and end-of-paper bibliographies. By giving an introduction to citing styles, this guide helps to ease students into their use, and, by showing how to avoid plagiarism, it shows writers how to use the styles most effectively.

Research and Documentation Online
dianahacker.com/resdoc

This companion website for the book *Research and Documentation in the Electronic Age* (Bedford/St. Martin's, 2002) by the noted textbook author and professor of English Diana Hacker offers many powerful features for new scholars. Scholars in any of 30 expertise areas can quickly navigate to the most appropriate sources for their research or diversify their sources if they find themselves over-emphasizing a single type. The guidelines for documenting print and online sources provide the most current advice available for MLA, APA, Chicago, and CSE styles, which are especially important because of the often perplexing differences among the citation approaches of the various styles. Researchers who are unfamiliar with these differences might find the list of style manuals organized by disciplines useful for comparing stylistic approaches; when writers have a choice in the style they can use, they might make a more informed decision about which style more closely meets the needs of their discipline, writing style, or citation needs. The sample papers with annotations for the various styles provide real world examples for new scholars to follow. The tips for evaluating print and online resources are an extremely valuable resource in a world in which anyone, scholarly or otherwise, can publish freely on the Web.

In addition to the style manual guide sites described, free interactive citation generator tool sites exist on the web. A few fairly well-known interactive MLA bibliography citation generators can be found at the Oregon School Library Information System (OSLIS) site and Damon and Debbie Abilock's NoodleTools site. At both websites, you choose a citation source located on the interactive page, fill in the fields as described with your citation information, and each of the free tools will generate and allow you to view your citation in the proper MLA style format. Of the two sites, the NoodleTools' section seems to be updated most frequently, but both are kept current.

Oregon School Library Information System (OSLIS): I Need to . . . Cite My Sources
secondary.oslis.org/cite-sources

OSLIS has specific MLA citation generators geared for the elementary, middle, and high school student. The link given takes you to the secondary school level page containing the Citation Maker it designed to help simplify the sometimes difficult task of creating an MLA works cited page. A similar APA citation generator is explained clearly, with many examples. The citations are not saved for later access, but copying and pasting into students' in-progress work is encouraged. The elementary portion of this great resource site (elementary.oslis.org/cite-sources/ mla) has a section of MLA citation examples appropriate for younger researchers; both primary and secondary citation guides provide a key for reviewing the biggest changes of the MLA, 7th edition. Use the drop-down arrow box on the upper right-hand corner of each page to easily switch between the "Elementary Student," "Elementary Educator," "Secondary Student," and "Secondary Educator" OSLIS sites.

NoodleTools' MLA Starter and NoodleBib Express
www.noodletools.com

The highly rated, comprehensive (formerly free) NoodleTools' Noodle-Bib software is available for a small fee to individuals and organizations to create advanced MLA works cited, APA reference, and Chicago/ Turabian bibliography citations, and it easily compiles the lists in formatted Word documents. However, NoodleTools also provides a few noted free tools: NoodleBib MLA Starter and NoodleBib Express. The free MLA Starter citation generator tool is designed for students in grades one through five, introducing very young scholars to the basics of citing sources and providing color-coded examples for sources commonly used by this age group (e.g., books, encyclopedias, magazines, and newspapers).

If students and/or educators just need one or two quick citations and not an entire list, NoodleBib Express provides access to all of the citation types available in the APA, MLA, and Chicago/Turabian advanced versions of the tool. Neither of the free tools compiles the citations into a source list or saves them for you, but you can just copy and paste from the screen. This author highly recommends these up-to-date, user-friendly, and useful teaching tools, as well as the other free resources that exist on the NoodleTools main page (www.noodletools.com)—they are all worth taking the time to explore.

Zotero Firefox Extension
www.zotero.com

Recently, a tool called Zotero has emerged as another great citation assistance resource. For users of the Web browser Firefox, Zotero is a Firefox extension (a free piece of software that extends Firefox's core functionality). After installing Zotero, when you visit websites that have bibliographic information included in their content, as hundreds of sites including the *New York Times*, Google Scholar, and Amazon already do, you can simply click on a Zotero icon in the address bar to collect a snapshot of the resource and its associated bibliographic data. After you have collected the resources you wish to use in your local Zotero database, you can click again to create a bibliography in many styles, including MLA, APA, and Chicago. Then, you can paste your properly formatted reference list right into your word processor application. Exciting future features include the ability for an organization, such as a library or university, to run their own Zotero server, where patrons or students and faculty can collect organization-specific citations en masse and share them across the organization.

A Mightier Pen: Web Resources for Building Stronger Writing Skills

In addition to steering our students toward excellent, free, web-based citation and documentation guides, we should also provide our students with supplementary quality research and writing assistance resources for use inside and outside of the classroom. Many highlighted plagiarism prevention strategies—such as educating students on the meaning of plagiarism, providing interactive quizzes and other resources to assist students on how to do proper research, and demonstrating how to properly write academic research papers—can be found in a very comprehensive and useful annotated listing of articles and websites regarding plagiarism recently compiled and updated by Sharon Stoerger (2009) at the Office of the Vice Chancellor for Research, University of Illinois at Urbana-Champaign.

In articles and professional presentations concerning plagiarism prevention, Rebecca Moore Howard (Howard, 2002; Howard, 2009; Howard and Davies, 2009), Associate Professor in the Writing Program at Syracuse University, in Syracuse, New York, and noted author and expert on the topic of plagiarism, stresses real pedagogical reform as a key plagiarism prevention strategy. However, she indicates that current working conditions may be preventing some professors from finding the time to prepare genuinely meaningful and useful writing assignments, teach the research process, and incrementally respond to their students' writing drafts. Schoolteachers often say this is intensified by the myriad of demands placed upon them in areas ranging from the cognitive to the affective domains. Fortunately, educators from all academic levels do not have to reinvent the wheel when it comes to assignment redesign and research writing support. Just as the web provides help in the form of style guides and tools that can be successfully used inside and outside of the classroom, the web also provides excellent support materials and interactive sites that can help us ensure that good teaching takes place along the way.

Obviously, many high school and college students are comfortable with using the web. Therefore, encouraging them to use the web as an additional guide to research and writing—rather than for intentional theft of papers—should not be a difficult task. Although many students may be well versed in locating certain types of information on the web—or using it to communicate with their friends—they may not be aware that it can be a valuable resource for both practicing with research and writing strategies and retrieving information on plagiarism prevention. Finding those accurate and reliable academic writing "hidden gem" sites can be difficult and time-consuming. Therefore, to save time for all concerned, librarians and educators should be capable of directing students to the best free online support material and interactive sites on the web for researching and writing academic papers. Then, when in conference with students, educators, with the possible assistance of librarians as well, should look at drafts and discuss the assignment progression with students to determine if more assistance with research and citing is required. If more help is required, classroom instructors and librarians will have the tools to assist in teaching good writing skills immediately at their disposal. Here are a few preferred research and writing sites, freely available on the web, that can help prevent plagiarism from becoming a reality for novice and/or frustrated writers.

The OWL at Purdue: Free Writing Help and Teaching Resources, Open 24/7
owl.english.purdue.edu

Mentioned earlier in this chapter specifically for its style manual assistance, Purdue University's OWL also has highly cited sections on writing research papers, including a step-by-step writing process guide, plagiarism prevention help, worthwhile quoting, paraphrasing, summarizing handouts, and more. There are guides for researching based on discipline, with some presented as handouts and others as PowerPoint presentations. OWL also has lengthy sections about general academic writing and teaching writing skills, which offer important assistance on database research, evaluating sources, guidelines for fair use, and conducting interviews, among others. Major headings are found on the main navigation page. Because this site has deep sections that cover professional, technical, and job search writing; English as a Second Language (ESL) literacy; and assistance with creative writing, grammar, and mechanics, the OWL Writing Resources Site Map (owl.english.purdue.edu/sitemap) is invaluable. For new scholars who are interested in getting a broad yet deep overview of writing with a scholarly purpose, the OWL site with its many resources is an ideal place to get started. This is why more than a few seasoned scholars keep it bookmarked, including this author.

The Writers' Workshop
www.engl.niu.edu/comskills

This award-winning site, created by Northern Illinois University, is a great resource for high school and college instructors, students, and tutors. Resources such as these allow writers to keep coming back to a trusted, known resource throughout their writing career. It is broken down into Students' Resources, Tutors' Resources, and Instructors' Resources sections, offering useful writing resources and quizzes for students to test themselves. The quiz function is an especially useful tool for students to help determine if they are ready to submit their formatted paper. The Students' Resources section has some particularly helpful information on grammar and mechanics, plagiarism, quotations, and the MLA style for citing resources.

ipl2: A+ Research and Writing
www.ipl.org/div/aplus

Originally created for the highly respected Internet Public Library (IPL) and their Teenspace site by Kathryn L. Schwartz, this is one of the best student-friendly explanatory guides to writing research papers on the web. It contains sections on step-by-step research and writing and on learning to research in the library and on the web as well as an annotated list of online resources for research and assistance with paraphrasing, summarizing, plagiarism, and using quotations. IPL, which started as a graduate seminar at the University of Michigan School of Information, has been a public service organization praised by librarians everywhere for its excellent teaching-learning assistance. Currently hosted by The iSchool at Drexel University's College of Information Science & Technology (with the valuable assistance of the College of Information at Florida State University as well as a growing consortium of other higher education institutions), IPL has very recently merged with another top-rated research site, the Librarians' Internet Index (www.lii.org) and updated its name to ipl2: Information You Can Trust. The merger of these two titans of quality web resource guides can only result in an even more impressive research and writing section for high school and college students—something to look forward to soon.

Nuts and Bolts of College Writing
nutsandbolts.washcoll.edu

Created by Professor Michael Harvey of Washington College, Maryland, this comprehensive writing guide site is one of the most popular on the web for students and teachers, covering the beginning stages of writing to the polishing of the finished product. Because this guide is meant for students and teachers in all types of college courses, not just research writing and literature courses, it also provides detailed help guides to common documentation styles such as APA, CMS, and CSE, in addition to MLA. In particular, this site covers topics such as thinking about writing (arguments and drafting), style (clarity, rhetoric, and conclusion), structure (design, beginning, middle, and end), evidence (research, plagiarism, and quoting), and mechanics (presentation, punctuation, and top ten mistakes). In the context of today's highly designed, interactive Web 2.0 sites and resources, this site immediately appears a bit dated, but look beyond its simple interface to the depth of knowledge and collection of key writing skill sets, and you will be rewarded as a writer and scholar.

Guide to Grammar and Writing
grammar.ccc.commnet.edu/grammar
Secondary and higher education English teachers, tutors, and instructors will find this site, maintained by Capital Community College Foundation, in memory of English Professor Charles Darling, is especially helpful, as it is chock full of instructional materials. It contains numerous interactive quizzes on grammar, copious PowerPoint presentations and guides on English usage, and a sizeable number of recommendations on writing essays and research papers—all provided free to the general public. The Principles of Composition and the annotated Online Resources for Writers sections of the site are valuable for students and teachers alike.

Additional Help with When and Why to Cite Sources

Although high school and college faculty and their students will find these recommended online style guides, interactive tools, and online research and writing sites to be handy and practical, sometimes more in-depth information is needed to help librarians and teachers educate themselves and/or teach others how to better avoid plagiarism. Particularly pleasing tutorial sites and unique online workshops on plagiarism prevention are freely available on the web—resources that offer additional discussions and lessons for educators to help them assist students in understanding and avoiding the perils of practicing plagiarism. Here are a few of these free web resources.

Synthesis: Using the Work of Others
plagiarism.umf.maine.edu
This detailed plagiarism prevention tutorial site from the University of Maine at Farmington's Writing Center details issues surrounding plagiarism, including what it is, why one should care about it, why it is difficult to avoid, what can be done to prevent it, and a practical interactive plagiarism game. Games like these can engage current generations of high school and college students (such as Generation M) in ways that are not necessarily obvious (Cvetkovic and Lackie, 2009). In addition, this site provides information on copyright; assistance on citing and giving credit for papers, presentations, and websites; and, conveniently, another interactive game, this time on copyright infringement. Given the ways in which peer-to-peer file sharing and digital media revolutions have muddied the understanding of many about when they are and are not infringing upon copyright, this topic is perhaps as important as plagiarism itself.

The Plagiarism Court: You Be the Judge
www.fairfield.edu/library/lib_plagiarismcourt.html

This excellent tutorial site by Reference and Educational Technology Librarian Ramona Islam of the Fairfield University DiMenna-Nyselius Library provides a Macromedia Flash movie with voiceovers as a part of the plagiarism avoidance lesson, ending with a short ten-question interactive quiz. Students and educators will find this tutorial stimulating and effective, and, if Flash is not available, they also offer two HTML versions of the tutorial. For some people, this may be the first time they've thought very seriously about the issues outside of their own experiences, and so this flash application may actually model the kind of critical thought and behavior required to truly combat plagiarism.

Cybercheats: Plagiarism and the Internet
cybercheats.blogspot.com

Steve Garwood, Staff Training and Development Coordinator at the Princeton University Library and an adjunct Assistant Professor in the Library and Information Science Department at the School of Communication and Information of Rutgers University, provides an instructive and engaging PowerPoint presentation on plagiarism, using "Timmy's Tragic Tale" as the centerpiece for the lesson. The entire site, to include the presentation, class website, and informative bibliography (all available free of charge), is worth exploring and sharing. In addition, Professor Garwood recommends on his blog a few citation generator sites (e.g., www.bibme.org, citationmachine.net, easybib.com, and noodle tools.com/tools), and he lists and describes a second presentation dealing with the topic, titled *Plagiarism Prevention for Research Projects*. This online lecture is more of a how-to on plagiarism prevention, focusing on the topics of academic integrity policies and assignment redesign.

Plagiarism Workshop
mail.nvnet.org/~cooper_j/plagiarism

Northern Valley Regional High School (Old Tappan, New Jersey) Media Specialist Janice Cooper designed this carefully planned and comprehensive workshop lesson plan for students in grades seven through ten, providing them with an introduction to plagiarism, copyright, and fair use. A focus of the workshop is to encourage students to consider issues of plagiarism from the perspective of the artists whose works are used unethically. It includes links to essential resources for students and teachers, including techniques, tips, and tools for paraphrasing, quoting, and citing, that they can employ to help avoid committing plagiarism. Again, by creating an experiential resource, Cooper potentially allows new scholars to think outside of their own personal experiences, which may allow for a shift away from false personal assumptions about plagiarism.

Final Comments from Noted Experts in the Field

It is no surprise that excellent free educational websites exist to help students, teaching faculty, and librarians to conduct research, to write educational reports and academic papers, and to attribute sources properly. As veteran librarians and educators, more than likely our experience and education have significantly assisted us in becoming more adept at research and writing. But recent books, reports, articles, and blog posts, such as the latest interesting and wide-ranging publications from plagiarism gurus Debbie Abilock (2008), Rebecca Moore Howard (2009), and Donald L. McCabe et al. (2008), not to mention the preliminary findings from the collaborative efforts of authors for The Citation Project: Preliminary Findings (Howard, Rodrigue, and Serviss, accessed 2010), all indicate that plagiarism has become one of society's most important and controversial topics, inside and outside of educational systems. Plagiarism-detecting companies and their services, such as the Turnitin.com plagiarism detection system, have become household names within thousands of educational institutions.

Robert Harris (2009), noted writer and educator on plagiarism, details on his VirtualSalt website why students sometimes plagiarize. He states that many students are "natural economizers" or procrastinators and may resort to plagiarism possibly because of their "poor time management and planning skills" (under "Understand Why Students Cheat"). Essentially, they make bad choices and do not allow themselves enough time to do all of the necessary recursive writing and research required.

Debbie Abilock, cofounder of the NoodleTools site, basically agrees but also remarks: "Let's face it—[creating a] citation isn't easy. Many adults can remember discarding a source they had actually used for research, because they were unable to figure out how to create the citation correctly. In order to create a citation for some of the trickier database sources one must understand and implement elements from several different sections of style manuals, a tedious and frustrating process" (Abilock, 2008: under "School Factors Contributing to Academic Dishonesty").

Additionally, plagiarism is a relatively *new* concept. Historically speaking, repeating one's work was grounded in the oral tradition and encouraged throughout the centuries. In fact, repetition of one's stories was not only encouraged but also necessary if customs and traditions were to be passed down. Imitation was the ultimate compliment. "This view was grounded in the belief that knowledge of the human condition should be shared by everyone, not owned or hoarded. The notion of individual authorship was much less important than it is today" (Hansen, 2003: 782).

Plagiarism prevention scholars continually point out that paraphrasing is difficult for native speakers and writers of English, in addition to ESL students. "Paraphrasing is arguably the highest and most synthetic language skill of all," notes Sharon Myers, Associate Professor and Director of the Academic English as a Second Language Program at Texas Tech University. "Not only does the student have to possess a large and sophisticated vocabulary, but must also recognize (so as not to repeat) sometimes very subtle stylistic features of writing" (Lackie and D'Angelo-Long, 2004: 41).

Rebecca Moore Howard writes (2009: 64), "Teachers warn students not to copy—or else—and present them with citation guides and the trinity of techniques to write using others' research without plagiarizing: quoting, paraphrasing, and summarizing. The onus then falls on the students, who are expected to use these techniques well, assuming that they know how to do so." Being consistent is important with both detection of and consequences for infractions. Most schools have handbooks and official policies detailing academic dishonesty, but the problem results from lip service to the procedures or at least perceived incongruency in effectuated policies. Perhaps follow-through with infractions will become as important as designing the ideals and even teaching the protocols. Statements of academic honesty detailing ownership of submitted work as well as agreeing to take the consequences of submitting plagiarized work are prolific on college campuses. Faculty need to get to the place where they realize and accept that detecting plagiarism is part of their job description and work toward limiting it and responding appropriately to it.

Conclusion

The advent of the (easily copied) web seems to have had a somewhat negative impact on the development of proficient research and writing skills for some high school and college students, as many of them use it to "borrow" someone else's ideas and words instead of conducting their own authentic research. Therefore, just as instructors must diligently provide explanations, strategies, tips, and resources for students to cultivate good-quality research and writing skills, librarians and all other educators should also endeavor to guide and teach students about information literacy, the issues surrounding plagiarism, and how to avoid it by properly citing and documenting attributions within their speeches and papers.

Librarians, teachers, and professors have only so much face-to-face time with students within their classrooms and libraries, so all educators need to direct students to those free, excellent supplementary resources and tutorials on the web to help them to develop more proficient research, writing, and documentation skills. Because of the expanding and constantly changing aspect of the evolved free web—with its current ability to engage, interact, converse, and collaborate—the roles of teachers, professors, and librarians are a bit more difficult in regard to efficiently and effectively locating those highly rated online tools and sites that make teaching, learning, and research easier. But those accurate and reliable sites do exist, and they can help educators to develop a curriculum that will prepare students for future research and writing opportunities, while possibly giving them an exciting addition to the traditional English composition and rhetoric curriculum.

A major goal for this chapter is to serve as a specific resource guide to these quality websites, enabling and facilitating the research and academic writing processes. It is important to review periodically the recommended web resources for citing, researching, and writing that are contained within this chapter. Also, check out some of the online workshops and presentations, experiment with some of the tutorials and quizzes, and play around with the various citation generators and interactive research and writing guides. Then, bookmark favorites within a favorite browser and/or social bookmarking site (e.g., delicious.com) and share them with other educators and students. Keeping up with changes to the sites highlighted in this chapter will sufficiently provide additional tools and guidelines for helping all educators to better teach others how to research and construct exemplary papers and speech outlines. Additionally, they adequately address the quandaries of how, when, and why to cite sources—something for which many students and even new scholars continuously need guidance.

Just remember that not all sections of every recommended site may be totally up to date for each type of information provided, so evaluate accordingly. Be advised that it may take a while for some sites to update their information regarding that style manual. However, the sites recommended in this chapter were chosen and recommended for their general currency, accuracy, ease of use, low cost, and interactivity, as well as the belief that the owners of the sites will strive to keep the information and materials as up to date as possible or lead to another site that does a better job at providing the best citing, researching, writing assistance. Many websites with outdated information on citation guides, for instance, did cite the Plagiarism.org website (sister site of the infamous Turnitin.com service mentioned above), which houses an excellent, free, comprehensive plagiarism prevention/research resource section for educators and students today—their FAQs subsection is thorough, and their Important Terms listing is useful. Anybody interested in plagiarism prevention will find value in their resource section, as well as within the many recommended tools, sites, articles, and advice from experts presented in this chapter.

Certainly, the idea that plagiarism is on the rise can be debated; however, the medium, i.e., the Internet, has changed the way many students plagiarize and has vastly increased the variety and availability of easily manipulated sources, putting a dangerous new spin on an age-old problem. As librarians and teaching faculty, it is important that we provide the resources, instruction, and guidance on ways to preserve the integrity of scholarly writing and combat the newer, easier specter of Internet-driven plagiarism.

References

Abilock, Debbie. 2008. "Guiding the Gifted to Honest Work." *Duke Gifted Letter* 9, no. 1 (Fall). Available: www.dukegiftedletter.com/articles/vol9no1_feature.html (accessed May 27, 2010).

Cvetkovic, Vibiana Bowman, and Robert J. Lackie, eds. 2009. *Teaching Generation M: A Handbook for Librarians and Educators*. New York: Neal-Schuman.

Hansen, Brian. 2003. "Combating Plagiarism." *CQ Researcher* 13, no. 2 (September 19): 773–796.

Harris, Robert. 2009. "Anti-Plagiarism Strategies for Research Papers." VirtualSalt (June 14). Available: www.virtualsalt.com/antiplag.htm (accessed May 27, 2010).

Howard, Rebecca Moore. 2002. "Don't Police Plagiarism: Just Teach!" *Education Digest* 67, no. 5 (January): 46–49.

———. 2009. "Writing from Sources versus Plagiarism: Setting Instructional Priorities." Keynote address given at the CONNECT Writing Conference, Bridgewater (MA) State College (May 21).

Howard, Rebecca Moore, and Laura J. Davies. 2009. "Plagiarism in the Internet Age." *Educational Leadership* 66, no. 6 (March): 64–67.

Howard, Rebecca Moore, Tanya K. Rodrigue, and Tricia C. Serviss. "Preliminary Findings." The Citation Project: Preventing Plagiarism, Teaching Writing. Available: citationproject.net/CitationProject-findings.html (accessed May 27, 2010).

Lackie, Robert J. 2004. "Where to Go for What They Need to Know: Style Sheets, Writing Guides, and Other Resources." In *The Plagiarism Plague: A Resource Guide and CD-ROM Tutorial for Educators and Librarians* (pp. 167–77), edited by Vibiana Bowman. New York: Neal-Schuman.

Lackie, Robert J., and Michele D'Angelo-Long. 2004. "It's a Small World? Cross-Cultural Perspectives and ESL Considerations." In *The Plagiarism Plague: A Resource Guide and CD-ROM Tutorial for Educators and Librarians* (pp. 35–48), edited by Vibiana Bowman. New York: Neal-Schuman.

McCabe, Donald L., Tony Feghali, and Hanin Abdallah. 2008. "Academic Dishonesty in the Middle East: Individual and Contextual Factors." *Research in Higher Education* 49, no. 5 (August): 451–467.

Stoerger, Sharon. 2009. "Plagiarism." University of Illinois at Urbana-Champaign (September 30). Available: www.web-miner.com/plagiarism (accessed May 27, 2010).

Recommended Readings

American Psychological Association. 2009. *Publication Manual of the American Psychological Association,* 6th ed. Washington, DC: APA. Available: apastyle .org (accessed April 23, 2010). (Note: make sure you purchase the revised, second printing of the 6th edition—there were many mistakes in the first printing, and the APA began allowing orders for free replacements as of November 2009.)

The Chicago Manual of Style, 15th ed. 2003. Chicago: University of Chicago Press. Available: www.chicagomanualofstyle.org (accessed April 23, 2010).

East, Julianne. 2009. "Review [of the Book]: *Pluralizing Plagiarism: Identities, Contexts, Pedagogies* [edited by Rebecca Moore Howard and Amy E. Robillard]." *International Journal for Educational Integrity* 5, no. 1 (June): 32–34.

Eisner, Caroline, and Martha Vicinus, eds. 2008. *Originality, Imitation, and Plagiarism: Teaching Writing in the Digital Age.* Ann Arbor: University of Michigan Press.

Gallup, George, Jr. 2005. "Cyber Cheating." In *Teens and Cheating* (pp. 39–54), edited by Hal Marcovitz. Broomall, PA: Mason Crest.

Howard, Rebecca Moore, and Amy E. Robillard, eds. 2008. *Pluralizing Plagiarism: Identities, Contexts, Pedagogies.* Portsmouth, NH: Boynton/Cook.

Kaminer, Wendy. 2007. "Word Crimes and Misdemeanors." *Wilson Quarterly* 31, no. 2 (Spring): 83–86.

Modern Language Association. 2009. *MLA Handbook for Writers of Research Papers,* 7th ed. New York: MLA. Available: www.mla.org/style (accessed April 23, 2010).

Posner, Richard A. 2007. *The Little Book of Plagiarism.* New York: Pantheon.

Reece, Tamekia. 2009. "Cheat Sheet." *Current Health 2* 35, no. 5 (January): 27–29.

Snyder, Gail. 2004. *Teens, Religion, and Values.* Broomall, PA: Mason Crest.

Yaccino, Steve. 2008. "Students Up the Ante, Too." *U.S. News & World Report* 145, no. 8 (October 13): 74.

Plagiarism: An Annotated Bibliography

Patience L. Simmonds

Introduction

Plagiarism and the issues associated with plagiarism, such as cheating, academic dishonesty, academic integrity, honor codes, self-plagiarism, etc., continue as topics of discussion in both the academic and publishing communities. Students in high school, colleges, and universities are often targeted as the people who are responsible for committing the most egregious acts of plagiarism and cheating. Most educational institutions have academic integrity policies and rules and regulations regarding intellectual honesty for students and faculty. Some colleges and universities mandate that their schools and departments provide their students with a "syllabus statement of academic integrity." An example of this can be found at the Penn State Policies on Academic Integrity site (tlt.its.psu.edu/plagiarism/facguide/policy). The Internet has contributed to the problem of plagiarism, but plagiarism existed long before the birth of the Internet. Most people have heard of the word "plagiarism," and plagiarism is also a word that has garnered a lot of interest globally. Some people know what it means; others think they know what it means. It is also very easy to commit plagiarism. What the Internet has done is to make more visible the immense number of resources available for people interested in the topic of plagiarism and the sources they can use to define, deter, prevent, detect, and educate people about plagiarism.

When one begins a search on the topic of plagiarism, one is confronted with an extraordinarily large number of resources. These include books, magazine and journal articles, products to detect and prevent plagiarism, plagiarism and antiplagiarism software, and network and cable television programs. This chapter will highlight resources from all of these categories that have not already been discussed in previous chapters. The sources listed provide further reading and examination for some of the topics discussed in the book.

The chapter begins with general resources on plagiarism in the form of books, periodical articles, workshops, seminars, and conferences. There are thousands of books and periodical articles on the issues of plagiarism and cheating among students discussed from many angles. Educators who are concerned about the plagiarism issue and academic integrity have approached the problem from various sides. There are resources targeted at students, teaching faculty, and administrators in general. The perennial nature of the plagiarism problem has also contributed to the difficulty of having a single comprehensive definition of plagiarism that is understood by all students without exception. The largest section of this chapter is the one that discusses websites aimed at defining, avoiding, deterring, and detecting plagiarism. Also included are studies and reports as well as specific sites for the humanities, social sciences, and sciences, and engineering. The final section discusses video sources ranging from YouTube videos to videocassettes.

Selected Books on Plagiarism and Cyber-Plagiarism

Bowman, Vibiana. 2004. *The Plagiarism Plague: A Resource Guide and CD-ROM Tutorial for Educators and Librarians*. New York: Neal-Schuman.

This is a compilation of book chapters dealing with various topics related to plagiarism, what it is, and ideas for combating it. The book is divided into three parts dealing with understanding the plagiarism problem and its causes and challenges, techniques for teaching citations, principles of academic honesty, and an annotated bibliography of professional resources and a CD-ROM tutorial for quick web access to links.

Harris, Robert A., and Vic Lockman. 2001. *The Plagiarism Handbook: Strategies for Preventing, Detecting, and Dealing with Plagiarism*. Los Angeles: Pyrczak.

The authors of this book tackle the causes of plagiarism and cheating and the many types of plagiarism that are possible. They offer materials and suggestions to help students deal with the issues related to plagiarism prevention and detection and the means of handling policy issues at the institutional and administrative levels. They provide sample definitions, policies, quizzes, activities, and handouts. They use cartoons to illustrate their points, make available about 24 reproducible handouts that can be used for teaching and discussion, and present faculty with practical ways to address plagiarism and cheating. The book is well organized, and the material is treated in a way that makes it easy to understand and apply the strategies Harris and Lockman suggest.

Haviland, Carol Peterson. 2009. *Who Owns This Text? Plagiarism, Authorship, and Disciplinary Cultures*. Logan: Utah State University Press.

The book focuses on ownership of text and collaboration. The author discusses "scholarly practice relating to intellectual property, plagiarism, and authorship" among various disciplines.

Lathrop, Ann, and Kathleen E. Foss. 2000. *Student Cheating and Plagiarism in the Internet Era: A Wake-Up Call for Educators and Parents.* Englewood, CO: LibrariesUnlimited.

Lathrop and Foss's book "is organized as a practical guide for educators and parents who want to reduce cheating and plagiarizing." The book includes "strategies to counter both high-tech and more traditional and 'low-tech' cheating and plagiarism in K–12 schools." The book also tackles electronic plagiarism, how parents can be "vigilant, informed, and involved," and stresses integrity, ethics, and character education among students. There are also some definitions of plagiarism in the book. The authors present tools for writing without plagiarizing, alternatives to writing assignments, and online sites for reports and research papers. It has references to print and online resources and a collection of articles at the end of the chapters to promote further discussion of the issues. The topics are well laid out, and the authors provide a thorough treatment of the issues.

Markman, Roberta H., Peter T. Markman, and Marie L. Waddell. 2001. *10 Steps in Writing the Research Paper,* 6th ed. Hauppauge, NY: Barron's.

The authors describe their book as a "succinct, easy-to-follow guide [that] gives students clear directions for writing papers in virtually all academic subjects." The authors also "describe how to determine a subject, formulate and outline a provisional thesis, prepare a bibliography, take notes from sources, write a draft, and then revise and edit the paper, bringing it to its final form. Added advice includes avoiding plagiarism and making the most of library resources."

Pattison, Tania, Trent University, and Academic Skills Centre. 2002. *Avoiding Plagiarism: A Guide for ESL Students.* Peterborough, Ont.: Academic Skills Centre, Trent University.

In this introduction to the subject of plagiarism, the author explains the differences between deliberate or intentional plagiarism and unintentional, accidental, or plain sloppy research. She provides strategies to show students how to do research and to learn proper paraphrasing and summarization. She also includes strategies for proper documentation using examples from the APA style manual.

Posner, Richard A. 2007. *The Little Book of Plagiarism.* New York: Pantheon Books.

The author defines plagiarism and presents side-by-side excerpts comparing original texts with plagiarized texts. He discusses copyright infringement, plagiarism, the intent to plagiarize, and some of the legal consequences of plagiarism-related cases.

Sutherland-Smith, Wendy. 2008. *Plagiarism, the Internet, and Student Learning: Improving Academic Integrity.* New York: Routledge.

This book tackles the moral and ethical aspects of plagiarism and student learning. Focus is on plagiarism and Internet plagiarism. The book is written for higher education educators, managers, and policymakers.

Selected Articles on Plagiarism and Cyber-Plagiarism

Numerous articles have been written on plagiarism and plagiarism-related topics. The articles selected and discussed here will give the reader a better and clearer understanding of what plagiarism is and what strategies can be used to prevent, detect, and deter plagiarism and to teach students not to plagiarize. This is only a selected list from the vast number of articles available on plagiarism.

Auer, Nicole J., and Ellen M. Krupar. 2001. "Mouse Click Plagiarism: The Role of Technology in Plagiarism and the Librarian's Role in Combating It." *Library Trends* 49, no. 3: 415.

The authors present a historical perspective on plagiarism and show how "views on plagiarism have changed over time," and they discuss how the Internet has contributed to the increase in plagiarism. They list different types of plagiarism, "plagiarism by copying, by paraphrasing, and by the theft of an idea." They discuss student and faculty attitudes about plagiarism and examine the role that librarians can play in tackling the plagiarism problem. The authors suggest that librarians should be informed and make faculty aware of resources that can help tackle the issues related to plagiarism.

Boehm, Pamela J., Madeline Justice, and Sandy Weeks. 2009. "Promoting Academic Integrity in Higher Education." *Community College Enterprise* 15, no. 1: 45–61.

This study identifies "best practice initiatives that contribute to academic integrity and reduce dishonesty in academic education." These initiatives include faculty training, effective classroom management strategies, clear definitions and examples of cheating, and placing an "XF" on official transcripts for students found cheating.

Breen, Lauren, and Margaret Maassen. 2005. "Reducing the Incidence of Plagiarism in an Undergraduate Course: The Role of Education." *Issues in Educational Research* 15, no.1: 1–16.

The article investigates students' perceptions of plagiarism and tries to develop learning materials to educate students about avoiding plagiarism.

Buranen, Lisa. 2009. "A Safe Place: The Role of Librarians and Writing Centers in Addressing Citation Practices and Plagiarism." *Knowledge Quest* 37, no. 3: 24–33.

The article discusses ways to help students learn how to incorporate sources into documents and cite properly. It also discusses what textual practice is and what it is not.

Chao, Chai-An, William J. Wilhelm, and Brian D. Neureuther. 2009. "A Study of Electronic Detection and Pedagogical Approaches for Reducing Plagiarism." *Delta Pi Epsilon Journal* 51, no. 1: 31–42.

This study discusses teaching students how not to plagiarize with a look at Turnitin.com. It discusses why students plagiarize and aims to teach students about proper quotation, citation, and paraphrasing techniques.

"Combating Plagiarism." 2003. *CQ Researcher* 13, no. 32 (September 19): 773–796.

CQ Researcher presents a comprehensive overview of plagiarism in its September 19, 2003, issue, "Combating Plagiarism," including a thorough treatment of plagiarism and plagiarism-related issues. Topics include a general overview, the pros and cons of plagiarism, a chronology of plagiarism, bibliographies to enable further research, and a list of contacts.

Gardiner, Steve. 2001. "Cyber Cheating: A New Twist on an Old Problem." *Phi Delta Kappan* 83, no. 2 (October): 172–174.

The growing problem of cybercheating is discussed in this article, and the author shows how he uses search engines on the web to track down sources that his students had copied word for word. He used engines such as AltaVista, Google, Yahoo, Netcrawler, and, more recently, Dogpile. Gardiner also provides a list of term paper sites to make faculty aware of some of the places where their students are getting their "research" papers. He also recognizes how the Internet can be a good tool for research if used properly.

Howard, Rebecca Moore. 2007. "Understanding Internet Plagiarism." *Computers and Composition* 24, no. 1: 3–15.

The author focuses on plagiarism, new media, the Internet, intertextuality, and plagiarism detecting services. She stresses the importance of revised institutional plagiarism policies.

Hulsart, Robyn, and Vikkie McCarthy. 2009. "Educators' Role in Promoting Academic Integrity." *Academy of Educational Leadership Journal* 13, no. 4: 49–69.

This article discusses the important role of ethics in the classroom and the role faculty has to play in taking the lead to create a climate of academic integrity in the classroom.

Jackson, Pamela A. 2006. "Plagiarism Instruction Online: Assessing Undergraduate Students' Ability to Avoid Plagiarism." *College and Research Libraries* 67, no. 2: 418–428.

This is a study of 2,829 students to assess their understanding of plagiarism and their learning through the use of an interactive web-based tutorial administered to them. The author also presents pre- and posttest results and improvements that the students made.

Klesser, Kate. 2003. "Helping High School Students Understand Academic Integrity." *English Journal* 92, no. 6 (July): 57–66.

The author recommends that teachers educate high school students about academic integrity before they make the transition to college. She suggests that professors in academic institutions should be invited to discuss with high school students what academic integrity is and why it is important to be fully knowledgeable about what academic integrity is and is not.

Lewis, Norman P. 2008. "Plagiarism Antecedents and Situational Influences." *Journalism and Mass Communication Quarterly* 85, no. 2: 353–370.

Lewis focuses on plagiarism in professional journalism over a ten-year period. The study includes interviews with some of the people accused of plagiarism and some of the reasons or excuses people use when they are accused of plagiarism.

McCabe, Donald. 2009. "Academic Dishonesty in Nursing Schools: An Empirical Investigation." *Journal of Nursing Education* 48, no. 11 (November): 614.

The author examines academic dishonesty in the field of nursing from students from 12 schools in the United States in the areas of plagiarism and cheating on tests.

Minkel, Walter. 2002. "Web of Deceit." *School Library Journal* 48, no. 4: 50.

This article highlights the problem of plagiarism in high schools. Christine Pelton, a high school teacher, was embroiled in a controversy when she flunked 28 of her sophomore students for cheating. She was forced to give up her position when her community attacked her actions against the students and when she failed to get the support of the school principal and the town sheriff. The article recommends discussing academic integrity with students in high school to help them learn how to define it and recognize it and how to cite and otherwise properly credit other people's work.

Owens, Trevor. 2001. "Learning with Technology: Plagiarism and the Internet: Turning the Tables." *English Journal* 90, no.4 (March): 101–104.

Owens discusses how the Internet as a technological tool can be used to combat plagiarism. He shows how one can select a document and use some of the Internet detection resources to tell whether that particular document has been plagiarized. He uses examples from texts taken from Martin Luther King's books and speeches.

Pincus, Holly Seirup, and Liora Pedhazur Schmelkin. 2003. "Faculty Perceptions of Academic Dishonesty: A Multidimensional Scaling Analysis." *Journal of Higher Education* 74, no. 2 (March/April): 196–209.

This article analyzes what faculty think about academic dishonesty (cheating and plagiarism). The authors discuss what plagiarism encompasses based on research they conducted. Their results indicate that "faculty perceives academically dishonest behavior in two dimensions: seriousness and papers versus Exams." The authors "recommend that policies be made more explicit as to differential sanctions."

Power, Lori G. 2009. "University Students' Perceptions of Plagiarism." *Journal of Higher Education* 80, no. 6 (November/December): 643–662.

This study explores freshman and sophmore students' perceptions and understanding of plagiarism. The author used interviews and focus group sessions.

Pricer, Wayne F. 2009. "At Issue: Academic Integrity, an Annotated Bibliography." *Community College Enterprise* 15, no. 1: 63–81.

The bibliography addresses a range of topics, including academic integrity, copyright, violating copyright, consequences of violating plagiarism and copyright fair use, proper documentation, and identifying plagiarized material.

Simmonds, Patience L. 2003. "Plagiarism and Cyber-Plagiarism." *College and Research Libraries News* 64, no. 6 (June): 385–389.

This article is a selected guide to plagiarism resources on the web. Created by Patience L. Simmonds, it offers a definition and statements on plagiarism and links to plagiarism detection and prevention sites, academic integrity sites and honor codes, and sites that sell term papers.

Willis, Dottie J. 2001. "High Tech Cheating: Plagiarism and the Internet." *Kentucky Libraries* 65, no. 4 (Fall): 28–30.

The author examines how technology has "dramatically changed the teaching and learning process in twenty-first century classrooms." She defines plagiarism and shows how flagrant plagiarism is in American society.

Yeo, Shelley. 2007. "First-Year University Science and Engineering Students' Understanding of Plagiarism." *Higher Education Research & Development* 26, no. 2 (June): 199–216.

This study of first-year science and engineering students and their understanding of plagiarism explores the issues of academic integrity, academic misconduct, and plagiarism. The study aims to find out what the students understand about the seriousness and consequences of plagiarism and academic misconduct.

Young, Jeffrey R. 2001. "The Cat-and-Mouse Game of Plagiarism Detection." *Chronicle of Higher Education* 47, no. 43: A26–A27.

This article describes how colleges and universities provide professors with web detection tools to tackle the problems of plagiarism and how professors should be vigilant.

Selected Websites on Plagiarism

Defining Plagiarism

Indiana University Bloomington Writing Tutorial Services. "Plagiarism: What It Is and How to Recognize and Avoid It." www.indiana.edu/~wts/pamphlets/plagiarism.html.

The guidelines in this pamphlet are taken from the *Student Code of Rights, Responsibilities, and Ethics Handbook* of the Writing Resource's pages of the Writing Tutorial Services at Indiana University, Bloomington. It teaches students the differences between acceptable and unacceptable paraphrasing, what is or is not common knowledge, and different strategies for avoiding plagiarism.

Plagiarism: What It Is and How to Avoid It. Montgomery College, Rockville, Maryland. www.montgomerycollege.edu/library/plagiarismintro.htm.

This site provides a tutorial that discusses what plagiarism is and how students can avoid it. It starts by defining plagiarism and then provides examples of what constitutes plagiarism and shows how and what sources should be cited. It gives examples of proper and improper paraphrasing and discusses plagiarism within the context of the Montgomery College Student Code of Conduct. It provides an evaluation and quiz section that, when completed and submitted, earns the student an extra credit.

What Is Plagiarism? Georgetown University, Washington, DC. www.georgetown .edu/honor/plagiarism.html.

This is a section of the Georgetown University Honor Code for students and crafted by the Honor Council. Nine questions related to plagiarism and cheating are discussed, and sample statements often given by student who plagiarize are provided, for example, "in my country/high school, using someone else's work is a sign of respect" and "I don't have time to do it right."

What Is Plagiarism? History News Network. hnn.us/articles/514.html.

The History News Network staff posted three definitions of plagiarism provided by the American Historical Association, the Modern Language Association, and the American Psychological Association. One of the definitions states that "plagiarism includes more subtle and perhaps more pernicious abuses than simply expropriating the exact wording of another author without attribution." The site encourages all scholars, especially students of history, to resist plagiarism.

What Is Plagiarism at Indiana University? Recognizing Plagiarism. Indiana University, Bloomington. education.indiana.edu/~frick/plagiarism/index2.html.

This tutorial site was developed by the Indiana University School of Education's Instructional Systems Technology (IST) Department. The tutorial defines what plagiarism is for the students, provides an overview of what it is and how to recognize it, and presents two types of text examples, one original and the other edited to show signs of possible plagiarism. After practicing the examples, the students can take a test on their knowledge of what plagiarism is and how they can recognize it and avoid it. Students are allowed to retake the tests until they get the required score and are given a confirmation certificate. Students are, however, not given a certificate until they score 100 percent on the tests.

Avoiding Plagiarism

Avoiding Plagiarism. Glendale Community College, Glendale, California. www .glendale.edu/library/research/plagiarism.html.

This site defines plagiarism for the students to help them recognize what it is and how to avoid it. It provides a list of relevant terms that students should know as well as information on what and how to quote, how to paraphrase, what to cite, when to cite, and how to cite.

Avoiding Plagiarism: Mastering the Art of Scholarship. University of California, Davis. sja.ucdavis.edu/files/plagiarism-001.html.

This handout from Student Judicial Affairs provides guidelines for avoiding plagiarism within the UC Davis code of academic conduct and presents examples of ethical scholarship. It also provides examples of proper citation of sources. Different versions of documents are presented to show instances of plagiarism, proper citation, and paraphrasing. The handout is also available in PDF format.

Documentation Guidelines. Duke University, Durham, North Carolina. www .lib.duke.edu/libguide/citing.htm and library.duke.edu/research/plagiarism.

Duke University Libraries has guidelines for citing sources and avoiding plagiarism. They include sections on citing sources in papers and on how to assemble a list of works cited in a paper. The purpose of these sites is to educate students about plagiarism and the consequences of plagiarism and to give them strategies for avoiding it. They allow students to use the citation style they want to and present them with an example of how to cite their sources. They also make available the Duke University honor code, which addresses plagiarism and other academic misconducts and how they are dealt with.

How to Avoid Plagiarism. Northwestern University, Evanston, Illinois. www .northwestern.edu/uacc/plagiar.html.

Northwestern University's academic integrity policies apply to both undergraduate and graduate research. This site provide strategies for students to avoid plagiarism.

What Is Plagiarism? Avoiding Plagiarism. Penn State. tlt.its.psu.edu/suggestions/cyberplag/cyberplagexamples.html.

Aspects of plagiarism and cyber-plagiarism are discussed at this Penn State site. The site provides examples of wholesale copying, cutting and pasting, inappropriate paraphrasing, when to cite, and sample citation guidelines to help students cite their work. Links to other relevant sites that provide similar information on plagiarism are provided.

WPA Statement on Avoiding Plagiarism: Best Practices. Council of Writing Program Administrators. www.wpacouncil.org/positions/WPAplagiarism.pdf.

This statement defines what plagiarism is according to the Council of Writing Program Administrators and outlines strategies for avoiding plagiarism. It has sections devoted to students, administrators, and teaching faculty who are involving with writing.

Deterring and Detecting Plagiarism

General Sites

Deterring Plagiarism: Some Strategies. University of Toronto. www.writing .utoronto.ca/faculty/deterring-plagiarism.

Margaret Proctor, Coordinator, and Writing Support at the University of Toronto created this site. It presents practical ways to deter plagiarism by "making assignments an integral part of the course, demonstrating the instructors' expectation for the course, and making the assignment a process rather than a onetime exercise." The site has available resources and examples for students, instructional resources for students, advice and resources for faculty, and advice and examples from other universities.

Plagiarism and Anti-Plagiarism. Rutgers University. newark.rutgers.edu/ ~ehrlich/plagiarism598.html.

This is a discussion of what plagiarism is and how to avoid it. Suggestions include becoming familiar with "the details of the plagiarism policies of your university, college, department, course, and assignment." Students are also encouraged to know the penalties for plagiarism and the ins and outs of plagiarism as they relate to computers, the Internet, and copyright laws. The site also lists useful webpages for detecting and deterring plagiarism.

Rutgers University Plagiarism Module. www.scc.rutgers.edu/douglass/sal/ plagiarism/intro.html.

Rutgers University's library skill plagiarism module is a mini-play that teaches students about proper citation, cheating, plagiarism, etc.

Plagiarism Detection Programs and Software

CCL Software Ltd. www.cflsoftware.com.

CCL Software "provides consultancy services and creates programs for automated Document Comparison. We also undertake research and development into what makes us recognize similarity between sentences, and how that human facility can be translated into computer programs." Under the umbrella of this company are products and services such as CopyCatch Gold, which "is primarily aimed at collusion detection, but can be used anywhere there is a requirement to check on the independent production of documents. It can handle large class sizes very quickly and provides immediate feedback, making it suitable for classroom or one-to-one use."

DupliChecker. www.duplichecker.com/preventingplagiarism.asp.

DupliChecker is a free online plagiarism tool to detect and prevent plagiarism.

EVE 2 (Essay Verification Engine). www.canexus.com/eve.

The creators of EVE 2 describe it as "a very powerful tool that allows professors and teachers at all levels of the education system to determine if students have plagiarized material from the World Wide Web. EVE 2 accepts essays in plain text, Microsoft Word, or Corel Word Perfect format and returns links to web pages from which a student may have plagiarized. EVE 2 has been developed to be powerful enough to find plagiarized material while not overwhelming the professor with false links." EVE 2 provides a full report "on each paper that contained plagiarism, including the percent of the essay plagiarized, and an annotated copy of the paper showing all plagiarism highlighted in red." Each professor who wishes to use EVE 2 must purchase a one-time license of $29.99 for all essays submitted in his or her class. The license is not transferable from one professor to another.

Glatt Plagiarism Services. www.plagiarism.com.
Glatt Plagiarism provides services to "help deter plagiarism and encourage academic honesty." Glatt offers three types of plagiarism services: Glatt Plagiarism Teaching Program (GPTeach), a tutorial that teaches students what plagiarism is, shows them how to avoid it, and acts as a self-detection tool with a practice section on proper paraphrasing and proper citation; Glatt Plagiarism Screening Program, a plagiarism detection procedure for teaching faculty; and Glatt Plagiarism Self-Detection Program, "a screening program to help deter inadvertent instances of plagiarism."

iThenticate. iThenticate.com.
iThenticate is a new service offered by iParadigms.com. It is intended for "publishers, corporations, law firms, and others" to check sources, prevent plagiarism, and protect their own intellectual property. iThenticate searches only the Internet.

JPlag. www.ipd.uni-karlsruhe.de/jplag.
This system "finds similarities among multiple sets of source code files" and "can detect software plagiarism." Its creator also claims that "JPlag does not merely compare bytes of text, but is aware of programming language syntax and program structure and hence is robust against many kinds of attempts to disguise similarities between plagiarized files. JPlag currently supports Java, C, C++, Scheme, and natural language text." Use of JPlag is free, but users must obtain an account by sending an e-mail to jplag@ira.uka.de and stating the purpose for which they are going to use it.

Moss (A Measure of Software Similarity). theory.stanford.edu/~aiken/moss.
This service is a tool that detects plagiarism in programming language. Moss is "an automatic system for determining the similarity of C, C++, Java, Pascal, Ada, ML, Lisp, or Scheme programs." Currently Moss is a free Internet service and is available to anyone who wishes to use it for educational purpose. To get a Moss account one has to send an e-mail to moss@moss.cs.berkeley.edu. Commercial use of the program is forbidden.

MyDropBox. www.mydropbox.com.

MyDropBox.com identifies itself as the provider of "the world's leading technology to detect and prevent cases of Internet plagiarism." It is geared toward administrators, faculty, and students. Its "goal is to use technology to help reduce academic dishonesty and keep your classroom a level playing field for all students." It provides a 30-day free trial pilot to all academic institutions. MyDropBox.com checks a student-submitted document against every possible source on the Internet" and does an "analysis of published works in password-protected electronic databases." It also checks their customers' own database of submitted papers to prevent "peer-to-peer cheating." The company offers both individual and institutional licenses for purchase.

Plagiarism Checker. www.plagiarismchecker.com.

Plagiarism Checker was created in 2005. It allows teachers and writers to type or cut and paste in phrases to check for instances of plagiarism. The student can send hard copies or e-mail copies of papers to their teachers to be scanned or downloaded to Plagiarism Checker.

Turnitin. www.Turnitin.com

iParadigms is the parent company behind which Turnitin.com operates. Other products under iParadigms LLC include Plagiarism.org. Turnitin plagiarism detection service claims to be "the leader in textual intellectual property protection and a pioneer of web-based services for collaborative, online educational support" and "the world's leading online plagiarism prevention resource." Turnitin.com also claims that it "has been helping millions of faculty and students in over 50 countries to improve writing and research skills, encourage collaborative online learning, ensure originality of student work, and save instructors' time—all at a very affordable price." Turnitin "checks student papers for originality by comparing them against over 100 million previously submitted student papers PLUS over 11 billion pages of web content and articles from more than 80,000 subscription-based journals and periodicals."

Products from Turnitin.com include a preventive tool that identifies unoriginal documents by students. Turnitin.com provides a one-month free trial to prospective users and individual licenses to instructors and staff from departments and schools. The cost of Turnitin.com is determined by school or institution type, the license plan chosen, and the total enrollment of the school.

Using Search Engines for Plagiarism Detection

A few search engines on the Internet are capable of detecting Internet plagiarism. Sometimes, all you have to do is take a few of the words from the text you think has been plagiarized and follow the instructions the particular search engine gives for detecting plagiarism. Here are a few of the engines that can be used effectively to detect plagiarism.

- Ask.com
  www.ask.com/web?q=plagiarism

- Bing.com
  www.bing.com/search?q=plagiarism
- Dogpile.com
  www.dogpile.com
  For a search in Dogpile, enclose your search in quotation marks. Dogpile will search for phrases by using various search engines, including Google.
- Google.com
  www.google.com
  The advanced search feature in Google can be used to determine if a section of a document has been plagiarized. If you enclose ten or fewer words in quotation marks and search in Google, the search engine should come up with similar phrases in documents on the web. Google will search for stop words to find similarities.
- Google Directory on Plagiarism
  directory.google.com/Top/Reference/Education/Educators/Academic_Dishonesty/Plagiarism
- Internet Essay Exposer
  www.mattclare.ca/essay
  To search for possible plagiarism in an essay using Internet Essay Exposer, select "Web Search" and insert one or two sentences between the quotation marks provided. This service checks about ten search engines, and users can select which search engines they prefer.
- Yahoo.com
  search.yahoo.com/bin/search?p=plagiarism

Studies and Reports about Plagiarism

Academic Misconduct: Guide for Instructors, Dean of Students Office, University of Wisconsin–Madison. students.wisc.edu/saja/misconduct/facstaff.html.

This site includes University of Wisconsin System (UWS) 14, the chapter in the UW System Administrative Code regulating academic misconduct. The document includes tips on preventing academic misconduct, defines academic misconduct, and describes the investigation process, penalties and procedures, and the students' right to a hearing. It also provides a sample procedure for instructors to follow if they suspect that a student has committed academic misconduct.

How the Ambrose Story Developed. History News Network. historynewsnetwork.org/articles/article.html?id=504.

The History News Network (HNN) provides a thorough examination of the Stephen E. Ambrose plagiarism controversy. It examines various accounts of the controversy from many news reports and touches on the difference between sloppiness in research and deliberate copying of other authors' work. The HNN also has links to other sites that discuss the Ambrose controversy.

Pearson, Gretchen. 2006. Electronic Plagiarism Seminar. Syracuse, New York: Noreen Reale Falcone Library, Le Moyne College. web.lemoyne.edu/~pearson/plagiarism/detection_sites.htm.

This is a comprehensive and well-organized site with a general bibliography on plagiarism and another bibliography on scientific misconduct. It provides definitions of plagiarism, tips on detecting and preventing plagiarism. and guides for educators and students. The site stays current on reports from various news organizations about plagiarism cases. Other sections present general strategies for preventing plagiarism, ethics and honor codes, and writing strategies to help prevent plagiarism.

Plagiarism. www.web-miner.com/plagiarism.

Sharon Stoerger is a librarian at the University of Illinois at Urbana-Champaign, and she prepared this comprehensive document. She examines selected articles relating to copyright and intellectual freedom targeted to instructors and students. She also discusses and provides links to topics such as plagiarism cases, plagiarism detection tools, term paper sites, and current articles on plagiarism cases in the news.

Plagiarism in Colleges in USA. www.rbs2.com/plag.htm.

This long and very comprehensive document was prepared in 2000 by Ronald B. Standler, who is an attorney and a consultant. He discusses plagiarism by students and faculty and legal cases involving plagiarism. Topics include plagiarism law, trademark law, copyright law, statutes, and court cases involving the sale of term papers. He has practical ideas about how faculty can detect plagiarism. He provides information on actual cases involving plagiarism in colleges, cases against commercial institutions, and legal actions that have been taken against people who report plagiarism. He also provides information on cases where degrees were revoked after evidence of plagiarism or academic misconduct was revealed after students had graduated.

Plagiarism in the Humanities and Social Sciences

Academic Fraud & Plagiarism. Faculty of Social Sciences, Undergraduate Studies, University of Ottawa. www.socialsciences.uottawa.ca/eng/ugrad_academic_fraud.asp.

This website contains information on plagiarism and how to avoid it and its consequences. It is targeted toward undergraduates in the social sciences and has links to documents on academic integrity and intellectual property. It includes the paper submission form (Personal Ethics Agreement Concerning University Assignments) that students have to sign.

Plagiarism: A Guide for Law Lecturers. www.ukcle.ac.uk/resources/trns/plagiarism/index.html.

This guide is available at the U.K. Centre for Legal Education and includes detailed information on defining plagiarism, preventing plagiarism, detecting plagiarism paraphrasing, and unintentional and intentional plagiarism. It provides a list of questions as to who plagiarizes and why, a guide for first-year students, a discussion of preventing plagiarism at school/department and institutional levels, and a description of the penalties for plagiarism.

Plagiarism Is Cheating. Department of English and Modern Languages, Purdue University North Central, Westville, Indiana. www.pnc.edu/engl/plagiarism.html.

This website provides information about what constitutes plagiarism and tips on avoiding plagiarism. The section "Public Domain Information versus Controversial or Specialized Information" distinguishes between information that needs a citation and information that does not.

Plagiarism Resources. College of Humanities, San Francisco State University. www.sfsu.edu/~collhum/?q=node/851.

This humanities website contains definitions of different kinds of plagiarism, reasons why students plagiarize, ways of preventing plagiarism, and procedures for dealing with plagiarism issues when they occur.

Understand Plagiarism and Avoid It. College of Arts and Sciences, Lawrence Technological University, Southfield, Michigan. www.ltu.edu/arts_sciences/humanities_ss_comm/plagiarism.asp.

This website has information on what constitutes plagiarism and ways to avoid it. It discusses degrees of plagiarism, including word-for-word plagiarism, patchwork plagiarism, and unacknowledged paraphrase. It includes side-by-side examples of original text and plagiarized work for comparison and analysis.

Plagiarism in the Sciences and Engineering

ACS Citation Examples and Plagiarism. Washington University Libraries, St. Louis. library.wustl.edu/subjects/chemistry/acscitation.htm.

This page provides examples of the American Chemical Society's citation style, defines plagiarism, and offers guidelines for avoiding plagiarism.

Authorship and Plagiarism in Science: A Bibliography of Primary and Secondary Sources. Compiled by Rebecca Howard, The Writing Program, Syracuse University, New York. wrt-howard.syr.edu/Bibs/PlagScience.htm.

This useful bibliography of primary and secondary sources on plagiarism in science was last updated in June 2009.

Introduction to the Guidelines for Handling Plagiarism Complaints. IEEE. www.ieee.org/web/publications/rights/Plagiarism_Guidelines_Intro.html.

This page on the IEEE website provides a definition of plagiarism and the IEEE guidelines for handling plagiarism complaints. It describes four levels of misconduct and includes a plagiarism FAQs section.

Plagiarism. Technical Communication in Civil Engineering. CE 333T: Engineering Communication. University of Texas, Austin. www.ce.utexas.edu/prof/hart/333t/plagiarism.cfm.

This is a resource for an engineering class at the University of Texas at Austin that provides a definition of plagiarism as well as guidelines to avoiding plagiarism. It discusses accountability and includes a link to the Student Judicial Services' Plagiarism page.

Plagiarism: Definitions, Examples and Penalties. Department of Chemistry, University of Toronto. www.chem.utoronto.ca/undergrad/plagiarism.php.

The department lays out for the student what plagiarism is and presents six illustrative examples: Case 1: Submitting Someone Else's Work; Case 2: Rewording a Sentence (Paraphrasing); 3: Direct Copying from Original Sources; Case 4: Direct Copying from Original Sources, but with Footnotes; Case 5: Borrowing Organization; Case 6: Failing to Reference/Footnote Source Material.

Student Plagiarism in an Online World. www.prism-magazine.org/december/html/student_plagiarism_in_an_onlin.htm.

This site, which is sponsored by the Society for Engineering Education, features resources and strategies to help detect plagiarism among students.

Resources on Self-Plagiarism

Bretag, Tracey, and Saadia Mahmud. 2009. "Self-Plagiarism or Appropriate Textual Re-use?" *Journal of Academic Ethics* 7, no. 3 (September): 193–205.

The authors discuss self-plagiarism, appropriateness of textual reuse, text recycling and self-copying, multiple submissions, and ethics.

Gibson, J. Paul. 2009. "Software Reuse and Plagiarism: A Code of Practice." *ACM SIGCSE Bulletin* 41, no. 3 (September): 55–59.

This article discusses plagiarism, software reuse, ethics, and testing student projects.

Roig, M. 2006. "Avoiding Plagiarism, Self-Plagiarism, and Other Questionable Writing Practices: A Guide to Ethical Writing." Available: facpub.stjohns .edu/~roigm/plagiarism/Index.html (accessed December 8, 2009).

Roig focuses on avoiding plagiarism and self-plagiarism and on ethical issues in professional and scientific writing. He states that "the ethical professional is expected to operate at the highest levels of scientific integrity and, therefore, must avoid all forms of writing that could be conceptualized as plagiarism." The article also provides exercises to distinguish between paraphrasing and plagiarism.

Scanlon, P. 2007. "Song from Myself: An Anatomy of Self-Plagiarism. Plagiary: Cross-Disciplinary Studies in Plagiarism, Fabrication, and Falsification." *Journal of Academic Ethics* 2: 57–66.

Scanlon addresses the issue of self-plagiarism across disciplines, research fabrication, and falsification.

SPLaT. University of Arizona, Tucson. splat.cs.arizona.edu.

This is a tool for detecting self-plagiarism. It allows an author to check current work against previous work.

Selected Audiovisual Resources

Copyright Perspectives: No, You Stole It. www.youtube.com/watch?v=TzV8GAtK0A0.

This video was created at Penn State and is "part of a joint effort between the College of Communications, Information Technology Services, Schreyer Honors College, Student Affairs, and University Libraries." It addresses "intellectual property issues in a student-centered way" and presents "some realistic alternatives that will encourage students to act in a responsible manner." The video is available on YouTube and easily accessible to students.

Crook, Bob, Bruce Deck, Dallas TeleLearning, and PBS Adult Learning Service. 2003. *Critical Challenges in Distance Education: Cheating and Plagiarism Using the Internet.* Videocassette, c. 90 minutes.

This video from the teleconference "Critical Challenges in Distance Education: Cheating and Plagiarism Using the Internet," which took place April 3, 2003, is a presentation of the PBS Adult Learning Service. It is about cheating and plagiarism, the role of the Internet in education, and intellectual property. The video recommends that faculty involve themselves in all aspects of the student writing process and offers solutions for cheating and plagiarism by showing the use of strategies such as teaching students to cite sources properly. It also encourages teaching faculty to be creative about assignments so that they are not predictable.

Egan, Clifton, Robert J. Rutland Center for Ethics, and Clemson University. 2002. *Academic Integrity Initiative Ethics Vignettes.* Videocassette, 21 minutes, 17 seconds.

This video was produced by the Robert J. Rutland Center for Ethics at Clemson University in South Carolina with the participation of Director Clifton Egan. It presents case studies involving student ethics, college student cheating, dealing with plagiarism, other types of academic dishonesty, and moral and ethical aspects in higher education. The viewer is presented with six vignettes in the university setting: "Cheating 101," "The Café," "The Lab Report," "The Paper," "Dream," and "Professor." A companion pamphlet contains discussion questions.

How to Avoid Plagiarism. library.camden.rutgers.edu/EducationalModule/Plagiarism.

This three-part suite of animated videos was created by the Reference Department of the Paul Robeson Library, Rutgers University, Camden, NJ. Included are "What Is Plagiarism?" "Plagiarism: Real Life Examples," and an interactive game show quiz, "The Cite Is Right."

Naphin, Deirdre, Morley Safer, Lou Bloomfield, CBS Video, CBS News Archives, and CBS Worldwide. 2002. *Cheaters*. Videocassette, 13 minutes.

This short video was a segment of the *CBS 60 Minutes* television program that originally aired November 10, 2002. CBS reporter Morley Safer discusses the topic of cheating in colleges and universities. His interviews feature Lou Bloomfield, a physics professor from the University of Virginia, and Donald L. McCabe, founder of the Center for Academic Integrity. The video examines why students cheat. It also touches on the sale of research papers on the web and on how plagiarism detection software can detect plagiarism in student papers.

Rather, Dan, Rob Klug, Barry Leibowitz, and CBS News. 2001. *Truth and Consequences*. Videocassette, c. 43 minutes.

This video was first broadcast as an episode of the television program *48 Hours*. Dan Rather is the host, with parts of the segment being presented by Rob Klug and Barry Leibowitz. The topic is cheating and plagiarism in the United States.

Rather, Dan, Erin Moriarty, B. Lagattuta, Steve Hartman, Harold Dow, Rob Klug, Barry Leibowitz, and CBS News. 2002. *Truth and Consequences*. Videocassette, 44 minutes.

This is an in-depth look at cheating, honesty, and plagiarism in education. It asks people whether they would cheat and under what circumstances who they would cheat. This video is part of the CBS *48 Hours* television program that was broadcast May 31, 2002. Other correspondents in the video include Erin Morriaty, Bill Lagattuta, Steve Hartman, and Harold Dow.

Rehm, Diane, WAMU-FM (radio station in Washington, DC), and American University, Washington, DC. 2002. *Plagiarism*. Sound cassette, 59 minutes.

Plagiarism is a sound recording by Diane Rehm for the Diane Rehm Show. The topic is plagiarism in the United States and cheating among high school and college students. Rehm leads a discussion with three panelists, Donald L. McCabe, James Sandefur, and Patricia Harned, about why students plagiarize, the relationship between the Internet and plagiarism, and the use of plagiarism detection software. The roles and responsibilities of both students and faculty as well as some penalties for plagiarism are also covered. The panel also discusses high-profile cases of plagiarism involving professional writers like Stephen Ambrose. Listeners were invited to phone in their questions on plagiarism.

Sanders, Bob Ray, Hope Burwell, William L. Kibler, Jessica A. Kier, LeCroy Center for Educational Telecommunication, Dallas County Community College District, and PBS Adult Learning Satellite Service. 2003. *Cheating and Plagiarism Using the Internet*. One videocassette, 90 minutes.

This video of a teleconference on cheating in education and cheating and plagiarism on the Internet was taped on April 3, 2003. It examines what constitutes cheating and plagiarism. It touches on the importance of honor codes and on the role faculty can play in requiring students to refrain from committing plagiarism, teaching them about plagiarism, and teaching them about proper ethical behavior. It presents effective strategies for detecting plagiarism and shows what methods can be used once plagiarism has been detected. Distinctions are made between what plagiarism and cheating are and what they are not. Interested persons can also listen to the audio version of the program at www.wamu.org/dr/shows/drarc_020218.html.

Stop, Thief! Avoiding Plagiarism by Paraphrasing. 2008. www.youtube.com/watch?v=9z3EHIoa9HI.
This video was created in 2008 and is available on YouTube. It is an instructional video on how to paraphrase in order to avoid plagiarism.

Wetherington, Kevin, Ronald Green, Ellen Grassie for Absalom Productions, and Educational Video Network, Inc. 2003. *Plagiarism: It's a Crime.* Videocassette, 22 minutes.
The videocassette discusses intellectual property rights, copyright infringements, and plagiarism. It includes definitions of plagiarism and what happens when people plagiarize, why people plagiarize, types of plagiarism, and strategies that can help prevent people from committing plagiarism.

Wetherington, Kevin, Shannon McWhirter, and Jude Lee Routh for Educational Video Network, Inc. 2002. *Research Skills: How to Find Information."* Videocassette, 22 minutes.
This video is about report writing, research methodology, information resources, and plagiarism and is targeted to high school and college students. It is divided into six sections: "What Is Research?," "Selecting a Topic," "Research Tools," "Organizing Research Information," "Plagiarism," and "Writing a Research Paper." Too much emphasis is placed on the presence of the card catalog, considering the fact that many students are now more familiar with the online catalog.

About the Editors and Contributors

Vibiana Bowman Cvetkovic is a Reference Librarian and the Web Administrator at the Paul Robeson Library, Rutgers University, in Camden, New Jersey. Her books include *The Plagiarism Plague: A Resource Guide and CD-ROM Tutorial for Educators and Librarians* (Neal-Schuman, 2004), *Scholarly Resources for Children and Childhood Studies: A Research Guide and Annotated Bibliography* (Scarecrow Press, 2007), and *Teaching Generation M: A Handbook for Librarians and Educators* (Neal-Schuman, 2009). She has also published in various refereed journals and library and information science publications. Ms. Cvetkovic is a past president of the Library Instruction Round Table of the American Library Association and is the current chair of the Children and Childhood Studies Area of the Mid-Atlantic Popular/American Culture Association.

Katie Elson Anderson is a Reference and Instruction Librarian at the Paul Robeson Library, Rutgers University, in Camden, New Jersey. Ms. Anderson holds an MLIS (2007) from Rutgers University and bachelor's degrees in Anthropology and German from Washington University, St. Louis, Missouri. Publications include chapters in *Scholarly Resources for Children and Childhood Studies: A Research Guide and Annotated Bibliography* (edited by Vibiana Bowman, Scarecrow Press, 2007) and *Teaching Generation M: A Handbook for Librarians and Educators* (edited by Vibiana Bowman and Robert Lackie, Neal Schuman, 2009). Other publications include contributions to ABC-CLIO's *World History Encyclopedia* and Sage's *21st Century Handbook of Anthropology.*

* * *

Dawn Amsberry is a Reference and Instruction Librarian at Penn State University Libraries. She has an MLS from San Jose State University, California, and an MA in Teaching English to Speakers of Other Languages from Hunter

College, New York. She has been a children's and reference librarian in public and academic libraries and has taught ESL and writing to adults in the New York City area. Her articles on plagiarism and academic library service to international students have been published in the *Journal of Academic Librarianship*, *The Reference Librarian*, and *Reference Services Review*. She is currently the chair of the Association of College and Research Libraries' Academic Library Service to International Students Interest Group.

Robert Berry is the Research Librarian for the Social and Behavioral Sciences at Sacred Heart University, in Fairfield, Connecticut. Rob completed a BA in Sociology at Edinboro University of Pennsylvania, an MA in Political Science at the New School for Social Research, a JD at Brooklyn Law School, and an MLS at Southern Connecticut State University. Rob's publications include *Civil Liberties Constraints on Tribal Sovereignty after the Indian Civil Rights Act of 1968*, 1 J.L. & Pol'y 1 (1993) and Note, *Indigenous Nations and International Trade*, 24 Brook. J. Int'l L. 239 (1998). A former litigator, Rob is admitted to practice in New York. Rob is an adjunct instructor at Southern Connecticut State University and is on the faculty of Lawline.com.

Sarah F. Brookover is a junior at Rutgers University in Camden, New Jersey. She will graduate in 2011 with a double major in History and African American Studies.

Nick Cvetkovic, still active as an author, teacher, and speaker, retired after nearly 40 years as a programmer and computer consultant. He operated his own computer consulting firm for 23 years. Mr. Cvetkovic has held a variety of leadership positions within the independent computer consulting and computer user group communities and has been a personal computer hobbyist since 1982. Mr. Cvetkovic is a former national board member of the Independent Computer Consultants Association and is a past president of the Association of Personal Computer Professionals in the Philadelphia area. He is one of the pioneer online users and is the founding "wizop" for CompuServe's Computer Consultants Forum. He was also the forum administrator for the Photography Forum.

John B. Gibson is the Instructional Technology Specialist for the Paul Robeson Library at Rutgers University in Camden, New Jersey. John is responsible for technical support, one-on-one training, and digital programming at the library. John completed his undergraduate degree at the Honor's College of Rutgers University and is currently pursuing a Master of Computer Science. He has taken courses on web development strategies, innovative web technologies, security, and more. While at Rutgers, John contributed to *The Plagiarism Plague: A Resource Guide and CD-ROM Tutorial for Educators and Librarians* (Neal-Schuman, 2004). He has also co-presented on the topic of plagiarism via the "Plagiarism Plague" at the local, state, and national levels. John contributes to various community blogs, technical writing forums, and web development committees, and he recently developed a software appliance for assisting libraries and patrons via touchscreen that includes audiovisual, web searching, and video conferencing features.

Frances Kaufmann is an independent research and academic librarian. She has served as Assistant Director of Libraries at Union County College, Cranford, New Jersey, and as Client Services Librarian at the Seton Hall University Library, South Orange, New Jersey. Her areas of expertise include reference services, information literacy, interlibrary cooperation, and library advocacy. She is active in local, state, and national library organizations, presently serving on the American Library Association's Committee on Library Advocacy, and she is past president of the New Jersey chapter of the Association of College and Research Libraries. She has presented at regional and state library conferences and has had poster sessions and roundtable discussions accepted for ACRL and ALA.

Robert J. Lackie is a Professor-Librarian at Rider University in New Jersey, where he co-leads the course-integrated Library Instruction Program. A frequent presenter at local, state, and national library, education, and technology conferences, Professor Lackie has presented over 500 workshops and seminars around the United States, and he has been published within various professional and scholarly works. His co-edited book, *Teaching Generation M: A Handbook for Librarians and Educators*, was published by Neal-Schuman in 2009.

Leslie Murtha is a public services librarian with 15 years of experience in academic libraries. Recently employed as a freelance researcher and technology coach, Ms. Murtha held an adjunct position for several years as Social Sciences and Humanities Librarian at Firestone Library at Princeton University. Previously, she was employed for over ten years in various capacities in the Rutgers University Libraries. Ms. Murtha holds an MLS and an EdM in Adult and Continuing Education, both from Rutgers University. Ms. Murtha has written and presented on a variety of topics relating to information literacy and academic integrity.

Gillian A. Newton is currently employed in Access and Interlibrary Loan services at Rutgers University Libraries. In addition she is a part-time Reference and Instruction Librarian at Union County College and holds an MLIS from Rutgers University. Ms. Newton has gained invaluable insight into the world of the college freshman while managing student employees at Alexander Library and closer to home, where her daughters have both completed their own first-year college experiences.

Dolores Pfeuffer-Scherer is the Interim Director of Writing Across the Curriculum and the Coordinator of Historical Understanding I at Philadelphia University, Philadelphia, Pennsylvania. She is currently a PhD candidate in American History at Temple University.

Luis F. Rodriguez is the University Librarian at the Nancy Thompson Library of Kean University. He is active in state and national organizations. Mr. Rodriguez is a past president of the New Jersey Library Association College and University Section/New Jersey Association of College and Research Libraries Chapter and received its Distinguished Service Award in 2007. He currently serves as the legislative representative for the group, and he is the New Jersey Legislative Advocate for the Association of College and Research Libraries. He also served on the national task force that created the Strategic Marketing Initiative for the Association of College and Research Libraries (2002).

Patience L. Simmonds is a Reference and Instruction Librarian at Penn State Erie, The Behrend College. She contributed a chapter in *The Plagiarism Plague: A Resource Guide and CD-ROM Tutorial for Educators and Librarians* (Neal-Schuman, 2004) and her article "Plagiarism and Cyber-Plagiarism: A Guide to Selected Resources on the Web" was published in the *College & Research Library News*, June 2003 (www.ala.org; search "plagiarism"). She has also published in various journals and information science publications on user satisfaction in academic libraries. Ms. Simmonds is currently a member of the Library Instruction Round Table's Transition to College Committee.

Laura B. Spencer is a Reference Librarian at the Paul Robeson Library, Rutgers University, in Camden, New Jersey. Her primary professional concern is to understand how the digital environment shapes thinking and learning for better, for worse, for indifferent. She pays particular attention to the hidden cognitive and emotional costs of that environment for both students and society.

Julie Still is a Reference Librarian at the Paul Robeson Library, Rutgers University in Camden, New Jersey. Her books include *The Accidental Fundraiser* (Information Today, 2007) and *The Accidental Webmaster* (Information Today, 2004). She has also written several book chapters and is published in various refereed journals and library and information science publications. In addition, she serves on the editorial board of *MP: A Feminist Online Journal*.

Jeffrey J. Teichmann is an Access Services Supervisor at the Alexander Library of Rutgers University. He brings over 20 years of experience working with college students to the discussion of first-year students and their interactions with academic libraries. In addition, he has "shepherded" two children of his own through their first-year experiences. Mr. Teichmann holds an MLIS from the School of Communication and Information, Rutgers University.

Index

Page numbers followed by the letter "i" indicate figures or sidebars.